NANCY HENLEY is Associate Professor of Psychology at the University of Lowell in Massachusetts. Coauthor of *Language and Sex: Difference and Dominance* and co-compiler of *She Said/He Said,* she has published many articles on language, social organization, and women's issues in professional journals.

BODY POLITICS
Power, Sex, and Nonverbal Communication

Nancy M. Henley

Drawings by Deirdre Patrick

A TOUCHSTONE BOOK
Published by Simon & Schuster, Inc.
NEW YORK

Copyright © 1977 by Simon & Schuster, Inc.

First Touchstone Edition, 1986

Published by Simon & Schuster, Inc.
Simon & Schuster Building
Rockefeller Center
1230 Avenue of the Americas
New York, New York 10020

Originally published by Prentice-Hall, Inc.

TOUCHSTONE and colophon are registered trademarks of
Simon & Schuster, Inc.

Manufactured in the United States of America

10 9 8 7 6 5   Pbk.

Library of Congress Cataloging in Publication Data

Henley, Nancy.
    Body politics.

    (A Touchstone book)
    Reprint. Originally published: Englewood Cliffs, N.J.:
Prentice-Hall, © 1977.
    Includes index.
    1. Nonverbal communication (Psychology)   2. Power
(Social sciences   3. Interpersonal relations.
I. Title.
[BF637.N66H46   1986]   153.6   86-6425
ISBN 0-671-62243-9 (pbk.)

CONTENTS

PREFACE
AND ACKNOWLEDGMENTS

If you care about power, if you care about how power is wielded *over you*, this book is for you. It describes how the way we sit, smile, take up space, stare, cock our heads, or touch others is bound to our power relationships. Body language is not composed only of messages about friendship and sex; it is *body politics* also.

This book is for those people who have felt oppressed by power, yet confused about some of the ways it is used to oppress them. It is especially for women who have been oppressed by power because of their sex and who are more affected by body politics than men are. And it is also especially for those who have been fighting the oppression of power over their own lives, while ignoring the meaning of much of their day-to-day interaction with the powerful.

This book is also for those who are deeply concerned about the injustices and inequities they see about them, though they may not be so much direct victims of injustice themselves. It is for those who have been reared and sustained on an intellectual malnourishment of lies and half-truths from our textbooks and media into believing that body language is trivial or is primarily for emotional expression, that it is based largely on innate differences between the sexes and between individuals, that people with powerful gestures are "born leaders," and so forth. These readers are well-meaning people who can be honest with themselves, perhaps at great cost, but who have not had access to alternatives to the prevailing ideology of "body talk."

Finally, the book is for people who are curious about nonverbal communication, who want to know what is passing between them and others on levels they aren't aware of. Some of these people are students and scholars who I hope will develop further the ideas I put forward. References are provided, often in detail, for those who wish to pursue them.

Though this book is the first to deal exclusively with power in nonverbal communication, no book can be all things to all people. This book can't be an introduction to nonverbal behavior; those who want to read about topics other than power will need to look elsewhere (Albert Scheflen's works are especially recommended for this). It is also not the thorough radical political analysis some will want; in part, I believe, because the knowledge is not sufficient to yield to such analysis—but I hope it is a step toward this. And finally, the book is not "objective" social science, because that doesn't exist. To lay out facts without drawing conclusions, to strip conclusions of their emotional content, to treat findings with vastly different social implications as equivalent—these are some of the biased methods of "objective social science." In this book when conclusions are based on solid research findings and clearly traced logical argument, they will be carried into social reality, and I trust readers to follow and judge.

My own bias, for a radical restructuring of our social organization to respond to those who labor to create its wealth, will be evident. My special concern with women's issues too is reflected in this book; but perhaps a note should be added that being pro-woman and anti-male supremacy does not necessarily mean being anti-man. The book is written for readers of all sexes and all backgrounds.

I hope you will learn as much about body politics as I did in surveying these studies—and I hope what you learn will change your life.

No book is written alone, no matter how sole the authorship. For me to say that what follows is a product of many people is not an attempt to avoid responsibility or to avoid, as some women are accused of doing, acknowledgment of achievement.

This book is truly the product of many persons. Some of them are easy to identify: Barrie Thorne has been my colleague, co-author, and critic through many projects in which we have known only mutual sharing, strength, and support; she has shown early and continuing interest in my ideas, and working with her has been the happiest professional collaboration of my career. She has given a careful and critical reading of this manuscript; not only has she clarified and strengthened it by the questions she raised, but I am sure many of the ideas expressed in it as my own have evolved through discussions with her. Craig Jackson similarly has been a constant, helpful critic and political comrade who has read the manuscript in earlier and later forms, and helped me clarify my understanding of many points. His unfailing support, both material and intangible, has sustained me through the long haul and in crises. There are other colleagues whose unwavering encouragement and belief in my ideas have bolstered me more than they realize. I count among them especially Jo-Ann Gardner, Robert Brannon, and Mary Parlee.

Zick Rubin, editor of this series, is another who has sustained me both with interest in my ideas and through concerned and helpful criticism and editing, with just enough pressure to make me keep going. I am also grateful to Shirley Weitz, who reviewed the entire manuscript, for suggestions which significantly improved the book; to Richard Heslin and Steve Ellyson, who read selected chapters of the manuscript; and to editors and other workers at Prentice-Hall who have brought my words to print.

Many of the theses advanced here, and much of the research behind them, were developed during a postdoctoral year at Harvard University, with the aid of a Special Research Fellowship (1 FO3 MH 35977-0 MTLH) from the National Institute of Mental Health, for which I have much appreciation. Roger Brown was my sponsor during that year, and I am grateful both for the inspiration of his own theories and for his interest in my furthering and expanding them in this fashion. Other research and writing have been done while on the faculty of the University of Maryland (Baltimore County) and of the University of Lowell, and I am grateful for the institutional assistance they provided.

When I could no longer face details one more time, Carol Woolfe painstakingly checked quotations and citations for accuracy; and Lisa and Larry Kuenning gave an intelligent and careful final typing of the manuscript. I thank them all for doing my work.

Finally, there are the persons who served as "subjects" in the various research projects reported here (including some of my own), who have given precious information from their own lives to educate and enhance researchers, often without being much enlightened in exchange. I hope this book will return some of that knowledge to them.

My indebtedness to scholars who have gone before me will be clear to readers—I follow a path blazed by Erving Goffman, Roger Brown, Ray Birdwhistell, and other known giants of social science. Less obvious, perhaps, will be my debt to two women who are less famous, but whose insights I have tried to carry on: Lynn O'Connor and Nicole Anthony, who undersood the sexual/political aspects of several realms of nonverbal communication when I was examining these for touching.

Naturally, any of these persons may disagree with points I make in the book, and I have not always followed others' suggestions. For the errors and weaknesses of the book I, of course, take full responsibility.

Excerpt from *Women and Madness* on page x by Phyllis Chesler. Copyright © 1972 by Phyllis Chesler. Reprinted by permission of Doubleday & Company, Inc. and Penguin Books, Allen Lane.

Quotations from Barry Schwartz, "Waiting, Exchange, and Power, *American Journal of Sociology*, vol. 79 (1974), pp. 841-70 are reprinted by permission of The University of Chicago Press. © 1974 The University of Chicago.

Quotation from Erving Goffman, "The Nature of Deference and Demeanor," *The American Anthropologist*, vol. 58, no. 3 (1956) are reproduced by permission of the American Anthropological Association.

Quotations from John Spiegel and Pavel Machotka, *Messages of the Body* are used by permission of Macmillan Publishing Co., Inc. © 1974 by The Free Press, a Division of Macmillan Publishing Co., Inc.

"Exercises for Men" is used by kind permission of the *Portland Scribe*, successor to the alternate newspaper the *Willamette Bridge*.

To those who think I am suggesting that we have a war between the sexes, I say: "But we've always had one—and women have always lost it."

PHYLLIS CHESLER
Women and Madness

chapter one
THE OTHER DIMENSION

"Dear Ann Landers," writes Straight Goods to (perhaps) our time's greatest arbiter and chronicler of social mores. "So often we hear people criticize women for looking sexy in their tight pants, see-through blouses, and short, short skirts. . . . One of your readers wrote, 'No wonder so many women get raped. The way they dress, they are asking for it.' " Straight Goods goes on to quote the director of a rape treatment center that "Rape is a crime of violence, not sex. . . . Many [rapists] have no idea what their victims looked like. For the most part, the rapist is an angry man who feels the need to abuse a woman in order to get even with a female he hates. . . ."

Straight Goods asks the advice columnist to clear up the old misconception that rape is invited by certain women's dress and demeanor. Ann, however, lets her correspondent down. The authority may be right about "the classic rapist," she acknowledges, but "There is another kind of rapist —the one who knows his victim, and most rapes fall into this category. These males DO know what the women look like and the rape is sometimes triggered by a see-through blouse, those short, short skirts and tight pants." [1]

Ann Landers is not the only authority who holds that women's sexual invitation is to be judged from their external appearance. In 1975 a Copenhagen court convicted a woman of soliciting in a public place, on a policeman's testimony that he determined her intention from her walk. The walk, like the clothing, is taken as a sign of sexual invitation that overrules one's words or other actions.

[1] Ann Landers' column, January 9, 1976, in the Boston *Globe*, p. 20.

1

What have these cases to do with nonverbal communication? They illustrate most dramatically the intersection of power, sex, and nonverbal communication, the intersection of concern in this book. Attacks on women have long been justified on the basis of "she was asking for it" and "she really meant 'yes,'" and women's nonverbal rather than verbal behavior is cited as justification for this interpretation.

The social consequences of (real or imagined) female nonverbal cues, and male interpretation of them, stand out sharply in these cases. Other consequences of our nonverbal behavior, while less drastic and not so immediately visible, can be shown to have major importance to our personal lives (whatever our sex) and to the social structure. This book is concerned not with sex or gender, but *power*. It attempts to demonstrate that the observed "sex differences," "race differences," and "class differences" in nonverbal behavior may be traced to differences in power; and that these are learned differences which serve to strengthen the system of power and privilege that exists.

TWO DIMENSIONS OF NONVERBAL COMMUNICATION

If you're looking at this book you must be interested in nonverbal communication—how we say things with our body postures and movements, facial expressions, gestures, touching, eye contact, use of space, and so on. You may have read other books, or articles, on the subject. If so, you may have noticed—or, with many authors, taken for granted—that most of the concerns of this field are ones such as closeness, like and dislike, intimacy, sexuality, expressions of emotion, or attempts to send or cover signals conveying positive or negative attitudes.

But there is another side to interpersonal relationship, one that affects us greatly but which we're encouraged to pay little attention to. This is the element of status, power, dominance, superiority—the vertical dimension of human relations, signalled by our spatial metaphor of "higher-ups," "underlings," "being over," and "looking up to" others. Friendship relations make up the horizontal dimension, and the corresponding spatial metaphor refers to closeness, "being near" and "being distant." The power relation is the "other" dimension in the study of nonverbal communication: important as it is in ordering human interaction, it has received little study from investigators of nonverbal behavior.*

* Albert Mehrabian has examined status relations in nonverbal behavior and has identified three dimensions along which nonverbal communication varies: evaluation, potency or status, and responsiveness (*Nonverbal Communication* [Chicago: Aldine-Atherton, 1972]). My naming of two dimensions is a reference to major conceptual dimensions that parallel other aspects of social behavior and is derived from the work of Roger Brown (*Social Psychology* [New York: Free Press, 1965]).

The "trivia" of everyday life—touching others, moving closer or farther away, dropping the eyes, smiling, interrupting—are commonly interpreted as facilitating social intercourse, but not recognized in their position as micropolitical gestures, defenders of the status quo—of the state, of the wealthy, of authority, of all those whose power may be challenged. Nevertheless these minutiae find their place on a continuum of social control which extends from internalized socialization at one end to sheer physical force at the other.

In front of, and defending, the political–economic structure that determines our lives and defines the context of human relationships, there is the micropolitical structure that helps maintain it. This micropolitical structure is the substance of our everyday experience. The humiliation of being a subordinate is often felt most sharply and painfully when one is ignored or interrupted while speaking, towered over or forced to move by another's bodily presence, or cowed unknowingly into dropping the eyes, the head, the shoulders. Conversely, the power to manipulate others' lives, to take graft, price gouge, or plan the bombing of far-off peasants is conferred in part by others' snapping to attention in one's presence, their smiling, fearing to touch or approach, their following one around for information and favors. These are the trivia that make up the batter for that great stratified waffle that we call our society.

There are some good anecdotal accounts that illustrate the working of nonverbal controls and point to truths about our unspoken power relationships that we can immediately recognize. One example is Jay Haley's tongue-in-cheek description of "The Art of Psychoanalysis," in which he analyzes the interaction between therapist and patient from the point of view of "gamesmanship." [2] Besides calling attention to behaviors of the analyst and patient which emphasize their superior–inferior relationship, Haley shows features of the setting which also reinforce a pattern of dominance:

> By placing the patient on a couch, the analyst gives the patient the feeling of having his feet up in the air and the knowledge that the analyst has both feet on the ground. Not only is the patient disconcerted by having to lie down while talking, but he finds himself literally below the analyst and so his one-down position is geographically emphasized. In addition, the analyst seats himself behind the couch where he can watch the patient but the patient cannot watch him. This gives the patient the sort of disconcerted feeling a person has when sparring with an opponent while blindfolded. Unable to see what response his ploys provoke, he is unsure when he is one-up

2 Jay Haley, "The Art of Psychoanalysis." In S. I. Hayakawa (ed.), *The Use and Misuse of Language* (Greenwich, Conn.: Fawcett, 1962), pp. 207–18.

and when one-down. . . . It is essential that the rare patient who gets an opportunity to observe the analyst see only an impassive demeanor.

Another purpose is served by the position behind the couch. Inevitably what the analyst says becomes exaggerated in importance since the patient lacks any other means of determining his effect on the analyst. The patient finds himself hanging on the analyst's every word, and by definition he who hangs on another's words is one-down.[3]

Superior or inferior spatial position . . . sitting or lying body posture . . . visibility or invisibilty . . . impassive or expressive demeanor . . . these unnoticed details of an encounter are strong determiners of one person's power over another.

Another anecdotal description that tells us much about nonverbal power cues is Erving Goffman's insightful essay, "The Nature of Deference and Demeanor." [4] Goffman draws a general principle from his many observations on a hospital ward: the principle of *symmetric relations between status equals and asymmetric ones between unequals*. That is, equals, such as co-workers on a job, can call each other by first name (e.g., Mike and Phil) and have equal rights to borrow each other's pen, sit in each other's chair, to touch one another or to invite each other out for a drink. Between unequals, though, one may be called by a title and the other by first name (e.g., Mrs. Updegraff and Debbie), and one may have privileges in the relationship that the other does not. This is a principle we'll return to often in our examination of nonverbal behavior. Goffman also cites subtle aspects of verbal behavior—voice quality, pitch, interruption, self-disclosure—that signal superiority and subordination.

Deferential pledges are frequently conveyed through spoken terms of address involving status-identifiers, as when a nurse responds to a rebuke in the operating room with the phrase, "yes, Doctor," signifying by term of address and tone of voice that the criticism has been understood and that, however unpalatable, it has not caused her to rebel.[5]

Between status equals we may expect to find interaction guided by symmetrical familiarity. Between superordinate and subordinate we may expect to find asymmetrical relations, the superordinate having the right to exercise certain familiarities which the subordinate is not allowed to reciprocate. Thus, in the research hospital, doctors tended to call nurses by their first name, while nurses responded with "polite" or "formal" address. Similarly, in American business organizations the boss may thoughtfully ask the elevator man how his children are, but this entrance into another's life may

[3] Haley, "Art of Psychoanalysis," pp. 208–10.
[4] Erving Goffman, *Interaction Ritual* (Garden City, N.Y.: Doubleday, 1967), pp. 47–95.
[5] Goffman, *Interaction Ritual*, pp. 60–61.

be blocked to the elevator man, who can appreciate the concern but not return it. Perhaps the clearest form of this is found in the psychiatrist-patient relation, where the psychiatrist has a right to touch on aspects of the patient's life that the patient might not even allow himself to touch upon, while of course this privilege is not reciprocated.[6]

Here we see that the psychoanalyst's one-up game described by Jay Haley extends even into the nature of the analyst's listening role—who tells all, and who listens, makes a power game too. What is sympathy when extended symmetrically becomes privilege when it is one-sided. In the same way, the homely gesture of touching may involve privilege:

> On Ward A, as in other wards in this hospital, there was a "touch system." . . . In addition to . . . symmetrical touch relations on the ward, there were also asymmetrical ones. The doctors touched other ranks as a means of conveying friendly support and comfort, but other ranks tended to feel that it would be presumptuous for them to reciprocate a doctor's touch, let alone initiate such a contact with a doctor.[7]

First names versus formal address . . . asking or answering personal questions . . . touching or being touched . . . status references . . . tone of voice . . . Goffman calls attention to other unobtrusive aspects of an encounter that go with status differences. And more, he shows them as aspects of a group structure, not just a one-to-one relationship. Nonverbal cues, as Haley and Goffman have illustrated, play an extremely important and complex role in the maintenance of the social order: as signs and symbols of dominance, as subtle messages of threat, as gestures of submission.

Nonverbal cues also play an important role among people at the same social level; gestures of recognition, of friendship, loving, disdain, rejection, all regulate and maintain behavior. However, our focus in this book will be on the power aspect of nonverbal communication, both on the interpersonal and intergroup level, with particular reference to male dominance as one dimension of power. Overall in the social sciences, race dominance is a better known and better studied power manifestation, but there is little in the nonverbal literature written on patterns of interaction among people of different races. To say anything about the use of nonverbal cues maintaining race dominance, we usually must extrapolate from other studies. There is, on the other hand, plenty on sex differences, though it's seldom interpreted in a political (i.e., power-oriented) context.

---

[6] Goffman, *Interaction Ritual*, p. 64. Roger Brown and his colleagues have also analyzed this symmetry/asymmetry pattern; their work is presented more fully in Chapter 5.

[7] Goffman, *Interaction Ritual*, pp. 73–74.

IF A BODY MEET A BODY . . .

The subject of nonverbal communication is a frightening one to a lot of people. They think that if you're interested in how they communicate nonverbally, you're suddenly privy to all their secrets, reading their minds, seeing the holes in their underwear. They get edgy, defensive, and restrained physically. And it's no wonder people think this way, considering the promotion that has accompanied some of the popular books on "body language":

"Learn to read the body as you read a book!" commands the cover of one paperback. Another book claims you can learn to "tell whether the person you're talking to is lying" or "spot the 'feigned gesture' that's meant to throw you off the track." The cover of the biggest seller features a picture of a longhaired, bare-footed woman sitting in a transparent chair, arms and legs crossed, surrounded by the questions: "Does her body say that she's a loose woman? Does her body say that she's a manipulator? Does her body say that she's a phoney? Does her body say that she's lonely?" Its back cover advises you to read it "so that you can penetrate the personal secrets, both of intimates and total strangers."

So every body is frightened and scurries to learn how to read other people's bodies; this knowledge is indeed power. But apart from the media bombardment, our fearful concern with nonverbal communication has other, more valid bases. Like our physiological functioning, it seems somehow a very important part of our lives, even though we often can't understand it ourselves. And like our physiological functioning, it seems like something we can't be trusted to interpret correctly either in ourselves or others.

Our culture places great emphasis on verbal communication: English is taught in our schools through all grades, with the dual aim of better understanding and better expression. But nonverbal communication isn't taught: we never learn to analyze what certain postures, gestures, and looks mean, or how to express ourselves better nonverbally. Of course, nonverbal communication is learned informally as a matter of survival, just as language is learned before we enter school to study it.

As children there are some things we are told to do with our bodies: for example, that staring and pointing (both gestures of dominance that adults feel are ill-suited to children) are impolite, that we should stand up or sit down at certain times, not scratch or pick certain places in public, to sit up straight, not make faces, and (particularly if male) shake hands on being introduced. But these are limited and specific directions, with little of the survival value our earliest language instruction has.

The fact that we're never formally tutored in nonverbal communication doesn't mean everybody doesn't know that looks and postures mean something, perhaps everything, especially in emotion-charged interaction. But looks and postures are illegitimate in analyzing communication: legal transcripts and newspaper accounts don't record them, and they are seldom allowed in personal argument ("What look? What tone of voice? Look, did I say o.k., or didn't I?").*

As we would guess, nonverbal communication is very important in the human context; it becomes the yardstick against which words and intentions are measured. Experiments have been done which can help us estimate the importance of nonverbal communication in human interaction. A team of British investigators, headed by Michael Argyle, devised an experiment which could, among other things, assess the importance of nonverbal cues compared with verbal ones.[8] Their 120 subjects made ratings of 18 videotapes which varied in the following ways: either of two female performers delivered a verbal message which implied superiority, equality, or inferiority, along with a nonverbal manner that implied superiority, neutrality, or inferiority, in all possible combinations. For example, a superior message was:

> It is probably quite a good thing for you subjects to come along to help in these experiments because it gives you a small glimpse of what psychological research is about. In fact, the whole process is far more complex than you would be able to appreciate without a considerable training in research methods, paralinguistics and kinesic analysis, and so on.[9]

This could be delivered with nonverbal cues of superiority (no smile, head raised, loud, dominating speech), of inferiority (deferential smile, head lowered, and nervous, eager-to-please speech), or of neutrality (light smile, head level, neutral-to-pleasant speech).

* When Richard Nixon sent transcripts, rather than tapes, of presidential conversations to the House Judiciary Committee investigating the question of his possible impeachment (April, 1974), members quite rightly complained that transcripts could not convey the full or correct meaning of an utterance, having no voice inflection, stress, or other such nuances, and demanded the tapes. This exchange is a landmark in recognizing the legitimacy of paralinguistic communication, those characteristics of speech that affect its interpretation but are not part of the usually recognized language.

8 Michael Argyle, et al., "The Communication of Inferior and Superior Attitudes by Verbal and Non-Verbal Signals," *British Journal of Social and Clinical Psychology*, 1970, 9, 222–31.

9 Argyle, et al., "Verbal and Non-Verbal Signals," p. 224.

Earlier ratings by other subjects had shown that the verbal and nonverbal messages, when presented separately, were given ratings of an almost identical range. A separate verbal message consisted of a typed message; for a nonverbal message, a performer merely counted aloud, but with the cues of one of the three nonverbal styles.

The subjects saw all 18 tapes, and rated their impressions for each performance on 10 scales of such qualities as "Hostile-Friendly," "Inferior-Superior," "Unpleasant-Pleasant," "Submissive-Dominant." Since each verbal manner was presented with each nonverbal manner, the effect of verbal and nonverbal components of the message could be assessed independently.

These researchers found that though the verbal variable significantly affected six of the ten scales, the nonverbal variable affected all the scales. Moreover, the size of the effect of the nonverbal variable was much greater than that of the verbal.*

Another clue to the salience of nonverbal cues comes from the work of Harvard psychologist Robert Rosenthal and his colleagues, who have developed a measure of sensitivity to nonverbal communication.[10] They too worked with film to make 200 segments showing an actress portraying various emotions in certain contexts. People were so accurate in recognizing the scene and emotion portrayed that the experimenters cut the exposure length again and again to see at what point accuracy was diminished. But even at an exposure of $\frac{1}{24}$ of a second, people were correct over $\frac{2}{3}$ of the time.

This finding tends to confirm Sapir's observation in 1927 that "we respond to gestures with an extreme alertness and, one might almost say, in accordance with an elaborate and secret code that is written nowhere, known by none and understood by all." [11] We turn next to some of the consequences of this fact.

---

* This was demonstrated in a couple of ways: first, the amount of total variation in the ratings people gave that was due to the nonverbal message was 21.7 times the variation due to the verbal one. Second, though verbal and nonverbal messages when used alone were equal in effect on the subject's ratings, when the two were combined, the impact of nonverbal cues jumped to 4.3 times that of the verbal message.

[10] Robert Rosenthal, et al., "Body Talk and Tone of Voice: The Language Without Words," Psychology Today, September 1974 (vol. 8, no. 4), 64–68. Also by the same authors, "Assessing Sensitivity to Nonverbal Communication: The PONS Test," Division 8 Newsletter, Division of Personality and Social Psychology of the American Psychological Association, January, 1974, 1–3.

[11] Edward Sapir, "The Unconscious Patterning of Behavior in Society," 1927. In D. G. Mandelbaum, ed., Selected Writings of Edward Sapir (Berkeley: University of California Press, 1949), pp. 544–59.

FROM SELF-FULFILLING PROPHECY TO
VICIOUS CIRCLE

If you are not a black man seeking employment, imagine for the moment that you are. You consider yourself well qualified, and observe all the proprieties: you are neatly dressed, cleanly shaven, you show what you consider an appropriate amount of respect to the interviewer, you are vital and interested. Yet something doesn't click with these interviewers, almost all of them white males. They don't seem as interested in the interview as you are, in fact they seem almost sloppy about it, and the interview doesn't last long. There was more, but you can't quite put your finger on it; maybe it's just the way you're used to being treated by whites, a vague feeling that you don't much exist. And afterwards you feel frustrated and unsatisfied about your own performance. A relatively self-assured man, you felt vaguely nervous and lacking in self-confidence during the interview. You wonder if your feelings were related to the interviewer's being so distant and distracted.

What was going on? Had they already made up their minds to hire somebody else before wasting your time with that interview? You feel you've been discriminated against, but not in a way that you could describe coherently. Here is racism, but what is this process by which it was working?

This hypothetical situation is far from mythical, though it is hard to document in real-life situations. Fortunately, we have an excellent experiment designed to help us examine and understand the processes in situations like this, carried out by a team of Princeton investigators, Word, Zanna and Cooper.[12] These researchers wished to study the part that nonverbal behavior plays in a particularly vicious circle in interracial interaction. They focused specifically on a form of the self-fulfilling prophecy: whites react to blacks in a stigmatizing way, leading to the blacks reciprocating their behavior, with the end result of whites devaluing black performance.

Word, Zanna and Cooper noted that black skin in a white culture is a stigma much as a physical disability is, and evokes similar treatment from those without that stigma.[13] The kinds of behaviors they wished to study

[12] Carl O. Word, Mark P. Zanna, and Joel Cooper, "The Nonverbal Mediation of Self-Fulfilling Prophecies in Interracial Interaction," *Journal of Experimental Social Psychology*, 1974, 10, 109–20.

[13] See Erving Goffman, *Stigma: Notes on the Management of Spoiled Identity* (Englewood Cliffs, N.J.: Prentice-Hall, 1963).

were those shown to stigmatized persons, generally avoidance behaviors, as we would expect, and have been detailed in a series of experiments by Kleck and his colleagues. They include the tendency to keep a greater distance, terminate interaction sooner, and to be inhibited in body movement.[14] Behaviors of avoidance or of approach ("immediacy") tend to be reciprocated.

However, since we are generally so unaware of our own nonverbal behavior, if we unwittingly give off such signs of liking or disliking another, we don't usually interpret the other person's subsequent behavior as a reaction to ours. Rather, we attribute it to some internal cause or inherent trait in the other. Positive cycles can be built up in this way, but so can negative ones. As Word, Zanna, and Cooper put their hypothesis:

> . . . whites interacting with blacks will emit nonverbal behaviors corresponding to negative evaluations and . . . blacks, in turn, will reciprocate with less immediate behaviors. If the context in which the interaction occurs involves a job interview, with the white interviewing the black, such reciprocated behavior may be interpreted as less adequate performance, thus confirming, in part, the interviewer's original attitude.[15]

To test this hypothesis, and investigate the nonverbal mediation of self-fulfilling prophecies in interracial interaction, they carried out two related experiments. The first sought to find out what behaviors were emitted differently to black and to white interviewees by white interviewers, and the second sought to test the theory that these behaviors affected the responses of the interviewees. In Experiment 1, white male subjects believed they were interviewing applicants for a team position in a group decision-making experiment. They interviewed a black and a white male applicant for the position while being surreptitiously recorded and observed through one-way mirrors. The "applicants" were really confederates, trained to act in a standard way, and performances of both black and white confederates were rehearsed until all applicants appeared equally qualifying.

This experiment found that the white interviewers did indeed behave differently to black and white applicants. They placed their chairs at a

---

[14] Robert E. Kleck, H. Ono, and A. H. Hastorf, "The Effects of Physical Deviance Upon Face-to-Face Interaction," *Human Relations,* 1966, 19, 425–36. Robert E. Kleck, "Physical Stigma and Nonverbal Cues Emitted in Face-to-Face Interactions," *Human Relations,* 1968, 21, 19–28. Robert Kleck, et al., "Effects of Stigmatizing Conditions on the Use of Personal Space," *Psychological Reports,* 1968, 23, 111–18. Robert E. Kleck and W. Nuessle, "Congruence Between the Indicative and Communicative Functions of Eye Contact in Interpersonal Relations," *British Journal of Social and Clinical Psychology,* 1968, 7, 241–46.

[15] Word, Zanna, Cooper, "Nonverbal Mediation," p. 111.

significantly greater distance from the blacks, and showed significantly less "total immediacy," a measure made up of combined scores for forward lean, eye contact, and shoulder orientation (directness). In addition, they ended the interview significantly sooner with blacks, and made more speech errors (such as stuttering, repeating, breaking off sentences—also related to non-immediacy). These behaviors not only demonstrated differential treatment of blacks and whites, but the non-immediate behaviors offered blacks were typical of behavior toward stigmatized individuals.

What effect does such non-immediate, negative behavior have on those to whom it's directed? Experiment 2 approached this question by reversing the setup of the first experiment: now, the "applicants" were the subjects, and the interviewers were the trained confederates. White male subjects believed they were being interviewed as part of a program to train interviewers, and were given a monetary incentive to encourage them to really compete for a job. The interviewers were trained to exhibit either immediate or non-immediate behaviors to the applicants, i.e., varying their proximity, speech errors, and interview length. In other words, they were to treat half the applicants as white and half the applicants as black, though all were white.

The naive applicants' reactions to this manipulation were revealing: they reciprocated the degree of immediacy of the interviewer, placing their own chairs either close or far during the course of the interview, according to the interviewer's previous behavior. Subjects receiving non-immediate behavior were rated by observing judges (who could not know which condition they were in) as showing less adequate performance overall and less composure during the interview. Moreover, these subjects rated their interviewers as less friendly and generally less adequate. (Their own self-rated moods were less positive than those of subjects in the immediacy condition, but not significantly so.)

A Process, Not a Cause.   Whites typically devalue black performance, a fact of overwhelming consequence to our society, since the distribution of jobs, salaries and other resources is almost totally in the hands of white evaluators. This experiment is a powerful demonstration of one of the mechanisms by which a self-fulfilling prophecy can work, and of how self-fulfilling prophecies in the interpersonal realm probably do work most often The investigators note the social science tendency to explain social problems by "victim analysis," Ryan's term for a preoccupation with the wounds, defects and personalities of the victimized.[16] Word, Zanna and Cooper point out from their results that analyses of black–white interaction could profit if the "problem" of black performance were sought within the interaction setting itself rather than in the black population.

In fact, not only has "blaming the victim" been a prominent weapon against blacks, poor, and minorities, but a nonverbal version has recently been polished up for use against women. This thesis (unfortunately, sometimes advanced by women) says that a major source of women's unequal situation is that they don't "present" themselves correctly, but communicate inadequacy and weakness by their nonverbal behavior (as well as their verbal). The above experiment demonstrates how such behavior, when it exists, is not simply emitted by one participant. Rather, it is cued by others' behavior, in an interactive process.

Moreover, this cueing process accomplishes more than simple discrimination, keeping the powerless in "their place." It is an education and affirmation process for both participants to the interaction: every such interview confirms the white interviewer's opinions, presenting further examples of inadequate blacks; every such interview reinforces (by repetition at least) black applicants' nonverbal reactions to white interviewers, and their negative opinion of themselves.

This study illuminates a process by which racism works, even in well-meaning whites. Obviously, the principles apply equally to other targets of discrimination, whether because of another skin color, Spanish surname, sex, sexual preference, age or other stigma. It's important to remember

---

[16] William Ryan, *Blaming the Victim* (New York: Random House, 1971), pp. 119–20.

that nonverbal communication is a mechanism, however, not a cause of prejudice. Unless prejudice is overthrown, retraining women to be non-verbally assertive will only result in their being evaluated as "castrating bitches." Similarly, a black who has successfully resisted the virulent attacks of racism on her psyche, and projects an image of accomplishment and confidence (or who has learned to exhibit white mannerisms) will now be called "an uppity nigger." For this reason, changing nonverbal be-haviors will not eliminate prejudice or oppression—these must be attacked at their political and economic roots. But we have here one part of the micropolitical structure, shown in detail. Understanding this pervasive pro-cess will suggest ways we can *begin* dealing with our interaction on a per-sonal level, to begin to change our and others' opportunities.

A CASTE OF MILLIONS [17]

Nonverbal behavior seems to play an especially important part in wom-en's lives: many studies have found women to be more sensitive to nonverbal cues than men are. For example, the British study that showed the effect of nonverbal communication to so outweigh that of verbal also found women to be more affected by the difference than men.[18] In other studies, women were better than men at identifying an emotion portrayed nonverbally by either a male or female instructor, were more sensitive than men to nonverbal communication through tones, and were superior to males in perceiving implications from dialogues.[19]

The studies of Rosenthal, et al., previously described, are probably the most comprehensive in exploring sensitivity to nonverbal communication.[20] These researchers showed their filmed scenes to over 130 samples of sub-jects, from many different cultures—from American and Canadian college students to Eskimos and Australian aborigines. Their subjects varied widely also in age, education, cultural background, professional training, and men-tal health; but consistently, females of all ages performed better at under-standing nonverbal signals than did males. In 81 out of 98 sample groups for which they had subjects of both sexes, females got higher total scores than males. Though the differences were not exceptionally large, they were consistent.

[17] This heading is copied after the jacket of *Mountain-Moving Day,* an album of women's liberation songs produced by Rounder Records.

[18] Argyle, et al., "Verbal and Non-Verbal Signals."

[19] These findings are all cited in Wayne N. Thompson, *Quantitative Research in Public Address and Communication* (New York: Random House, 1967), pp. 47–48.

[20] Robert Rosenthal, et al., "Body Talk and Tone of Voice," 64–68.

Because this finding could have been biased by the fact that their stimulus person was female (as were those of Argyle et al.), the researchers made a partial version of the test with a male actor, and still found female subjects performing better at recognizing nonverbal cues. Moreover, female superiority at the task held at all seven grade levels tested (from grade five through college), though the difference decreased with age. This greater sensitivity to nonverbal communication may be seen as one aspect of a high orientation among females to social stimuli in general, a repeated finding in social psychological research.[21]

Greater social sensitivity itself may well be the special gift—or burden— of subordinates, for example, women in a male-dominated society, or blacks in a white-dominated one. Pam English has noted that slaves were described by early writers as having an acute judgment in discriminating the character of others, and believes this quality may refer to an aptitude for interpreting nonverbal signals, common to slaves and women alike.[22]

There is more recent evidence of blacks' nonverbal sensitivity: in a 1972 Boston study, actors ("expressors") portrayed seven emotions, and their photos were shown to others ("perceivers") who were asked to tell which emotion was being portrayed.[23] Both expressors and perceivers were black or white, female or male. Black perceivers were found to be more accurate at decoding these nonverbal emotions than were whites, whether the expressors were white or black, male or female (sex differences were not found in this experiment). Certainly it makes sense that when an oppressive social situation makes life a struggle, one becomes finely tuned to the nuances of that struggle.

The application of this sensitivity in the case of women has been demonstrated in the studies of Shirley Weitz, who has proposed a "female monitoring mechanism" attuned to male characteristics.[24] In Weitz's research,

---

[21] See, for example, such studies as Sam Witryol and Walter Kaess, "Sex Differences in Social Memory Tasks," *Journal of Abnormal and Social Psychology*, 1957, 54, 343–46; and those cited by Julia Sherman in *On the Psychology of Women* (Springfield, Ill.: C. C. Thomas, 1971), p. 18. Eleanor Maccoby and Carol Jacklin hold, however, in *The Psychology of Sex Differences* (Stanford: Stanford Univ. Press, 1974) that greater female social sensitivity has not been conclusively shown, at least among young people (pp. 213–14).

[22] Pam English, "Behavioral Concomitants of Dependent and Subservient Roles," 1972 paper, unpublished, Harvard University.

[23] A. George Gitter, Harvey Black, and David Mostofsky, "Race and Sex in the Communication of Emotion," *Journal of Social Psychology*, 1972, 88, 273–76.

[24] Shirley Weitz, "Sex Role Attitudes and Nonverbal Communication in Same and Opposite-Sex Interactions," presented at American Psychological Association, 1974; and "Sex Roles and Nonverbal Communication," presented at American Sociological Association, 1975.

males and females were filmed in interaction with the same or other sex, and raters made judgments of what was conveyed by their face and body (without knowing the sex of their partner). Females when with males adjusted their behaviors to the males' personality characteristics (such as dominance and affiliation), and showed more facial focus on high-dominant males than on low-dominant ones. We will see other evidence of female sensitivity and attentiveness in later chapters.

There are other factors that make micropolitical cues of particular importance in the study of woman's place in our society. If nonverbal cues are so vital in maintaining the status quo, they are a vital clue to changing that status quo. Women moving to fight their oppression will want to examine all the chains binding them, whether physical, legal or psychological. There are, furthermore, two reasons to suspect that nonverbal controls are the method of choice to keep women "in their place." First, as a group deliberately socialized to docility and passivity, women are the most likely targets for this milder form of social control. Second, their physical integration around centers of power (as wives, secretaries, etc.) makes frequent interaction—verbal and nonverbal—with women necessary for those in power. This is not so in large part for other oppressed groups in our society, who are often physically separated, by geography, ghettoes, and labor hierarchies, from power centers. (Personal servants, of course, are also physically integrated around power.) It is likely that in such cases of close and frequent contact nonverbal control is most called into play.

The contradictions surrounding nonverbal communication (the primary one being that it is so important and at the same time so unknown) make problems for us all. For women, being more involved in and affected by the nonverbal drama, there are extra hazards. They are told at times, especially when they reject sexual advances, that they were "sending signals," were "coming on" sexually. Were they? And exactly what *were* they doing? Many women wonder. When a stimulus situation is this vague and unstructured, we are more susceptible to social influence in interpreting it.[25] Thus when confronted with ambiguous nonverbal cues we are apt to accept any proffered interpretation of them, including all-purpose status quo explanations like sex stereotypes, for example, of "female" seductiveness.

Little matter that women do or don't intend seductiveness. As we saw earlier, popular belief puts great stock in women's clothing and movement as indicators of sexual invitation, and tends to disregard the women's own

[25] See Muzafer Sherif and Carolyn W. Sherif, *Social Psychology* (New York: Harper & Row, 1969), Proposition 10, p. 70: "The more unstructured the stimulus situation, the greater the effectiveness of (external) social influences. . . ."

stated intentions.* This tendency, we noted, may be used to justify rape.
Let's look at two other 1975 court rulings that illustrate the institutional-
ization of this belief.

The effect of one was aptly summarized by the *Los Angeles Times* writer
who wrote, "The ancient male notion that when a woman says 'no' she
really means 'yes' may now be a part of Britain's laws on rape." In this
case, three Royal Air Force men had initially been convicted of raping
the wife of a sergeant; the husband had invited them to have intercourse
with her and had told them to ignore her protests, which he said she produced for her own sexual stimulation. On appeal, the British law lords
ruled that a man can't be convicted of rape if he sincerely believed his
victim had consented, no matter how unreasonable that belief, and despite
any protests she might make.

In another case, this time in New York, a judge ruled that a man charged
with raping a woman was actually on the other side of that thin line of
consent—he had committed *seduction,* not rape. Though intercourse was
against her will, she had been naive and had not fought back *enough.* The
court, the judge said, couldn't protect women from their own naiveté
(though it is sympathetic to people whose naiveté loses them money or
property). Females in our society are trained to be physically weak, naive,
and passive, and rewarded for seductive walk and clothing, but then blamed
for these behaviors when men attack them. If women are intimidated by
these accusations made in an atmosphere of ignorance, it will help them to
learn all they can about nonverbal behavior—while at the same time fighting the power basis of the situation that makes them so vulnerable.

I assume none of the readers of this book condone sexual violence
against women (or anybody). But many may wonder if some women do
not in truth invite attack with their bodies, perhaps unconsciously, or
through naiveté give off unintended sexual signals. Whether women may be
sexually inviting is irrelevant to responsibility for rape, which is a crime
not of sex but of violence. Men are often much more openly seductive but
do not risk being attacked, beaten, and killed by women because of their
sexuality. Or one may suspect that men and women have different body

* That popular belief disregards women's own stated intentions fits in with the
general pattern that subordinates (e.g., children, mental inmates) are often denied
the right to state their own motives. This is part of the power of psychiatry: to ascribe
motives that people don't claim for themselves. To deny individuals the right to
declare their own intentions seems an ultimate stripping of human dignity. [I am
indebted to Barrie Thorne for this comment.] For a thorough analysis of rape as an
institution, see Susan Brownmiller, *Against Our Will* (New York: Simon & Schuster,
1975).

language, with consequent honest misunderstandings between them. In a sense, men and women do seem to know different languages (or dialects) nonverbally, but interpret each other's actions as if they spoke the same language. This "problem in communication," however, woven into the context of sexual dominance and exploitation, is often carried to its extreme, as a basis and justification for rape.

There is another confusion we face when looking at the workings of both sex and power: they are often confounded. That is, males are more likely to have power, females to be out of it. If we identify a particular behavior as more associated with one sex, how can we know whether the basis of the association lies in the sex difference or in the power difference? For example, do male bosses touch female secretaries more than vice versa because they are male or because they are bosses? To speak of touching or being touched as a "sex role" behavior here would obscure the fact that two social hierarchies are involved—one of labor and one of gender.* One way that can help us de-confound sex and power is to look at other sources of power than sex, for example wealth and race. If a behavior that's associated with sex dominance is also associated with economic or race dominance, we have evidence that dominance is the underlying factor. Looking for parallel behaviors in different dominance situations is a practice we'll use often in our investigation of nonverbal power.

There is no reason to assume that the sex differences we will discuss here are immutable, or more specifically, that they are innate and gender-linked. Women's greater sensitivity to people, for instance, can easily be traced to their socialization to a sex role which carries rewards for social awareness and punishments for the lack of it. Likewise, body language like vocal language is learned, not innate. There are aspects of body movement and vocal pitch that are related to anatomical differences between individuals and between the sexes, but they are greatly overshadowed by the learned aspects.

Unfortunately, most of us assign to biology a much greater responsibility for observed sex differences than it can carry. This is a mistake we should avoid from the very beginning in the study of nonverbal communication. In fact, males and females are not as different as they are cracked up to be. Birdwhistell writes that when different animal species are rated on a spectrum by the extent to which their sexes are differentiated, on the basis of secondary sexual characteristics, human beings seem far closer to the

---

* Individual tendencies and biological sex may be involved also; these will be discussed further in this chapter and later in the book.

undifferentiated end of the spectrum than they might like to believe.[26] He states that his work in kinesics (the science of body movement) leads him to postulate "that [humans] and probably a number of other weakly dimorphic species necessarily organize much of gender display and recognition at the level of position, movement, and expression." [27] Thus we realize that most of our nonverbal behavior, far from being "natural," has probably been developed and modified to emphasize and display sex and class differences, much as have our clothing and shelter.

A 1943 article in the journal *Psychiatry* [28] makes a related point; its author traces sexual evolution and concludes, "the *either–or* type of sexual behavior demanded of man and woman by the mores of Western culture under threat of severe penalty is not in line with the trend of sexual adjustment as it has developed throughout biological evolution." [29] The work of psychologist Sandra Bem verifies the maladaptive nature of extreme sexual polarization: in her experiments, neither "masculine" men nor "feminine" women have been as flexible and capable in varied situations and tasks as those "androgynous" people of both sexes who are not rigidly shackled to sex roles.[30]

Thus we have seen several aspects of the relationship between gender and nonverbal behavior: female sensitivity and the importance of nonverbal cues in women's lives; how women's nonverbal behavior may be used against them to justify attack; that females and males seem to bodyspeak different nonverbal languages; but that these differences are learned, and may be maladaptive. We will keep these points in mind as we review the many sex differences that have been found in nonverbal interaction, and compare them with the differences that have been found between the actions of the powerful and powerless.

[26] Ray L. Birdwhistell, "Masculinity and Femininity as Display," in *Kinesics and Context* (Philadelphia: University of Pennsylvania Press, 1970), pp. 39–46. On "the moderate physical dimorphism exhibited in Hominidae compared with, say, the seal family," see D. G. Freedman, "A Biological View of Man's Social Behavior," in William Etkin, *Social Behavior from Fish to Man* (Chicago: University of Chicago Press, 1967), especially pp. 160–61.

[27] Birdwhistell, *Kinesics and Context,* pp. 41–42.

[28] William E. Galt, "The Male–Female Dichotomy in Human Behavior," *Psychiatry,* 1943, 6, 1–14.

[29] Galt, "Male–Female Dichotomy," p. 9.

[30] Sandra L. Bem, "Sex Role Adaptability: One Consequence of Psychological Androgyny," *Journal of Personality and Social Psychology,* 1975, 31, 634–43; and "Androgyny vs. the Tight Little Lives of Fluffy Women and Chesty Men," in *Psychology Today,* September, 1975 (vol. 9, no. 4) 58–62

THE CHICKEN IS POWER

What do we mean by power? Social scientists usually define it in terms of the ability to influence other persons to do what one wants. This influence is generally understood as an asymmetric thing; when two persons shift back and forth in their ability to influence one another, but on the whole succeed about equally, neither is considered to have more power. Moreover, the attempts at exercising power have to work, and work regularly.

People can exert control over others because they have something— either rewards or punishments—the others don't have. Power is thus based on the control of resources, and on their defense: in down-to-earth terms, we know that people in power have the goods and/or the guns that force people to do their bidding. While brute force is seldom faced (by most of us) in daily life, it is nevertheless the ultimate source of power, whether between the state and an individual, or between a man and a woman.[31] The person with these resources has less to gain from a relationship and is consequently freer to move within it.*

How important is power in our daily lives? We may think of power as orders, threats, and coercion, and see little evidence of its use on or by us. But as sociologist George Homans has pointed out, the noncoercive form of power is probably far more common than the coercive.[33] These noncoercions of everyday life are often, as we shall see, in the form of gestures which signal power and assert dominance.

Dominance is sometimes used to mean power in the way I have defined it, but it has a connotation of more blatancy, and refers more often to individuals and individual relationships. In psychological usage it often

---

[31] See Peter M. Blau, *Exchange and Power in Social Life* (New York: Wiley, 1964): ". . . unilateral services that meet basic needs are the penultimate source of power. Its ultimate source, of course, is physical coercion" (p. 22).

* This is the Principle of Least Interest, articulated by Waller in 1938 as follows: "That person is able to dictate the conditions of association whose interest in the continuation of the affair is least." [32] Waller's Principle can be seen to be working against women in male/female relationships: besides their economic dependence, women's socialization typically leads them to care more about relationships.

[32] Willard Waller, *The Family* (New York: Drydan, 1938), p. 275. George Homans, in *Social Behavior: Its Elementary Forms* (New York: Harcourt Brace Jovanovich, 1974), identifies Least Interest as the principle according to which power is actually exercised, and incorporates it in his general definition of power.

[33] Homans, *Social Behavior*, p. 83.

describes a personality tendency, to seek to influence and control others. *Authority* suggests power that is legitimate in some way, such as through law or tradition. But it is power nonetheless, and its supposed legitimacy may be a screen for ruthless power, for example, in the patriarch, teacher, or doctor.

Status is not the same as power, though the two terms are often confused, and sometimes used more or less interchangeably. Status refers to a person's social position, the judgment of that person by the social group (however that's defined, and however it's measured). While status often goes with power and authority, there are times we can recognize them separately, as when an impoverished English lord "commands" a certain respect locally, though he can no longer *literally* command services. Brown states that status ("social value") goes with the possession of characteristics valued by the society, such as good looks, male sex, greater age.[34] Sherif and Sherif, however, place status closer to power, defining it as "a member's position in a hierarchy of power relations in a social unit." [35] Whatever status is, it is at least the *appearance* of power. But that may be all that it is; status accoutrements can give a false impression of power. On this point, I agree with Mills, who wrote, "The chicken is power, and comes first, the egg is status." [36]

In most cases in our experience, power and status are confounded, i.e., a person who has one is likely to have the other. Power is the concern of this book, and a more interesting topic of study in general, but it's harder for social scientists to assess than its outward and visible sign, status. Status has therefore more often been studied as an index of social influence. In our discussion of findings relating nonverbal behavior to power, we will at times review studies involving status, and must draw our conclusions according to our knowledge of the relationship between status and power. (In describing the studies, I'll identify which variable the authors looked at.)

Most discussions of power deal with broad scenarios, the power distribution within communities, the nation, the world. They are apt to be written by political scientists, and focus on control of wealth, industries, political bodies, and armies. Or at the opposite extreme, if they're written by psychologists they're apt to center on individual differences in power motivation. Psychologists often concentrate on dominating and submissive personality "types," with macro-analysis consisting largely of observations of the ways nations behave like (neurotic) people. The approach of social

---

[34] Roger Brown, *Social Psychology* (New York: Free Press, 1965), pp. 55, 73–74.
[35] Sherif and Sherif, *Social Psychology*, p. 140.
[36] C. Wright Mills, *The Power Elite* (New York: Oxford University Press, 1956), p. 264.

psychology has been to look at how *situations* rather than persons are arranged to foster or suppress dominance, and to ask what different factors contribute to overall social organization, for example, how the status quo, with its power relationships, is maintained. My approach is that of social psychology: to look at the everyday social relationships that glue together the social superstructure, to try to see what the glue is and what it's doing there.

This is not to say that the economic and political analyses of macro-structure aren't necessary, or are wrong; but it is to say that they aren't sufficient. In the same way, this book, while it attempts to fill in a neglected area, also deals with only one facet of the whole picture, and is not itself sufficient for an approach to understanding social structure. But it is neces-sary: that neglected area is a huge gap in our knowledge of power—the nonverbal behavior that speaks our truths while our words tell lies of nonpower.

THE LAST GREAT AMERICAN MYTH

I have noted that the power relation has received little notice from stu-dents of nonverbal behavior. This is not surprising, since we tend to sup-press suggestions of inequality in our supposedly egalitarian society. There has been in American social science a strong tendency to assume the Great American Myth of the classless society, to operate in that sterile "middle-class" world of so many movies and television commercials. Particularly in psychology has there been the tendency to deny the social context and see human problems as internally caused, to see the basis for human conflicts in some version of "human nature." Psychologists most often write of hu-man relations as relations between equals, complicated more by failures in communication than by unjust living conditions.

A prime example of this tendency may be seen in Freudian psycho-analysis, whose thrust is (in the words of Ronald Sampson) "to reduce all political conflict to the level of psychic conflict displaced from the private to the public sphere." [37] Freud's patients did not live in inner worlds devoid of status and power; in fact, his patients' problems were quite concerned with issues of status. Sampson points out:

> . . . as we follow Freud through the mass of evidence accumulated in his interpretation of dreams, we notice the important role played again and

[37] Ronald Sampson, *The Psychology of Power* (New York: Random House, 1965); see especially Chapter 2.

again in latent dream thoughts by status anxieties and ambitions arising out of membership of professional or social class groups.[38]

It was Freud's own interpretation that obscured the issue of inequality.

Sampson also calls attention to Freud's inability to "grasp that equality is even desirable in the field of sexual relations." Equality is in fact desirable everywhere—Sampson paints a disturbing picture of the psychic costs of inequality, particularly to the subordinate. We may consciously behave in a manner that will not arouse hostility in the powerful, and in so doing conceal and modify our true thoughts. But as this practice becomes habitual, the suppression becomes unconscious—we lose track of those original thoughts, and there is "a gradual erosion of the ability to formulate and live with a truthful picture of reality." When we recognize our psychic oppression by another and attempt to challenge it by modifying our behavior, tremendous effort is required to overcome the falsified reality, our own fears, and the other's defenses. Much of this struggle takes place, as we shall see, on the nonverbal level, the one we know least about; and of what we know, little helps us understand inequality.

Against all the literature psychology has produced on such topics as achievement motivation, sexual repression, or birth order, there is very little to help us understand the psychological effects of social class, the minutiae of social control, the nitty-gritty of the workings of sex privilege.[39] Little wonder that this is so, for there are strong forces built into a social system to make all its aspects help maintain the status quo, and the academic/intellectual sphere is no exception; it serves as both reflection and justification of the system. The history of social science, as of science in general (and of other fields of study), has been one of service to the prevailing ideology.[40] Many of the early writings in American psychology tended to rationalize, or at least accept, racism, as today many of them rationalize sexism and class privilege (and racism). In Germany, for another example, Nazism needed no better philosophical basis than that offered by its social science apologists, and indeed the Nazis did not need to carry out their own policies of mass murder of mental patients, as the psychiatrists fell over themselves rushing to do it for them.[41]

[38] Sampson, *Psychology of Power,* p. 203.

[39] There are of course exceptions, for instance, in the literature on racial prejudice, or in *Blaming the Victim* (William Ryan, Random House, 1971), or *The Hidden Injuries of Class* (Richard Sennett and Jonathan Cobb, Knopf, 1972).

[40] See Loren Baritz, *The Servants of Power* (Middletown, Conn.: Wesleyan University Press, 1960), for a good analysis of this.

[41] For documentation of both these points, see Fredric Wertham, *A Sign for Cain* (New York: Macmillan, 1966), especially Chapter 9.

If this book scratches off some of the veneer hiding a seldom-faced social reality, it does so in order to help the reader see beneath the veneer and grasp that reality. My emphasis throughout is not on the individual psychic factors in behavior (most often associated with the psychological approach), but on the societal factors more often ignored and avoided. To point to societal factors in human relations is not to say that people don't have any problems of their own making, or interpersonal conflicts largely unrelated to external social conditions. It is to say there are strong external factors, and to make us look at what our beloved social myths would cover up. This is done as both a contribution to scientific advancement—it is bad science to ignore or falsify reality—and as a first step toward changing that reality. To continue pretending there are no effects of social class, indeed no inequality worth looking at, is to take part in a gross and vicious conspiracy of denial, and to help perpetuate the injustices of class and caste.

NONVERBAL BEHAVIOR—THE FIELD OF STUDY

It's not within this book's compass to present an introduction to the study of nonverbal communication, though I shall try to give some minimal knowledge necessary for understanding the phenomena I want to discuss. Interested readers are referred to books I've cited in the area, for a fuller background in nonverbalization. There are a few introductory remarks that may be made, however, lest there be some misinterpretation of what my points are in this presentation.

A Systems Approach. First, though we will be isolating nonverbal communication in order to examine it more closely, I am not suggesting that it *is* isolated in the flow of events and communication. Communication is integral, carried on at many levels and in many channels simultaneously. The artificial divisions of communication created by traditions of study, and by this particular account, are only conventions.

More important, though at times our attention is focused on interactors or behaviors, the overall emphasis—and the essential context for understanding these phenomena—is the total communication situation. As Scheflen has put it, not a "things-and-forces" approach, but a systems, or field, approach. Scheflen has described the way our understanding of nonverbal communication, as of various fields of study, has moved in recent years, from an Aristotelian conceptualization to a field theory (Einsteinian) one.[42] What this means in discussing nonverbal behavior is that, rather than falling into the trap of seeing behaviors as the result of unseen forces such as "emotions" or "drives" and locating these forces in the individual interactors, we focus instead upon the total field, or configuration of events, and the totality of organization and changes within that field. The old approach created part-truth dogmas ("useful for political activities such as concealing how things work or shifting blame," writes Scheflen) which led to warring doctrinal schools, a belief in explanations as the cause of the thing explained, and "unknowables that only an 'expert' can 'see.' "[43] While this sort of enterprise proliferates research and researchers, it diverts attention from the total field which contains (among other things) power differences, social structure, the economy, race, gender, age, and their concomitant expectations.

In this approach, though we may isolate units for examination and clearer understanding, they are not seen as the forces themselves in the interaction—they are best understood when integrated back into the total picture, as units *within a system*.

Problems, Pitfalls, or Possibilities. Second, we must recognize the limitations of this early stage of a field of study. Terminology has been hazy,[44] and at times thinking has been fuzzy. Wiener and his colleagues raise such questions as: Is all nonverbal *behavior* to be taken as nonverbal *communication?* If nonverbal behavior is *interpreted* as communicative (by observers), does that make it so? If a message is "received" but the "sender" claims no intention of sending it (as happens often in psychoanalytic interpretation), can we nevertheless claim that it was sent, albeit unconsciously? Can we talk about *communication* in such a circumstance, especially when there is no known or accepted nonverbal code in the interacting community (except that code used by interpreting "experts")?[45]

Dealing with an area, then, that has such problems in terminology and conceptualization, we must be cautious in interpretation, but not totally rejecting. There is plenty to learn from what has been done even at this early stage of development, and it's hoped that a review such as this can lead both to new conclusions and to new questions. Certainly, focusing on

[42] Albert E. Scheflen, *How Behavior Means* (Garden City, N.Y.: Doubleday Anchor, 1974), particularly chap. 12. See also Scheflen's *Communicational Structure: Analysis of a Psychotherapy Transaction* (Bloomington, Ind.: Indiana University Press, 1973), written in a less popular style. And Starkey Duncan's paper "Nonverbal Communication," *Psychological Bulletin*, 1969, 72, 118–37.
[43] Scheflen, *How Behavior Means*, pp. 187–88.
[44] See Mehrabian, *Nonverbal Communication*, chap. 1, on this.
[45] Morton Wiener, et al., "Nonverbal Behavior and Nonverbal Communication," *Psychological Review*, 1972, 79, 185–214.

power and status should point toward a new direction for nonverbal research, and raise questions about old directions and assumptions. As Wiener, et al., have pointed out, the strange constriction of this area by overattention to affect (emotion) has unnecessarily hindered the exploration of other forms of significance.

Finally, related to some of the above problems, is the fact that much research, perhaps most, in this area has been correlational. That is, investigators have looked at a nonverbal behavior, and noted either the situations in which it occurs, or personality traits of the behavers, and reported it when they found a reliable relation: X and Y are co-occurring. We can't know if X (a situation or trait) causes Y (a behavior), if Y causes X in some way, or if a third factor causes both. For this reason, psychologists have long preferred the experimental method, in which they have some control over the occurrence of factors, as a superior investigative tool.*

Nevertheless, this problem is not so bad in this field as some people make it to be. A good amount of research, such as that in the interracial interview study reported above, is experimental in such a way as to deal with the correlational question. In some other cases, information external to the study can give us clues to causality. In other cases, it simply is helpful to know that certain relationships exist, that certain events co-occur. People armed with this knowledge are ready to test hypotheses about causality through experimentation and in practical experience.

Whether the behaviors we are concerned with are seen as simply *associated* with power, *affecting* it, or *resulting* from it; as *symbols* or *expressions;* as *describing, establishing* or *maintaining* power; we can observe that power and nonverbal behavior are intimately and fruitfully linked, and that their association deserves closer examination.

THE QUESTION OF INDIVIDUAL DIFFERENCES

When the subject of touching is discussed, many persons, even psychologists, tend to dismiss any generalizations about circumstances by reference to individual differences: "I'm a person who just touches others a lot; it has nothing to do with power." It would be foolish to deny that there are individual differences in the tendency to touch, or in any nonverbal behavior, since everyday experience tells us this is so. However, it would be just as foolish to deny that there are differences in extrapersonal factors

* Of course, there are other limitations on experimental method, most notably the question of its translatability to "real world" occurrences.

also—relationships, settings, etc.—which act independently of these individual differences, and may interact with them.

For example, person A may be characterized as a "toucher," while person B may be called a "non-toucher." In relationships with others in which one of these persons is dominant, the amount of touching on the part of both A and B may increase, though A's frequency of touching will remain higher than B's still. In a setting which inhibits the tendency to touch, A's frequency of touching drops, as does B's, but B's remains lower than A's. Thus the presence of individual differences doesn't preclude the presence of variation due to circumstances.* The examination of differences in behavior attributable to social situations has traditionally been the subject matter of social psychology, as the examination of differences attributable to individuals has been the subject matter of personality study. A truly comprehensive psychology will consider both these approaches and integrate them.

ORGANIZATION OF THE BOOK

Out of convenience and a certain amount of logic, I have divided the nonverbal behavior to be reviewed into nine areas of study: we shall begin with the grand schemes of *space, time, and environment,* proceeding from the impersonal to the personal through the subtler aspects of *language* and the global dimension of *demeanor,* finally into *touch, body movement, eye contact,* and *facial expression;* and will then sum up the evidence and it͡ implications.

* It may also be the case, of course, that certain individual differences or tendencies interact with certain social situations in such a way that people's actions are not predictable from knowledge of either factor alone, but this is a subject for research.

chapter two

DON'T FENCE ME IN:

Space

Excerpt from the First Venusian Anthropological Expedition to Earth:

> The most notable feature of their hierarchy is what we have named the "space bubble." All Earthlings have a space bubble around them, the amount of space belonging to their own bodies. (It is slightly variable according to situations and to apparently internal fluctuations.) Dominants have larger space bubbles, whether the innermost "person space" or their larger utilitarian and protective areas, such as vehicles, dwellings, etc.
>
> One need only watch the Earthlings moving about in their bubbles of different sizes, approaching bubble to bubble, to know immediately who is the superior, and who the inferior in an interaction. . . .

Any discussion of spatial division would do well to begin with the concept of territoriality, now widely known and in fact written to death in recent articles and books. Territoriality is a comparatively new concept in biological science, and refers to the behavior of staking out an area, i.e., marking it in some way, and defending it against others of one's species. Territoriality is seen in a complementary relationship with dominance; they are alternative systems for limiting aggression within a species. By these organized relationships, each member of the group is to know its place, both literally and figuratively.

It's not necessary to believe in an innate drive for territory in order to discuss territoriality as a human phenomenon, and the same goes for other aspects of animal behavior. But observing animal behavior, which we can see so much more clearly, in the same way we see other societies with the anthropologist's eye, will illuminate for us various aspects of human non-verbal behavior. Seeing the threatening stare, the appeasing smile, and the territorial defense in animals makes it harder to pass off such behaviors in humans as "individual differences," when they appear under such similar circumstances.*

Spaced-Out Animals. Not only are territoriality and dominance complementary systems for regulating drives, but they are seen to act concurrently. There are both spatial correlates of status levels and status correlates of spatial positions. Sommer [1] describes one example: "In the barnyard the top chickens have the greatest freedom of space and can walk anywhere, whereas lower birds are restricted to small areas and can be pecked by other birds wherever they go." [2] Hall relates the same phenomenon among Norway rats: "High-ranking rats do not have to defer to other rats as much as low-ranking rats. Their status is indicated in part by those areas within the territory which are open to them. The higher the status, the greater the number of areas they may visit." [3]

Freedom of space for locomotion and for one's bodily integrity are not, of course, the same as what is usually discussed as territoriality, but they reflect related aspects of spatial organization correlated with dominance. Another such aspect is what Hall has referred to as animals' "personal distance," that distance normally kept between members of the same species: dominant animals generally have larger personal distances than subordinate ones, and subordinate animals will yield space to dominant ones. Hall remarks that this correlation of personal distance and status in one form or another seems to occur throughout the vertebrate kingdom.[4]

Yielding space to dominants was also observed by Washburn and Devore: "The most dominant males . . . occupy feeding and resting positions of their choice. When a dominant animal approaches a subordinate one, the lesser animal moves out of the way. The observer can determine

* What conclusions may be drawn from the study of naturalistic animal behavior is of course a matter of some controversy at present. Many times in discussion of this issue, data are misused and the tremendous importance of culture overlooked. For further discussion on this topic, see Chapter 11.

[1] Robert Sommer, *Personal Space: The Behavioral Basis of Design* (Englewood Cliffs, N.J.: Prentice-Hall, 1969), p. 17.
[2] Sommer cites Glen McBride, *A General Theory of Social Organization and Behaviour* (St. Lucia: University of Queensland Press, 1964), for this comment.
[3] Edward T. Hall, *The Hidden Dimension* (Garden City, N.Y.: Doubleday, 1966), p. 26.
[4] Hall, *The Hidden Dimension*, p. 13.

the order of dominance simply by watching the reactions of the baboons as they move past each other." [5]

In still another aspect of spatial dominance, *where* one's space is can be as important as the size of it. We're all familiar with the game "King of the Mountain," in which children play at becoming dominant "mountain goat," by achieving the top of some heap. The relation between superior spatial and social position works the other way too, since the superior position gives greater visibility and therefore superior attack and defense capabilities. Horizontal spatial position is just as important as vertical, when it varies with access to an important commodity such as food or (like the hill) information. An example is one scientist's observation of birds' dominance relations, which changed as a feeding station was shifted through different territories. The closer a bird's territory to the feeder, the more dominant it became.[6]

There are several ways, then, in which space reflects dominance in animals:

1. Dominant animals control greater territory.
2. They are freer to move in other animals', or common, territory.
3. They are accorded greater personal (bodily) space.
4. Subordinates yield space to dominants when approached, or in passing.
5. Dominants occupy positions associated with, and/or controlling, desired resources.

Let's now look at how human spatial relations are affected by their hierarchical relations.

VERY SPATIAL PEOPLE

We can observe the same patterns in humans as in animals, but far less research has been done on spatial behavior in human dominance hierarchies. We must therefore examine evidence from diverse sources and piece the picture together.

[5] S. L. Washburn and Irven Devore, "The Social Life of Baboons," *Scientific American*, 1961, 204, no. 6, 62–71. Reprinted in *Primate Social Behavior*, Charles H. Southwick, ed. (Princeton, N.J.: Van Nostrand, 1963); quotation on p. 107.

[6] A. D. Bain, "Dominance in the Great Tit, Parus Major," *Scottish Naturalist*, 1949, 61, 369–472. (Cited in Hall, *The Hidden Dimension*, p. 9.)

Our first observation can be that the social elite is the spatial elite. Privileged people just plain own more space than the less privileged. And they own it in many ways. "In human society," writes Sommer,

the social elite possess more space in the form of larger home sites, more rooms per house, and vacation homes. In addition, they have greater spatial mobility and more opportunities to escape when they become tense, uncomfortable, or bored.[7]

Space is indeed the prerogative of the rich and the powerful; it is the poor who must live in crowded rooms, without yards, in crowded cities; whose schools, hospitals, and even cemeteries must tightly jam bodies together in the meager space allotted.

The territories controlled by the privileged extend from huge parcels of land down to private personal space. Goffman has made the connection between territory control and personal space in his categorization of eight types of "preserves," areas both literally and metaphorically spatial, which describe situational and personal territoriality.

Goffman, too, writes that the extensivity of preserves may vary greatly according to power and rank; those of higher rank not only have greater territories, but have greater control beyond their territorial boundaries. He cites the example that within a given household, "adults tend to have vastly larger territorial claims than do children." [8]

Gaining this extra space, especially symbolically marked territory, can take place in a competitive situation, the greatest prestige accruing to the most successful space-grabber. Freedman writes that in human beings, territoriality, possessiveness, and social status are inextricably interlinked. An example of what he calls "the unclear delineation between territoriality and status in hominid adaptation" [9] may be seen in this communication from a faculty member of a major university (who wishes to remain anonymous):

Last year I had the uncertain privilege of being placed on my department's Space Committee. Never having been on a Space Committee before, I imagined that it was going to be another of those petty bureaucratic assignments that no one cared much about. In fact, I found the first few meetings of the committee to be rather mystifying—it seemed that we were making maps of the department's space in the building and coloring it in four differ-

[7] Sommer, *Personal Space*, p. 17.

[8] Erving Goffman, *Relations in Public: Microstudies of the Public Order* (New York: Basic Books, 1971), Chapter 2.

[9] D. G. Freedman, "A Biological View of Man's Social Behavior," in William Etkin, *Social Behavior from Fish to Man* (Chicago: University of Chicago Press, 967) 8

ent colors—for individual office space, individual laboratory space, shared laboratory space, and the like. It was only gradually that it dawned on me that I was taking part in no mere exercise, but rather in the renegotiation of treaties in a newly reorganized department, in the manner of Truman, Churchill, and Stalin at Potsdam, and with a comparable degree of emotion on the part of all concerned parties. The arguments had relatively little to do with who really needed the space (e.g., for research or animal cages or whatever), and more to do with feelings about how much space they had had in the past, how much they had been promised, and how much they deserved—the assignment of offices, laboratories, and the like was taken as central to their status and worth as human beings.

We will see further mention of the effects of spatial acquisition when we discuss the environmental aspects of power in the pages ahead. As a final example of the thoroughness with which greater space is taken up by the privileged in every way, high status people even take up more space with their signatures. The higher your place on the academic ladder, from undergrad to professor, one study found, the bigger your signature is likely to be! [10]

Analogous to the freedom dominant animals have to be abroad in other animals' territories is the control that ranking humans have beyond their territorial limits. The boss may freely walk into lesser employees' offices and desk areas, but the subordinates don't have the same privilege of entering the boss's office. The dominant gang in a city area may tread with impunity the turf of rival gangs, but the reverse is not true.

As among animals, not only do the spatial elite own more space, but they own the most *desirable* spatial positions, too, whether they be the beachfront home or the seat on the 50-yard line, the farm with fertile land or the hotel suite with a fantastic view. Even in such seeming trivia as positions at the dining table, elaborate protocol determines that VIPs will sit in varying positions of privilege determined by their relative rank. While such positions have little real advantage in access to resources (they have some), their main function is symbolic.

Higher status persons take and are ceded positions of privilege or command in informal seating arrangements as well. In a series of studies of this phenomenon, Lott and Sommer had students indicate, by questionnaire response or by action, where they would locate themselves at a rectangular table, in relation to another (hypothetical) person. The other was designated as of higher, lower or equal status, male or female. There was a clear tendency for subjects when of superior status to take the "head" position

[10] K. Zweigenhaft, "Signature Size: Key to Status Awareness," *Journ* of *Social Psychology*, 1970, 81, 49–54.

(short end of the table) and when subordinate, to assign it to the other.[11] In small groups, leaders tend to take the head positions. For example, in experimentally-created juries, not only were those at the head positions more likely to be elected "foreman," but persons of higher socioeconomic status (e.g., proprietors and managers) also tended to select those head seats for themselves when entering the room.[12]

Thus, control of greater territory, control of more desirable territory, and freer mobility, three ways we saw among animals in which space reflects dominance, characterize humans high in the social hierarchy. What of hierarchies and human personal distance? First let us see how social scientists have looked at the use of space between and among humans; this study has been termed *proxemics*.

Zoning Restrictions.   Several writers have suggested systems of zones or interpersonal distances, which characterize the relationship and business of an interaction. Different cultures will have similar zones, but the distances will vary between cultures, with Anglo-Saxon-derived cultures, as usual, being the most distant. Here is the system proposed by Hall; it is presented in full because we will have reason to refer to it later. There are four divisions of "informal space," with typical American distances as follows: [13]

Intimate Distance
> Close phase: 0–6 inches. For very intimate (usually non-public) interaction, often involving body contact, such as love-making, wrestling, comforting, protecting.
> Far phase: 6–18 inches. For less intense but still intimate interaction; usually considered improper in public (except in impersonal situations like crowded subways, where defensive devices counteract it), although seen among younger people.

Personal Distance (the usual distance we maintain between ourselves and others)
> Close phase: 1½–2½ feet. For people bonded in some way, such as wife and husband, parent and child.
> Far phase: 2½–4 feet. The limit of physical domination; used for discussing subjects of personal interest and involvement.

Social Distance
> Close phase: 4–7 feet. For impersonal business; used by people who work together, or at a casual social gathering.

[11] Dale F. Lott and Robert Sommer, "Seating Arrangements and Status," *Journal of Personality and Social Psychology*, 1967, 7, 90–95.
[12] Fred L. Strodtbeck and L. H. Hook, "The Social Dimensions of a Twelve Man Jury Table," *Sociometry*, 1961, 24, 397–415.
[13] Hall, *The Hidden Dimension*, Chap. 10, especially pp. 110–22.

Far phase: 7–12 feet. For formal business and social discourse, as in offices, or in a home when the occupants are uninvolved.

Public Distance

Close phase: 12–25 feet. Possible to take action if threatened. More formal speech and occasions involved, such as a presentation to a small audience, brief impersonal messages such as requests to get something.

Far phase: 25 feet or more. Nonverbal gestures become more important (e.g., for actors), or speech amplification is used. When between non-strangers, it's generally because of necessity, as when one shouts to another from house to yard, or across a playing field.

We have, then, distances appropriate to certain types of interaction, and we adjust our positions accordingly. Or, if our positions are set, they may influence the nature of the interaction. These zones also affect and are affected by our social hierarchies, as Goffman pointed out with his notion of "preserves." The "proper" distance to be kept in an interaction is under the control of the more powerful person; thus, too, the nature of the interaction may be affected.

It's not hard to think of examples in which dominant individuals are given more personal space: such situations are even codified into certain social systems. For instance, in the military, junior officers approach to three paces from a senior officer—too deferent, as Hall points out, for comfortable conversation.[14] And Indian caste distances, the prescribed distances maintained between members of different castes, have been similarly specified.[15]

Hall suggests that "Thirty feet is the distance that is automatically set around important public figures," citing the example in White's *The Making of the President 1960:* When John Kennedy's nomination for president became a certainty, "others in the room surged forward on impulse to join him. Then they halted. A distance of perhaps 30 feet separated them from him, but it was impassable." [16] (Many times, personal space isn't automatically ceded to public figures, but is created by bodyguards or a retinue of friends, employees, and hangers-on.)

Those examples show the correlation of *status* and personal space. The relationship to *dominance* is less well researched, but King, who demonstrated a correlation of individual distance and dominance among chickens, has done the same among children. He found that pre-schoolers kept a

14 Edward T. Hall, *The Silent Language* (Garden City, N.Y.: Doubleday, 1959), p. 163.

15 See Goffman, *Relations in Public*, p. 44.

16 Hall, *The Hidden Dimension*, p. 117. Theodore H. White, *The Making of the President 1960* (New York: Atheneum, 1961).

greater distance from another child who had previously established dominance over them.[17]

Yielding space to dominants is a phenomenon studied less in humans than it has been in animals. One researcher who has looked at street proxemics suggests that for young American males, passing on the street may be the occasion for an abbreviated aggressive display. He found that males in his real-life observational study passed other males at a much closer distance (mean 4.6 inches) than they did females (12.8 inches) or than females passed each other (mean 12.0).[18] If this situation is indeed the setting for aggressive display, it may also be the setting for the exchange of gestures of dominance and submission, as tokens of the social structure. We shall see later that females yield space to males. Personal space then is affected by dominance, certainly in the amount of space typically accorded another person and apparently in the fact of a subordinate's yielding space to a dominant person. In all five ways in which dominance and space are related in animals, they are related in humans.

[17] Murray G. King, "Interpersonal Relations in Preschool Children and Average Approach Distance," *Journal of Genetic Psychology*, 1966, 109, 109–16.
[18] Dean C. Ing, "Sex Differences and Street Proxemics," talk given at Western Speech Communication Association, November 1974. Ing demonstrated the validity and reliability of such observer judgments of passing proximity in his dissertation, "Proxemics Simulation: A Validation Study of Observer Error," University of Oregon, 1974.

SPACE/RACE

We would expect space distribution to be affected by racial and ethnic factors, which are correlated with class and power, but there is not a great deal of solid information here. In the first place, some findings on ethnic factors in spacing are ambiguous. For example, measuring how close people came to each other to speak, Willis found a Caucasian (within-race) median approach distance of 22.5 inches, and a Negro median distance of 24 inches, indicating that blacks tend to prefer greater interpersonal distances than whites. Connolly, with a different technique, found the opposite tendency. Blacks in Connolly's study, judging pictures of men facing each other at varying distances, preferred *less* space between speakers (21-24 inches) than did whites (26-28 inches).[19]

As would be expected, cross-race interpersonal distances are greater than those within race. Willis found in one group that whites approached whites to a median 22 inches, and approached blacks to a median 28 inches.* There is undoubtedly here an effect of stigma, which was previously discussed. We would expect greater interracial distance, where it occurs, to be learned distance, and this is supported by research: one investigation of black-white dyads in schools showed a steady growth of interpersonal distances, from primary grades through intermediate and junior high.[20]

Speculations about other subcultural spacing differences have not been uniformly supported. In an observational study at the Houston Zoo, Baxter did observe large and significant † differences in spacing among ethnic groups: Mexican-Americans stood closest, followed by Anglo-Americans and Black-Americans.[21] But Jones reports two studies of Black, Puerto

19 Frank N. Willis, Jr., "Initial Speaking Distance as a Function of the Speakers' Relationship," *Psychonomic Science*, 1966, 5, 221–22. Patrick Connolly, doctoral dissertation, University of Iowa, 1974.

* Looking at it from another angle, however (not how close whites approach others, but how close others approach whites), the difference between blacks and whites approaching whites was not significant. (Such findings don't support previous suggestions of greater space accorded to higher-status persons, but in this study there were probably few status differences, despite the racial differences, since most subjects were college students. Also, the number of subjects here was small, and the significance of the findings marginal.)

20 Virginia C. Dennis and Eva R. Powell, "Nonverbal Communication in Across-Race Dyads," *Proceedings, 80th Annual Convention*, American Psychological Association, 1972, 7, Part 2, 557–58.

† Psychologists determine the statistical significance of a finding by calculating the probability that it might have happened just through chance alone. If that probability is a long shot, less than one in 20 (.05), they are generally willing to accept the finding as valid, unlikely to be due to chance.

21 James C. Baxter, "Interpersonal Spacing in Natural Settings," *Sociometry*, 1970 33 444–56.

Rican, Italian and Chinese subcultures in six areas of New York City,[22] in neither of which were found significant differences between cultures, either in standing distance or in body orientation angle (directness). In fact 80 percent of the people in his second study stood about 1½-2½ feet from one another, Hall's "close" phase of Personal Distance for middle-class Eastern Americans.

Jones suggests that this cultural homogeneity in distance, closer than persons of the dominant culture would be expected to stand, may reflect a "culture of poverty," i.e., that class differences override ethnic differences in spacing. This possibility underscores again the importance of status and power factors in nonverbal communication, compared with the ethnic differences which have been so highly touted.

THE INCREDIBLE SHRINKING WOMAN

Comparing female/male space use with that of subordinate/superior among animals and humans, we can observe that in general, females in our society have control over less territory, and less desirable territory, than do males. This is so largely because of the privileges many men obtain by virtue of their status. Of course, as we have already noted, sex and status are confounded variables in our society—males are likely to have higher status, and those spaces that come with it—such as roomy offices, private dens, more spacious possessions (boats, cars, airplanes, extra homes, etc.). As professionals and managers they retain privileged space at the centers of power—sumptuously-outfitted offices in strategic locations, with picture windows, private elevators, and private washrooms. Their female secretaries have less space, less fancy furnishings, common washrooms and elevators, and perhaps no window (depending on their and their boss's status). Women's consignment to poorer spatial positions, the windowless office, because of status has been immortalized in *Rooms with No View,* a collection of essays by women in the media. An anonymous writer describes the situation at one TV network:

> The NBC Spot Sales Department has sixteen male salesmen and sixteen female sales assistants. The salesmen hustle television spots (sixty- thirty- and ten-second commercial breaks) to advertisers. They sit in individual windowed offices. The women are crowded (all sixteen of them) on to the outer-office floor. The noise of sixteen typewriters, telephones, and voices on that outer floor is almost deafening.[23]

[22] Stanley E. Jones, "A Comparative Proxemics Analysis of Dyadic Interaction in Selected Subcultures of New York City," *Journal of Social Psychology,* 1971, 84, ?5–44.

[23] Ethel Strainchamps, ed., *Rooms with No View: A Woman's Guide to the Man' World of the Media* (New York: Harper & Row, 1974), p. 12.

Who gets the preferred space, and who the less preferred, is not a function of hierarchical position alone; sex is also a determinant even when other aspects of status are held constant. In one series of studies, students were given diagrams of rectangular tables and asked to indicate where they would sit if meeting another person in the cafeteria, and where they thought the other would sit.[24] The other person was described as either female or male, and at one of three status levels relative to the student: a professor (higher), a fellow student (equal), or a first-year student "who wasn't doing well in school" (lower). Females were more likely than males to choose a side-by-side seating arrangement, which was also characteristic of lower status persons. Professors were most often assigned to the head chair, but some students chose the head chair for themselves; of these, 37 chose it vis-à-vis "Professor *Susan* Smith," while about half as many chose it vis-à-vis "Professor *Henry* Smith."

Irene Frieze has reviewed the literature relating space and sex, and notes a survey of lower middle-class homes that found mothers were less likely to have a special room in the home than fathers, and any personal area they might have was more public than fathers' areas. Frieze adds her own observation that fathers are more likely to have a "special chair" than mothers. Moreover, she speculates that men take up more space than women when a man and a woman sleep together on a double bed, space beyond that proportional to men's larger size.[25]

A number of studies indicate that, as in other situations of dominance, males have larger personal space than females do.[26] A general finding for closeness within dyads has been that female-female pairs are spaced closer than male-male pairs, while female-male pairs are either intermediate or closer than female pairs.[27] This tendency has been shown not only in real human interaction, but in people's perceptions during experiments—e.g., in estimating on a diagram how close people would approach, or in placing small figures in a field.[28]

24 Dale F. Lott and Robert Sommer, "Seating Arrangements and Status."

25 Irene Frieze, "Nonverbal Aspects of Femininity and Masculinity which Perpetuate Sex-Role Stereotypes," presented to Eastern Psychological Association, 1974. The survey cited by Frieze is "The Ecology of Home Environments," by I. Altman and P. A. Nelson (Technical Report, Project No. 0-0502, U.S. Department of Health, Education and Welfare, Office of Education, January, 1972).

26 Gary W. Evans and Roger B. Howard have reviewed these studies in "Personal Space," *Psychological Bulletin*, 1973, 80, 334–44.

27 See, for example, Baxter, "Interpersonal Spacing in Natural Settings"; Robert Sommer, "Studies in Personal Space," *Sociometry*, 1959, 22, 247–60; R. J. Pellegrini and J. Empey, "Interpersonal Spatial Orientation in Dyads," *Journal of Psychology*, 1970, 76, 67–70.

28 For example, Darhl M. Pedersen and Anne B. Heaston, "The Effects of Sex of Subject, Sex of Approaching Person, and Angle of Approach Upon Personal Space," *Journal of Psychology*, 1972, 82, 277–86.

These studies have largely been done with white subjects, however; the same results may not be found in the case of other cultures or inter-cultural contact. For example, Dennis and Powell found that black female pupils interacted with white classmates at a much *greater* distance than did black males (about 12 cm. average, vs. about 4.8 cm., respectively). This difference grew over the years in school, affecting female contacts more heavily than male ones: black male interactions involving touch or physical contact with white classmates decreased from 63 percent to 61 percent to 53 percent from primary to intermediate to junior high grades; but black females' contact interactions with whites went from 50 percent to 38 percent to 0! We do not know from this study whether one or both interactants determined the distance between them (and if one, which), nor do we know if the interaction distance varied with white interactants' sex also. Thus we cannot know whether the greater distance between black females and white classmates is due to (say) stigmatizing, deference, or other factors.

Not only women's territory and personal space, but their very bodily demeanor must be restrained and restricted spatially. Their femininity is gauged, in fact, by how little space they take up, while men's masculinity is judged by their expansiveness and the strength of their flamboyant gestures. The novelist Marge Piercy has captured this contrast in describing what Wanda, the organizer of a theater group, teaches the members about movement:

> Wanda made them aware how they moved, how they rested, how they occupied space. She demonstrated how men sat and how women sat on the subway, on benches. Men expanded into available space. They sprawled, or they sat with spread legs. They put their arms on the arms of chairs. They crossed their legs by putting a foot on the other knee. They dominated space expansively.
>
> Women condensed. Women crossed their legs by putting one leg over the other and alongside. Women kept their elbows to their sides, taking up as little space as possible. They behaved as if it were their duty not to rub against, not to touch, not to bump a man. If contact occurred, the woman shrank back. If a woman bumped a man, he might choose to interpret it as a come-on. Women sat protectively using elbows not to dominate space, not to mark territory, but to protect their soft tissues.[29]

These observations go beyond the discussion of the space one occupies, into how we move our bodies to occupy less or more space. A later chapter will examine these differences in female/male "body language" (and essentially verify Piercy's observations).

[29] Marge Piercy, *Small Changes* (New York: Doubleday, 1973), p. 438

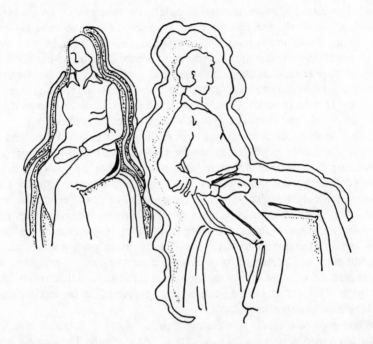

Despite the fact that women take up less space in many ways, there is evidence that what space they do have is violated more than men's is. For example, both females and males have been found to approach females more closely than they approach males.[30]

Phyllis Chesler has commented on the violability of women's space—particularly by their children. At the same time, she makes an astute observation on children's territory rights:

> Most children in contemporary American culture invade their mother's privacy, life space, sanity, and selves to such an extent that she must give up these things in order not to commit violence. (Invasion of a boundary into deserted territory is perhaps less painful than one into occupied and functional territory. Of course, such invasion is practiced by mothers against children. Fathers invade children too, but not as frequently. They don't have to: they already own the entire territory and need only make occasional forays to check on their holdings.) [31]

Crowding is a context of frequent, and mutual, spatial invasion, and a subject of some social concern as our cities become more densely popu-

[30] Willis, "Initial Speaking Distance," pp. 221–22.
[31] Phyllis Chesler, *Women and Madness* (New York: Doubleday, 1972), p. 294.

lated. Do men and women respond differently to crowds? To study this question, Marshall and Heslin created various kinds of crowds—large and small, dense and sparse, same-sex and mixed-sex. Females and males were asked their preference for different kinds of groups, but their responses were somewhat complex: while males preferred mixed-sex groups, females preferred mixed-sex groups if they were large, and same-sex groups if they were small. Females also preferred mixed-sex groups if they were crowded, and same-sex groups if they were uncrowded.

These findings differ somewhat from findings in similar studies, and the authors discuss the possible reasons for these differences. In a particularly interesting theoretical contribution, they point out that the loss of individuality (deindividuation) that comes with anonymity in group situations can release not only inhibited negative behaviors, but positive ones as well. Since women are traditionally more inhibited in their behavior than men, the effects of deindividuation in groups will be more pronounced on them. This explains the preference for mixed-sex groups only when large: mixed-sex situations are presumed to be more arousing of various emotions, and the expression of these emotions is released through deindividuation when the groups are large; in same-sex groups, presumed to be less arousing, such release was not necessary.[32]

When women's space is unilaterally invaded, their reaction seems to differ from men's, in ways that indicate their violability. In sidewalk invasions of personal space in Atlanta, Georgia, female subjects were found more likely than males to move out of the way when their space was invaded while they were waiting for a traffic light.[33] In Eugene, Oregon, Jeanette Silveira observed people passing on the sidewalk, and noted who got out of the other's way. In 12 out of 19 mixed-sex encounters she observed, it was the woman who moved; in four cases both moved, and in three cases the man did. (In single-sex encounters, about 50 percent of the time both persons moved; the other half of the time only one moved.)[34]

Similarly a student at Michigan State University made sidewalk observations in the Lansing, Michigan area involving over 100 subjects.[35] She

[32] Joan E. Marshall and Richard Heslin, "Boys ano Girls Together: Sexual Composition and the Effect of Density and Group Size on Cohesiveness," Journal of Personality and Social Psychology, 1975, 31, 952–61.

[33] James M. Dabbs, Jr., "Sex, Setting and Reactions to Crowding on Sidewalks," Proceedings, 80th Annual Convention, American Psychological Association, 1972, 205–06; Nancy Felipe and Robert Sommer, "Invasions of Personal Space," Social Problems, 1966, 14, 206–14.

[34] Jeanette Silveira, "Thoughts on the Politics of Touch," Women's Press (Eugene, Ore.), 1972, 1, 13 (Feb.), 13.

[35] Katherine McKinney, paper for Sociology of Sex Roles (Barrie Thorne, teacner), Michigan State University, 1974.

found not only that women tended to move out of the way more frequently than men did, but also that women moved earlier in the encounter (and younger people also tended to yield to older). And in Sidney, Australia, researchers made observations of human crowd motion; from their analysis they suggested that in a crosswalk "female pedestrians are much more easily perturbed [by cars] in their motion than males." [36]

A number of studies have also shown a difference in men's and women's preference for the direction in which someone may approach them, men showing more anxiety in head-on approach and women, in side approach.[37] Though we cannot know the reasons for this difference, it is possibly related to different threatening experiences for the two sexes: for men, face-to-face competition; for women, sexual threat from one who may jump from the alley or sit beside them in the movie.

The reactions in which women move to accommodate others (even cars) more than men do parallel human and animal findings that subordinates are more likely to yield personal space when approached than are dominants. Greater female deference may explain certain discrepant findings, for example, that black females interacted at a greater distance from white classmates than did black males; or that female subjects in a doll-placing experiment, when asked to depict interaction with authority, saw interactions of the dolls with authority figures (both dolls female) as taking place at a greater distance than men viewed similar transactions between male figures.[38] Unfortunately, there has not been systematic study of spatial deference. Many studies of human spacing fail to note that spatial approach is not necessarily a reciprocal variable socially; i.e., A may not approach B to the same distance that B may approach A.

There have been other apparent inconsistencies in the findings on space and sex, which have been discussed by several authors.[39] Some reason for the discrepancies can easily be found in the different methods and conceptualizations used in the various studies. In addition, sex difference findings may be unclear because in reality they are not so simple and clearcut, as, for example, always smaller personal distance among females.

[36] L. F. Henderson and D. J. Lyons, "Sexual Differences in Human Crowd Motion," *Nature*, 1972, 240, 353–55.

[37] Jeffrey D. Fisher and Donn Byrne, "Too Close for Comfort: Sex Differences in Response to Invasions of Personal Space," *Journal of Personality and Social Psychology*, 1975, 32, 15–21.

[38] Kenneth B. Little, "Cultural Variations in Social Schemata," *Journal of Personality and Social Psychology*, 1968, 10, 1–7.

[39] See Evans and Howard, "Personal Space," pp. 334–44; Baxter, "Interpersonal Spacing," pp. 444–56; and Nancy M. Henley, "Women and Men: the Silent Power Struggle," paper presented at Seventh Annual Conference on Applied Linguistics, 1976.

The truer sex difference may be in the *way* in which females and males respond to situations. Several studies illustrate, for example, that females respond (more) to differences which males fail to (or hardly) recognize nonverbally. In one, females differentiated spatially between the sexes in approaching them, while males did not. In another, spacing in public dyads containing females was greatly affected by the relationship between the two, while spacing in all-male dyads was not. And in a third, female subjects placed drawn figures significantly differently according to the background setting, though male subjects did not.*

We are not surprised to find, again, that females show more nonverbal response to social factors such as relationship, or that space is the medium for this response. Space is a factor, it would seem, capable of much manipulation, more perhaps than many of our body language "parts of speech."

Our discussion of the relation of spatial and hierarchical orders in humans shows that the same factors prevail here as in the animal world. Though little aware of it we may be, our world is set up so that powerful humans own more territory, move through common areas and others' territory more freely, and take up more space with their bodies, possessions and symbols. We yield space to them and they grab it from us, either openly or covertly as the occasion (and our acquiescence) allow. Even that corner of the world we call our own is less desirable, as space is evaluated, if we are not of the spatial elite. It will not gain us the resources, the privileges, the pleasures, even the survival possibilities, that come with the space of the powerful. This is what "position" means in life.

* In the first study, subjects in a group situation approached each other one at a time. Females approached other females more closely than they did males; but the male subjects did not differentiate spatially between the sexes. (Interestingly, participants subjected to a stress condition, in this and other experiments, also approached others less closely; could stress be a factor in this sex difference?) Michael A. Dosey and Murray Meisels, "Personal Space and Self-Protection," *Journal of Personality and Social Psychology,* 1969, 11, 93–97.

In the second study, Stanley Heshka and Yona Nelson took candid photos of public dyads in London and found that dyads of males stood at the same general distance, regardless of their relationship to each other. In female-male or all-female dyads, however, strangers stood farther apart than friends. "Interpersonal Speaking Distance as a Function of Age, Sex, and Relationship," *Sociometry,* 1972, 35, 491–98.

In the third study, female and male subjects placed drawn figures (of the same sex as the subject) on drawn backgrounds to represent interaction for different degrees of acquaintance. Females placed figures in the street at a greater distance than those in an office. Kenneth B. Little, "Personal Space," *Journal of Experimental Social Psychology,* 1965, 1, 237–47.

chapter three

DON'T CLOCK ME IN:

Time

"I have to wait?"

It was more of a wail than a question. Should the Secretary of State, Henry Kissinger, destiny's own man, be asked to cool his heels while the African Affairs Subcommittee went off to the Senate floor for a vote? It seemed unconscionable, but it was happening.[1]

Thus Mary McGrory describes the affront shown to the Secretary of State when he appeared before a Congressional subcommittee at the time when his Superman suit was beginning to wear thin. The committee chose a fitting way to demonstrate his lack of importance to them—keeping someone waiting probably does more to reduce someone's stature than telling the person verbally how you feel. Time is far from a neutral philosophical/physical concept in our society: it is a political weapon.

Before we examine the explicit power aspects of time, it will help to re-orient our understanding of it by looking at the parallels between time and space.

The Space–Time Continuum. Our language speaks of time in spatial metaphor, so everyone uses the space–time analogy: we would all understand the statement, "I like to space out my time," for instance. We make such a translation all the time, as when a queue (space order) is formed to signify order of arrival (time order). Hall shows that such a translation exists in other animals also, in describing reactions to a "behavioral sink," a pathology of social organization and behavior that develops when ani-

[1] "Congress Keeps Kissinger Waiting," Boston *Globe,* January 31, 1976, p. 8.

mals are collected together in unusually large numbers. In one such sink, three groups of rats developed, led by three dominant males. These rats staked out and defended territories of *time* at the feeding place rather than of space, since there was no space.[2] This is among humans also the manner of allocating space too valuable for a single (ordinary) person to own: time-limited "ownership" is used with such luxuries as resort accommodations.*

Carrying the space–time analogy farther, we may think of time-segments which are appropriate to particular types of encounters, as we have characterized space segments in this way. The most impersonal and most "distant" encounters, as with a stranger asking directions, are handled in the briefest way. But those with whom we spend large blocks of time voluntarily are those with whom we are most intimate and for whom we feel affection. It's apparent, then, that the extent of "time zones" is *directly* proportional to the intimacy of the situation, unlike that of space zones, which is *inversely* proportional.

Though I make no claim to having conducted a formal survey of time zones in American culture, I will speculate on the zones analogous to Hall's four space zones, discussed in the previous chapter.

Public Time, that engaged in anonymous and/or uninvolved interaction such as asking directions, checking out library books, etc., would seem to last from a few seconds to a few minutes. Corresponding to the 30-foot space bumper around VIPs is a time bumper: we get a few tenths of a second of their handshake in a receiving line. (People who represent institutions, or events, such as the Easter Seal poster child, may have 15 minutes of a president's time, but I suspect that little of their 15 minutes is actually engaged in personal interaction.)

Social Time, for impersonal business, as in making purchases or inquiring about services, may be from a few up to 15 or so minutes.

Personal Time, that amount by which members of our species ordinarily present ("space") themselves, may be from 15–30 minutes. I arrive at this in considering the rate at which we choose to be among a succession of people (a time queue, like a space queue). It seems that despite the gross diversities in the type of business to be conducted, from job interviews to doctor and dentist appointments to college advising or seeing constituents, appointments are set a either 15 or 30 minutes apart.

Intimate Time is the most extensive (as Intimate Space is the least ex-

[2] Edward T. Hall, *The Hidden Dimension* (Garden City, N.Y.: Doubleday, 1966), pp. 26–27.
* Humans may make this time–space trade-off in ways detrimental to them. Hall has suggested that Americans' misuse of space, and lack of proper planning for it, re balanced by an overemphasis on time planning.

tensive). When longer appointments are kept, such as the typical 50 minutes for therapy, marriage counseling, and other forms of consultation, the encounter clearly takes on an intimate aspect, evidenced by the personal nature of the information passed. This is the "far" zone for Intimate Time; the "close" zone, the amount of time spent with true intimates, is limited only by our tolerance for each other. Though couples and families on vacation, or retired, may find themselves spending 24 hours a day together, I believe there is still a preferred limit, which may be no more than a few hours (even on honeymoons!). One or the other may invoke the limit kindly or violently, but it will be invoked.

For all these time zones, as with space zones, violations are perceived when the boundaries are exceeded. We grow irritated with loved ones we've been with for too long, and we grow irritated with the stranger who takes up more than a minute of our time (this is like coming too close). To spend an hour in impersonal business is an imposition also. On the other hand, we are hurt when a loved one gives us too little time, or offended when a business contact does the same.

Temporal imposition may be handled by the manipulation of space: a long engagement with one person, as with a receptionist or social worker, is best handled at a great distance. Thus large waiting rooms may make long waits more bearable; being close-quartered with someone with whom you have long impersonal business would be uncomfortable. Close up, social relations would tend to develop in that space of time. Brief encounters, of course, may be handled, and generally are, at a fairly close distance.

As with space, the more powerful person in an encounter will control the length of the interaction and its nature. Just as the powerful have the privilege of getting as close as they wish to us, they have the privilege of taking up as much of our time as they wish. As we must stand at a greater distance from them, so must we also ask for only small periods of their time.

Finally, we see with time, as with space, touching, and other aspects of social organization, the dual system of power and intimacy. Between peers, time is equally shared—short periods for the unacquainted or distant, long periods for the close and intimate. But time is asymmetrically distributed between nonequals: the powerful share as little of their time as possible with the powerless while the powerless must give up time as the powerful demand it.

Barry Schwartz has provided a telling political analysis of an important aspect of time in our society, waiting. He devastates the simplistic analysis of waiting which suggests that delay is caused merely by scarcities of goods and services. His main proposition is "that the distribution of waiting time

coincides with the distribution of power."[3] Schwartz notes too the parallel of social distance and "temporal distance," both of which serve the elevation of those who impose them. Without distance barriers between them, strata would tend to erode: making people wait, like keeping them spatially removed, serves to maintain the boundaries of hierarchy.

Though usually we expend time only for the sake of a benefit we desire, Schwartz points out, in waiting our time is transformed into a resource governed only by the one we're waiting for. And though such waiting is negative to us, it often furthers the interests of the one keeping us waiting. Schwartz's comment on the psychological aspects of delay is especially noteworthy:

> The person who is delayed is not merely in a condition of objective dependence and subordination; because his only duty is to attend the call of a server, the waiter feels dependent and subordinate. To be kept waiting—especially to be kept waiting an unusually long while—is to be the subject of an assertion that one's own time (and, therefore, one's social worth) is less valuable than the time and worth of the one who imposes the wait. . . . Of course, waiting does not create the sense of subordination but only ac-

[3] Barry Schwartz, "Waiting, Exchange, and Power: The Distribution of Time in Social Systems," *American Journal of Sociology*, 1974, 79, 841–70. See also his *Queueing and Waiting: Studies in the Social Organization of Access and Delay* (Chicago: Univ. of Chicago Press, 1975).

centuates an initial inferiority, which is often presupposed by the fact that one is waiting in the first place. It needs to be said that this same sentiment has its parallel on the other side of the relationship, for the server calls out in himself the responses that he elicits in the ones he keeps waiting, which enables him not only to be conscious of his own power—to see himself from the point of view of his clients—but also to feel within himself the independent power that he extracts from those who wait for him.[4]

"Ritual waiting," which Schwartz defines as that imposed without reference to scarcity of server time, is a form of mystification. A server's inaccessibility itself promotes awe of his or her scarcity and social value, and finally attending to a client after a long waiting period in itself confers some immediate relief. The more important the person, the longer we will ungrudgingly wait for the service or the honor of attention. Waiting may even be offered up, in a ceremonial fashion, solely to express deference to another.

BUYING TIME

To illustrate and expand on Schwartz's observations, it will help again to compare time distribution to space distribution. At first glance it seems that the political use of time is different from such use of space. After all, it is those in power who have the *least* time, isn't it? And those most powerless who have "time on their hands"—for example, children, the aged, the unemployed, mental patients, other prisoners. And we all have 24 given hours a day, don't we, rich or poor?

No, contrary to outside appearances, time hogging is little different from space hogging. Time, like space, is in the control of those with more power, and they soak it up from the rest of us like so much virgin territory to be claimed. Unfortunately, time, unlike space, has few legal restrictions, and it is thus all the more vulnerable to rampant colonization and annexation.

First let's review the outside-appearances evidence. People of power are usually so time-tied that their days are boxed in minute for minute. "I can't call my time my own," they will say. Their time is so valuable ("Time is Money") they often will share it with others only at a dear price, in whatever is the commodity of the moment (for example, $100 per hour, or acceptance of guilt feelings for taking their precious time). They are not expected to wait for anyone, but others expect to be kept waiting for them. At places where they go others may wait in line, but these powerful are led through first. More often, for things that others wait in line for,

4 Schwartz, "Waiting, Exchange, and Power," p. 856.

they can afford to go where there is no waiting, or to have someone else wait in line for them. Alas, they have no time to spare.

Poor and powerless people, on the other hand, often find themselves with too much "time to spare." As a prisoner will often write, "Time is the one thing I have plenty of." And working people in low echelon positions are through when they punch out of the job—they're not on call day and night as many upper-level company managers are. They can call their nights and weekends their own, at least. A 40-hour week, despite the difference in earnings, must be a time boon over someone with an 80-hour week.

Yes, this is the way we are taught to look at it, and No, that's not the way it is at all.

The poor may "have plenty of time," but they had better have time, since a great portion of their time is spent waiting. Their lives are filled with waiting—in hospital emergency rooms and clinics, for unemployment or welfare benefits, for food stamps; in courts, in discount stores, for every service they have claim to. They wait. This waiting can cost them much of their wages. Since many services aren't available in non-working hours, working people paid by the day or hour lose money having to take time off from work for these necessities. But those in managerial positions and upwards can take an hour or half day for court, dentists, sick children, car repairs, and so on without penalty, or have someone else obtain these services for them.[5] For really important people, as Schwartz points out, servers will bring their services to them. And on those rare occasions when they must wait, as in airports, VIPs will have superior facilities to wait in—like "VIP lounges." Indeed, time is money to all of us, rich or poor.

There is another aspect to the relation between social class and use of time. Occasional writers have claimed that the shortened work week and work day have created a new "leisure class" of working people, who have both the time and the savings to engage in virtually the same recreational activities as the rich—skiing, sailing, luxury cruises—the works. (Of course, as these become recreational activities for the working class, the rich vacate them, or have grander versions.) How to spend leisure time, they say, is the problem of the future; thus the old class distinctions are breaking down.

But socialist scholars go beyond this one-eyed analysis and note two sides to the trend in working-class time allocation. There has developed a dramatic contrast in the relationship of the working class to the process

[5] D. H. J. Morgan has written, "the lower one gets in a workplace, the clearer the distinction between work time and personal time," and has further discussion of time use at different levels of an industrial setting, in "Autonomy and negotiation in an industrial setting," *Sociology of Work and Occupations,* 1975, 2, 203–226.

of production and to that of consumption. On the one hand, workers are still dominated and constrained in the *production* process, and classes as defined by their relation to production remain unchanged. But on the other hand, workers have a new freedom and independence as *consumers* such that class distinctions are somewhat obscured in consumption.[6] You can still tell the working class from the petit bourgeois by the clothes they wear to work and the settings they are seen in on the job, but you may not be able to tell them apart at the football game on Sundays. Rather than obliterating class distinctions, the trend in leisure development shows the further workings of a capitalist economy whose emphasis has shifted from problems of production to ones of consumption. Workers must be pressed into consumption with their new leisure time, rather than be allowed to keep their hard-won hours. (Women, of course, most exemplify this trend in our society of being pressed into frenzied consumption.)

To understand the political use of time, make the complete analogy to space. There is a limited amount of time, as there is of space, and only one 24-hour period is given to all of us each day, not separate packages of 24 hours to each. Some people have the power to annex other people's time, and the more they can annex, the more powerful they become; the more powerful they are, the more of others' time they can annex.

This time-stealing is equivalent to a territorial invasion; the extent of the incursion may be measured by the time annexed. It is not the less privileged who have more control over their time; rather, they have less. As workers, their labor is sold, and punched in and out on a time clock. At piece-work rates (where quotas are set higher than normal work outputs) or on a sped-up assembly line, their time is manipulated to suck their labor power from them. Those who can come and go as they please without having to account to anybody (such as employers of large numbers of people) do have control over their time. They manipulate their own time, like their workers', to extract the last ounce of profit from it.

Taking—literally—another's time is easily understood when we consider simple one-to-one interaction. We all know that a higher-status person can keep a lower-status one waiting, and very often will, solely to assert dominance. Time accrues to prestige. This clear time-stealing is reacted to as such—privately. The resentment felt when made to cool the heels can't generally be expressed directly, because the person who can make you do it has already got more power over you—if not control over your job or some aspect of it, perhaps over your health (a doctor) or welfare (a social worker)

6 T. B. Bottomore discusses this in *Classes in Modern Society* (New York: Random House, 1966), p. 31 ff. He cites Serge Mallet, *La Nouvelle Classe ouvriere* (Paris, Editions du Seuil, 1963) for this distinction.

Generally, the more powerful and important the person, the more likely others must make an appointment for that person's time; and the more likely the powerful person to violate even that appointed time by keeping them waiting. The less important the person, on the other hand, the more likely his or her time and work may be invaded without notice, often by summons from the powerful at their own convenience. In addition, when subordinates do spend time with a superior, that time may be violated— interrupted for other, more "important" people who wish audience, or even on the superior's own initiation. The psychological effect of this situation is, like so many nonverbal indicators of power, to reinforce the hierarchical relationship, to exalt the superior and demean the subordinate: "The assumption that the client correctly makes," writes Schwartz,

> is that his own worth is not sufficient to permit the superior to renounce other engagements; being unworthy of full engagement, he is seen, so to speak, between the superior's other appointments. In this way, the client is compelled to bear witness to the mortification of his own worthiness for proper social interaction.[7]

The correlation of status and waiting is neatly demonstrated in an experiment described by Sommer, in which audiences rated the status of two men shown in filmed interaction. Ten different one-minute films showed the same scene—one man working at a desk, then another who knocks at his office door, enters the office, and approaches to speak with him. The time between knocking and entry, and the time between the knock and the first man's response, were both related to their relative status: the longer the office worker took to respond to the knock, the higher the status.[8]

Professional people are, of course, notorious for making clients wait. Schwartz mentions the overscheduling practiced by both physicians and courts. A doctor may have four or five consulting rooms, keeping patients waiting in various states of undress and bewilderment in all of them, while the doctor pops in and out of the rooms like a horizontal jack-in-the-box, using time oh-so-efficiently. The doctor's time, that is. In the same way, institutions such as courts or clinics (especially those in hospitals serving low-income clients) will often give *all* clients for one day an appointment for the opening hour, so that a pool of ready clients will be ever-available for the professional staff. Again an efficient use of time for the professionals, but not for their clients.

Organized service-delivery institutions are generally gigantic time-

[7] Schwartz, "Waiting, Exchange, and Power," p. 847.

[8] Robert Sommer, *Personal Space: The Behavioral Basis of Design* (Englewood Cliffs, N.J.: Prentice-Hall, 1969), p. 19.

gobblers for society. They are time funnelers, too; they take away from the poor and give to the rich (along with other institutions and corporations). They are time sinks, sucking up time from thousands and literally giving it to those at the top.

We may think of time-gobblers in personal interaction as those boors who talk incessantly and take up our time when we don't want to give it. They are not generally the powerful. Well, be assured that the rich and powerful don't have their time absorbed in this way; they have triple-thick walls of protection from such intrusion, except from their peers. Among peers, there are still those who can terminate conversations with others they don't wish to spend time with. We can consider that those who refuse time-gobbling are dominant in that situation; and also, that private peer-level time-gobbling may be an attempt at interpersonal dominance which can't be achieved in other ways, as lint-picking and tie-straightening may be.

The issues in a temporal political analysis are *control over one's time* and *access to other people's time* (and thus to their labor potential), as well as the *quality of one's time*. As Schwartz points out, these issues are far from trivial:

> time itself [is] a generalized resource whose distribution affects life chances with regard to the attainment of other, more specific kinds of rewards. . . . Far from being a coincidental by-product of power, then, control of time comes into view as one of its essential properties.[9]

From this discussion it is clear that a philosophy that encourages us to think of time as an interesting abstraction, apolitical and affected only by one's personal management or mismanagement, can only serve to obscure the pervasive power relations by which it is organized.

WOMEN-IN-WAITING

Just as the political examination of time is just beginning, so the examination of sex differences in time is yet to start. One aspect has been most noted, in various places: women spend much of their time waiting. Penelope of Greek mythology best exemplifies this aspect of women's life: though her husband Odysseus was long gone and thought dead, she faithfully waited his return (fighting off suitors) for ten years. But do women do more waiting than men? What about the stereotype of the woman who is always late (with beauty preparation), keeping a man waiting when going on a date? I don't know of any research that can tell us whether

[9] Schwartz, "Waiting, Exchange, and Power," pp. 868–869.

this image is true or not, but our analysis of the political aspects of time would suggest it is unlikely.

There is a form of waiting between the sexes that is built into the system, though: waiting to be asked out. The tradition lingers on that the (active) male pursues the (passive) female and must be the one to propose a date. Thus women wait to be asked—"all alone by the telephone," as the song puts it. They must keep their time open and available for this possibility, and their female friends must accept the fact that *their* time is less valued, and appointments with them may be canceled at a moment's notice.

Waiting is built into women's social role as subservient providers of services and support for others. Since in general, males in their lives—either at work or in the family—are defined as more important, women's time is to be given over to them. On the job, women's time, while it is far from unoccupied, is at the disposal of (generally male) bosses. Much of it is spent in inordinately time-wasting tasks such as running errands, going for coffee, etc. Transcribing tape-recorded material, another "woman's job," is inherently time-consuming, as anyone knows who has ever had to do it; transcribing from written material is faster since the same message may be read silently at a much greater speed than read aloud, and may be rechecked faster than when one must run a recording machine back and forward to find and try to understand some obscure phrase.

The picture at home is no more comforting than in the paid workplace, though more confusing: women in families are depicted both as 24-hour-a-day servants and as going crazy from having time on their hands. Since both portraits may be true, depending on circumstances, it is difficult to defend either image as a criticism of women's position within the family. What is common to both, however, and the crux of the matter, is that *women's time is unimportant.* When they are overworked, their time is considered to be at the disposal of others; time for their own interests or needs is not considered a right. When they have "nothing" to do (more a malady of women of higher social class, and of those at a relatively late stage in family development), it is because their possible contribution to the family welfare or to society is considered so negligible, the time they could contribute so worthless, as to demonstrate their personal worthlessness. In both cases, the unimportance of women's time is shown by its easy violability. Mother's time, like mother's space, can always be interrupted. She is less likely to have a time to call her own within the family (or a "night out") than is father. Since her work is less valued, anyone can intrude on a woman's cooking, cleaning, sewing, paying bills, tending children; and in fact she is often expected to add jobs on (especially child-tending) while doing another, since she is "not doing anything" in the first place.

Part of the mythology of women's swimming in free time may come from advertising campaigns of recent years and the ideology they support, of the "pampered" American woman. New appliances and other products are hyped as "labor-saving" devices and short-cut conveniences, and the U.S. homemaker is touted as having been liberated from housework. In fact, over the past fifty years, time spent by nonemployed American women on housework has not decreased at all, staying within a narrow range of an average 51–56 hours in that time span.[10]

Margolis examined the operation of Parkinson's Law in housework, including a survey of 200 household hints offered by the columnist Heloise. She found that 37.5% of the hints were needlessly time-consuming, only 7.5% were time-saving, and 40% were time-neutral.[11] Thus hints to homemakers work more often to absorb their time (with little or no benefit in return) than to save it.

Women's time, again like women's space, is constricted as well as invaded. There has traditionally been greater control over the hours women keep. For example, college dormitory parietal hours have been applied more strongly to women than to men; family curfews have been more frequently and forcefully applied to young girls than to boys. Fox has provided an analysis of temporal restrictions on women as a means of social control—"nice girls" (of any age) may go out alone in public only in daytime hours.[12]

When it comes to intruding on women's time, other women tend to do it as well as members of their own families. From time to time various women's magazines have carried accounts of devices women have employed to preserve themselves from other women's demands on their time. One woman lied to her kaffee-klatsching neighbors that she was writing a book, and thus achieved the respect for her time that allowed her to use it for housework and for her personal needs.

Some of the intrusions that women may have to escape from are by women who are excessive talkers. There is a deeply-ingrained mythology that claims women talk more than men, and this falsification has probably supported more comic sketches, cartoons and jokes than have ethnic slurs: women-and-telephone jokes are always good for a laugh. Controlled studies, observational and experimental, don't confirm this myth, but

10 Joann Vanek, "Time Spent in Housework," *Scientific American,* 1974 (November), 231, 5, 116–20.
11 Maxine Margolis, "In Hartford, Hannibal, and (New) Hampshire, Heloise is hardly helpful," *Ms.,* 1976 (June), IV, no. 12, 28–36.
12 Greer Litton Fox, "Nice Girl: The Behavioral Legacy of a Value Construct." Paper presented at meeting of National Council on Family Relations, 1973.

rather have most often found men to be greater talkers.[13] The impression of women's talkativeness may come from certain circumstances, such as loneliness or the often-cited case of a woman left to infant companionship all day who starves for an adult listener by night. Though when with men women are generally found to do less talking, and women apparently talk less in mixed-sex groups than men do, it is still possible that with their own sex, some women attempt to achieve domination (or attention) by talkativeness. It is also likely, however, that any such temporal intrusion is more likely to be noticed, and resented, when it is by another woman than by any others in women's lives, since they are supposed to be sub-servient to men and children, but not to other women.

Since men are more often professionals and women more often con-sumers of professional services (again as part of their prescribed social and economic roles), women are more likely to be kept waiting in these service situations. Ninety-two percent of physicians are men, for example, but women account for approximately two-thirds of visits to doctors. Not only do women obtain these services for themselves, but they must bring other members of the family for them (e.g., medical and dental services, purchasing clothing) and must act as the family's representative in obtain-ing other services (e.g., welfare benefits, food stamps, paying bills, pur-chasing household goods).

It may seem that women are also the perpetrators of much time-stealing, especially by institutions, in their roles as screeners for executives and professionals, as hospital personnel, or as social service workers. Many of us have been kept waiting by female secretaries and assistants who seem to take a perverse pleasure, and gain superiority, in making us wait un-necessarily. It is true that some status may be gained (relative to their co-workers) in this way, but it is ultimately derived from the position of the professional they serve. Women as gatekeepers for services are acting as agents for professionals and institutions, and the temporal inferiority they thus impose accrues more to the professional and institutional director than to their servants. In fact, utilizing women as screeners in this manner is a way of demonstrating how unimportant the waiting person is—too worthless even to be demeaned by a male.

[13] See Nancy Henley and Barrie Thorne, She Said/He Said: An Annotated Bibli-ography of Language, Sex, and Nonverbal Communication (Pittsburgh: KNOW, Inc., 1975). This bibliography is also in Barrie Thorne and Nancy Henley (eds.), Lan-guage and Sex: Difference and Dominance (Rowley, Mass.: Newbury House, 1975).

chapter four

PAINTING THE POWERSCAPE:
Environment

We live in a world that tells us what to do—moves us through it in preordained fashion, tells us what to think of others and ourselves, and indicates how to act in each setting. There are silent messages in the nonhuman environment as well as the human one, and the division of space is here, too, one carrier of such messages—but now it is not the space pertaining just to us and our bodies that concerns us, but that space through which we must move in our work and life: the arrangements of offices and homes, the physical props that come with certain settings, the advertising pictures (and real-life vignettes) we view, the extensiveness of our environments and how we move through them, their hostile or friendly atmospheres, their associations. The imposing height and space of courtrooms and governmental buildings intimidate, as they are meant to, the people whose lives are affected there. A storefront structure is designed to draw people in; a courthouse or library, with distant stone facade and discouraging high steps, is designed to turn people away. This distribution of space—in quantity and quality—as we remarked earlier, is a clear indicator of hierarchy.

But space is only one such cue. Order is another. It is no accident that neat lines and ordered ranks are demanded for moving certain groups from one place to another—children, soldiers, prisoners, but not, say, touring business executives. Externally imposed order signifies the low status of the controlled and powerless. The neat rows of desks and chairs, the right-angle order of traditional classrooms, are powerful forces in keeping students' bodies and minds functioning in straight-line fashion.

Superior height always intimidates, either as a personal characteristic or as a sign of office. The judge, the police desk sergeant, the rabbi, priest or minister (not to mention Mommy and Daddy)—all tell us what to do from several feet over our heads. I have long suspected that a simple experiment would show people to be more influenced by a loudspeaker on the ceiling than by one on the floor! This respect and awe for height are a thread that

weaves through all human language (in terms like *superior* and *subordinate,* for example—there are many more) and religions ("higher" beings most often appear from, and disappear into, the sky, for one example). We rank order, beauty, wealth, talent, intelligence, power, and athletic skill (to name a few) from top to bottom, and our (linear) logical thinking apparently uses this arrangement, as studies by DeSoto, et al. have shown.[1] The connection of height with superior quality may have its roots in the physical advantage height gave to hand-to-hand combatants in our earliest prehistory; in the military advantage that geographical height gave to the nobility in later days; in religious imagery; or in some nativistic (e.g., Jungian or Chomskian) inborn arrangement of brain structure. Whatever its roots, it is apparently a human universal.[2]

In the struggle for more power among those that already have some, environmental cues play an important part also. Markers, especially, are

[1] See Clinton B. De Soto, M. London, and S. Handel, "Social Reasoning and Spatial Paralogic," *Journal of Personality and Social Psychology,* 1965, 2, 513–21.

[2] Joseph Campbell has written about this in *The Mythic Image* (Princeton: Princeton University Press, 1974).

used to designate one's turf when this struggle involves expanding territory. Chief Justice Warren Burger was said to be particularly high-handed in this way after assuming that office, columnist Jack Anderson wrote:

> For example, he has now annexed to his personal offices the court's con ference room, the inner sanctum where the justices meet in secret to thrash out their decisions. He has even installed a desk so there can be no mistaking that the court convenes in Burger's lair.[3]

Though emphasizing his own sovereignty, Burger also took pains to elevate the other justices, installing such trappings as a gold carpet leading to their bench, and requesting from Congress cars for their use, for the first time.

INTERIOR DESIGNS—ON POWER

An excellent analysis of power landscaping in offices has been made by Michael Korda, and we can learn a lot about power arrangements in general by studying his observations.[4] (Note that Korda's analysis is not a report of systematic study, but rather consists of informal and anecdotal evidence.) "To the person for whom work is the exercise of power," he writes, "the place where it is done becomes the board on which power games are played, the central source from which power is derived." According to Korda (and our own observations will bear this out), offices are based upon a corner power system, not a central one: corner offices are usually the powerful ones, and the power lines run between them in an X. Side offices, no matter how roomy and view-equipped, are out of the power nexus.

Proximity to power does count, of course, as does a position controlling the flow of some commodity, such as information. A high-level executive usually prefers to be isolated from access by others, and gains power thereby; the secretary to one, on the other hand, needs to have broad visual possibility, to see all who are coming and going and to be prepared to act. In coffee-break socializing, "power players" will emerge from their own offices to join the group, but will stand off from it and away from other power players; their backs will be against the wall near a doorway if pos-

[3] Jack Anderson, "Burger's Highhandedness," Buffalo *Courier-Express*, July 6, 1971.
[4] Michael Korda, "Office Power—You Are Where You Sit," *New York*, January 13, 1975, 8, no. 2, 36–44. See also his *Power! How to Get It, How to Use It* (New York: Random House, 1975).

sible, for control over others' approach, and for quick escape when the situation calls for it.

Korda states that a working layout in which the senior executives are on the floor below their junior staff is one in which the seniors have relinquished day-to-day authority. When on the upper floor, senior executives "tend to exercise a tighter control over the organization, and the hierarchy is usually more rigid. . . ." Describing an organization that has its senior executives segregated in a luxurious garden-penthouse reached only by a private elevator, he remarks that "Indeed, sharp divisions like this are partly *intended* to keep the lower echelons in their places, and to make the access to power mysterious, difficult, and impressive."

Control from above is also manifested in the "open office" plan, ostensibly introduced to promote interaction. However, employees are not really there for the purpose of free and open communication, and in such a setting cannot work for themselves but must work for an audience of fellow workers and superiors. An open office is excellent for keeping employees under surveillance.

Territoriality, naturally, comes under Korda's survey also. He describes power ploys in which executives, starting from a buffer zone of subordinates on either side, attempt to establish a beachhead some distance away and gradually secure the space in between. Large filing complexes are especially valuable as holders for space, to be moved around like chess pieces; but hall space also identifies ownership of territory, by bulletin boards, posters, even decor, including common paint colors. A single identifiable color can spread out from its home office and threaten other executives without their own power color, as it takes on symbolic meaning and indicates a spreading dominion. Other things can serve as such symbols, so long as they are clearly identified with the owner.

The desk of the player is the intense core of the power area. These cores are deliberately engineered to intimidate, and Korda presents some for our examination. In these real-life executive offices, visitors have to walk a considerable distance across the room, around impeding furniture, blinded by the window light, to reach the desk; or sit at an angle from the executive rather than directly across, or sit separated by desk trivia, facing a clock reminding them the executive is a busy person; or view such signs of importance as multi-buttoned call-director phones, murals, photos and models of grand possessions of the office-owner, or ultra-simplistic, dramatic and expensive furniture which simultaneously impresses and focuses attention on the executive.

A companion piece to Korda's article, in the same magazine, shows several executive desks, candidates for power manipulanda.[5] One wrapped almost completely around the executive vice president who had it installed, like a small fortress, and angered his colleagues. Another is designed like a slightly reduced boardroom table, an eight-foot expanse of smooth board. Others were a stand-up desk and an ostentatious Louis XVI rolltop, alternative ways to intimidate. Perhaps the desk of desks was described by someone who interviewed Nelson Rockefeller:

> I couldn't believe how simple his New York office was. But the big thing was his trick desk. It had a large pull-out drawer with steps on it. Rockefeller would strut up and step onto the top of his desk in order to address any assembled group.[6]

Here is a clear demonstration that having tremendous personal wealth and political power, as well as a position of command, do not suffice to maintain the security of the power-hungry. The very furniture, and the ability literally to look down on people, must stoke that fire too.

WOMAN'S PLACE

Every woman as she walks through her environment sees, whether aware of it or not, the images of a boss dictating while the secretary writes, head bent; or the doctor operating with the nurse assisting him; or sees the difference between her office and that of the man she works for. She sees the restaurants populated with waitresses serving men, and banks with women behind, men in front of the counter. These images are in their three-dimensional real world, as well as in their two-dimensional world of pictures—in magazines, newspapers, books, indoor and outdoor displays. The ads don't let her forget that care of the house and the children are her responsibilities, not her husband's, or that she is first and foremost a sexual object and has an obligation to nurture that image of herself. Along with the image goes an environment that is restricted in its settings and, because of the nature of the image, often hostile.

Women are restricted not only in their personal space and territory, but in the areas they may move freely in. There has been stricter control over

[5] Joan Kron, "Executive Sweeteners," *New York*, January 13, 1975, 8, no. 2 pp. 66–67.
[6] Felicia Roosevelt, quoted by Marian Christy, "Famous Doors, Doers Open Up to a Roosevelt," Boston Sunday *Globe*, May 4, 1975, p. D4.

women's spatial freedom (as over their time)—for example, certain areas of the city, certain movie theaters, food and drink establishments, or stores are deemed "not suitable for ladies," primarily because they would be exposed to explicit sexual material (or molestation, if not in the protection of a male) in these areas.

But there are other factors limiting women's spatial mobility—the expectations for their sex, and their socialization to fit these expectations. Such expectations are displayed in many media, including advertising and cartoons, two areas which have been studied for sex differences in spatial settings. David Lee, a geographer, examined men's and women's magazines from 1963 to 1973, for the settings depicted in advertisements. He categorized magazine ad illustrations as occurring in one of four spatial levels of setting: home, neighborhood and office, district or region, and "the far country"—the more interesting, but rarely visited places distant in space, time, and imagination. Out of 700 ads in women's magazines, 71% had the home as a setting; only 34% of the over 600 ads in men's magazines pictured the home. At the other extreme, men's ads pictured the "far country" (like Marlboro country) over 17% of the time, while women's ads showed it only 7% of the time. "The other side of the woman-in-the-home convention is a man-in-the-world convention," Lee writes.[7] A similar study by Cheris Kramer of cartoons in *Ladies Home Journal, Playboy, Cosmopolitan,* and the *New Yorker* found women pictured in fewer places than men were, and a study of women's image in television commercials had similar results.[8]

The effects of these expectations and restrictions on women are poignantly illustrated in the lives of women like Homebody, who wrote to "Dear Abby," another advice column, that her husband

> can't go to a movie because he hates to sit still for that long. He won't go to church, for the same reason. He won't take me dancing because he thinks dancing is foolish. He doesn't like to go out to dinner because it's too expensive. He refuses to go to band concerts because he doesn't like that kind of music.
>
> Camping is too rough and fishing is boring. He *will* go deer hunting, but

---

[7] D. R. Lee, "Spatial Setting of Advertisements: Some Sexist Observations," mimeo (Dept. of Geography, Florida Atlantic University), 1974. There is a positive note to this study: ads from both types of magazines seemed to be moving toward an environmental equality over the years 1963–1973.

[8] C. Kramer, "Stereotypes of Women's Speech: The Word from Cartoons," *Journal of Popular Culture,* 1975, 8, 624–30; Joseph R. Dominick and Gail E. Rauch, "The Image of Women in Network TV Commercials," *Journal of Broadcasting,* 1972, 16, 259–65.

he won't take me because "men don't take their wives." He won't go for a
walk with me because he might miss his favorite TV programs. . . .
I'm 38 and tired of staying home all the time. Any suggestions?

Homebody

Abby, a woman that other women turn to when in need, betrays her com-
plicity with the status quo; in her reply, she advocates women's confinement (and adds to their guilt for complaining):

> Dear Homebody: Count your blessings. A man with a "peach of a dis-
> position" and who is a good father can't be all bad. Build a social life by
> inviting a few friends in. You don't have to go "out" to have a good time.[9]

Even when women do escape from home into the slightly larger world
of the office, they gain little environmentally. Those spaces described by
Korda, the manipulation of which gave "office power," have only peripheral
meaning to the great majority of women who work in offices. Though they
may even take part in planning and manipulating those spaces, the women
themselves are mere agents for the power they serve, often pawns to be
moved into space-holding positions, or whose possession adds more power
to their owner. The open office appreciated by bosses who like a lot of
control is most often employed for the corralling of women, such as in the
steno pool.

While a good number of women may be thought of as environment cre-
ators, being interior decorators, they cannot be thought of as moving freely,
able to create a "woman-influenced" space. Rather, their assigned task is
often, in office buildings or grand hotels, to design space that males will
feel comfortable and reflected in. Some women have managed to create
their own living space in their homes or apartments, though it is often one
which is a nurturing center for the whole family. As we mentioned previously, they are not as likely to create a space of their own equivalent to
the male den.

In addition, women's most sacred preserve, the kitchen—the place
women in families can most truly call their own turf—is not created for
them. Periodically editorial attention is given to women's oppression by
kitchens: cabinets are built beyond their reach, counters are not scaled to
their height, floor plans don't take their kitchen movements or logistics into
account, and so on. They are spaces designed by men as if for men. The
reason for such concern with the kitchen, of course, is that it is the focus

[9] *Chicago Tribune*, August 31, 1975, section 5, p. 6.

of supportive household work, the nurturance core which keeps the whole family functioning through the day. Inefficiency here can keep women from effectively performing their function as service-provider to the family.

Since the kitchen is often accepted as woman's turf, it is no wonder that many conflicts between women take place in the kitchen. When one woman comes into another woman's kitchen, and begins to perform there the duties appropriate to the one whose territory it is, this constitutes a territorial invasion.[10] The kitchen is all the more defended because it is often the only sovereignty a woman has (though often she has a certain amount of command over activities of the common areas of the whole house). Women who want to respect these territorial rights could explicitly ask permission for every act they perform in another woman's kitchen, and more specifically, ask first what the owner would have them do.

Although when women kill their husbands it is usually in the kitchen,[11] I think the territorial defense is generally not made against men invaders, because they are more powerful in the first place. And their invasion, while it may change the territory for the worse, does not generally involve activities typical to women, i.e., providing for others. Men have no interest in expanding territorial rights into the kitchen as other women might; it is, after all, a factory whose "ownership" entails work.*

Women's environment is largely man-made and male-controlled, and it is often threatening. Some threat comes in the form of powerful, often dangerous machinery (e.g., large vehicles) whose use and control is mainly out of female hands; other is from the possibility of seeing that which is taboo to them, especially sexual material; other threat is of direct attack, made possible by their learned weakness; and in the form of suggested attack, harassment by men staring at, commenting on, or accosting their bodies. The environmental threat to women is so great as to occasion informal but real curfews on many: in few families are women of any age, but particularly young ones, "allowed" to walk freely in city streets, or use public transportation, after dark. Many single and independent women also observe this curtailment of activities.

It cannot be called self-imposed, however. It is imposed by the real

[10] Edward T. Hall, *The Silent Language* (Garden City, N.Y.: Doubleday, 1959), p. 148.

[11] *Psychology Today*, 1975 (July), 9, 2, 35–42.

* It's interesting to note that the upsurge in men's recreational cooking in the last two decades has been largely confined to cookouts. This choice of setting is possibly due to the twin forces of women's territorial defense of the kitchen and men's desire to avoid being associated with that workshop. Perhaps also their masculinity is enhanced by being associated with the outdoors; their egos are certainly enhanced by the attention given this special occasion (as compared with the little attention paid women's routine cooking).

forces that threaten women's freedom of movement. Since the threat is
mainly one of attack by men, and since the main defense is a male escort,
such an arrangement has been called a "protection racket" of the type
employed by criminal gangs. The situation has also been well illuminated
by Golda Meir's response when a curfew was proposed for women in
Israel because of the danger of attack: the curfew should be imposed on
men, not women, since the streets are safe when women alone walk them.
Analysis of attacks on women has ever been characterized by blaming the
victim,[12] and the solutions have ever been ones that follow the social pattern of restricting women's movement. Women's mobility has been so
curtailed that the admonishment "women's place is in the home" has much
more realization in practice than people realize.

[12] Articles by Florence Rush have provided excellent examples and analysis of this
phenomenon, particularly with respect to young females. See "The Sexual Abuse of
Children," *Radical Therapist*, 1971 (Dec.), 2, 4, 9–10; and "The Myth of Sexual
Delinquency," *Rough Times*, 1972 (June), 2, 7, 10–11. These are available in reprint form from KNOW, Inc., P.O. Box 86031, Pittsburgh, Pa. 15221.

Greer Fox claims that of three patterns of control used in different societies to regulate women's freedom, the *normative* type—self-control through the internalization of values and norms, as in our own society—covers a larger sphere of activity than does either *confinement* or *protection* (e.g., chaperones). Normative restrictions for women's venturing into the world apply to the means, the destination, and the time of travel. And the restrictions interact with economic and employment barriers for further curtailment of women's life experience. Since women have less knowledge of their environment, they have less power in it and over it.[13] Coser draws a similar conclusion, in showing how opportunities for spatial movement, including travel, are socially patterned so as not to interfere with the class structure.[14]

There has existed in our society, and still does in some pockets, a tradition of chivalry that shapes the world of women and keeps it an alien environment to them. The overall practice of chivalry keeps women from coming into contact with any of the life-moving functions and machinery of the world—such as opening doors,[15] carrying bundles, or driving vehicles. Although it takes credit for insulating them from the dirtier part of their environment, it takes no pains to save them from the drudge and filth of their own work. It has been a class-bound hidden message that women are to be ignorant and dependent except in the efficient execution of household management, a message spared working-class women because much more of their labor was desired. Our heritage of women's writings show that chivalry has not always been appreciated by women but rather has been exposed as the oppressive tool that it is (and another "protection" racket).[16]

An attitude study in 1959 documented the psychological connection between chivalry and misogyny: attitudes favoring chivalry went hand in hand with those favoring the open subordination of women—and both were posi-

---

[13] Greer Litton Fox, " 'Nice Girl': The Behavioral Legacy of a Value Construct," paper presented at meeting of National Council on Family Relations, 1973.

[14] Rose Laub Coser, "Stay Home, Little Sheba: On Placement, Displacement, and Social Change," *Social Problems*, 1975, 22, 470–480.

[15] For an interesting analysis of "The Changing Door Ceremony," see Laurel Walum's article by that title in *Urban Life and Culture*, 1974, 2, 506–15.

[16] For example, George Eliot wrote of her character Dorothea (in *Middlemarch*, first published in 1871–73), "there was the stifling oppression of that gentlewoman's world, where everything was done for her and none asked for her aid—where the sense of connection with a manifold pregnant existence had to be kept up painfully as an inward vision, instead of coming from without in claims that would have shaped her energies" (New York: Macmillan, 1939, 268–69). Or see Lucy Stone's speech of 1855, which states that women "mistake the politeness of men for rights." "Disappointment is the Lot of Woman," originally in *The History of Woman Suffrage*, excerpted in Leslie B. Tanner, *Voices from Women's Liberation* (New York: New American Library, 1971), pp. 75–77.

tively correlated with antidemocratic attitudes.[17] Not only does the practice of keeping women passive, doing things in the physical world for them such as opening doors and moving heavy furniture, give them a (true) feeling of inability to cope, it alienates them from the physical world. This separation is one historical reason for women's feeling in an alien environment. A famous psychological experiment of some years back used a contraption called the "kitten carousel": newborn kittens were strapped into it, one walking and the other riding round the track in a gondola. Both got the same visual experience of the environment, but the walking kitten had additional active physical experience so that it could coordinate sight and movement. This experience gave normal development of motor abilities to the walking cat, but left the passive one—with the "soft life"— deficient in such development.[18] In an analogous way, passive women are taken for a ride—chivalrous treatment of women puts them into that crippling gondola.

This point is well illustrated in this account by Jan Morris of her response to others' treatment of her after her change from male to female:

> The more I was treated as a woman, the more woman I became. I adapted willy-nilly. If I was assumed to be incompetent at reversing cars, or opening bottles, oddly incompetent I found myself becoming. If a case was thought too heavy for me, inexplicably I found it so myself.[19]

Another aspect of women's environment is the frilly "feminized" atmosphere they are subjected to, most notably in areas designed for women only. (Men would not put up with it.) Beauty parlors, women's rest rooms, bedrooms for teenage girls, often have the most nauseating abundance of frills, lace, ruffles, pink ribbons, frail materials, and of ballerina motifs exemplifying all these. Men's clubs and bars, on the other hand, project the masculine image of hardness and toughness with heavy materials and leather, dark colors, and angular, sterile furniture.

Male decor in fact predominates in settings designed for both sexes. A student research project at Michigan State University examined sex differentiation in interior design shown in magazines. Of course, leather, wood, and plain no-frills material were the rule for male settings, and frills, ruffles, pastel colors for female ones. "Family" settings, however, which

[17] Eugene B. Nadler and W. R. Morrow, "Authoritarian Attitudes Toward Women, and Their Correlates," *Journal of Social Psychology*, 1959, 49, 113–23.

[18] R. Held and A. Hein, "Movement Produced Stimulation in the Development of Visually Guided Behavior," *Journal of Comparative and Physiological Psychology*, 1963, 56, 872–76.

[19] Jan Morris, *Conundrum.* New York: Harcourt Brace Jovanovich, 1974, p. 165.

serve both sexes, fell closer to the male pattern of plainness and formality.[20]
Just as men's clothing may not imitate the female in the way women's may
imitate the male, so men may not risk association with the feminine in environments—in the decoration of space as of the body, power is coded.

Feminine atmosphere projects the image of immobility; these accoutrements are ones that one can only look beautiful in, not move, feel strong,
or be active in. (Ballerinas are of course fantastically active and athletic,
but such decor typically depicts them in repose.) What is most frightening
to contemplate is that the symbolic surroundings of women's imposed
paralysis are the same as those of the funeral parlor.[21] It is no accident that
coffins puff out with satin pads, lace, and frills (in which dead *men* look
extremely uncomfortable), and the funeral parlor is filled with flowers.
These signs of femininity, common also to the beauty parlor, are symbolic
of the powerlessness of the dead, as they are of the powerlessness of women.
But it is *living* women who must try to create life out of these pale pompons
of death.

[20] Kathryn Civitello, paper for Sociology of Sex Roles (Barrie Thorne, teacher),
Michigan State University, 1976.

[21] See Nancy M. Henley, "The American Way of Beauty," *The Paper* (Baltimore,
Md.), 1970, 1, 15, 7+. Available in reprint form from KNOW, Inc., P.O. Box 86031,
Pittsburgh, Pa. 15221.

chapter five

TINKLING SYMBOLS:

Language

Strictly speaking, language, being verbal communication, is out of the scope of this book. Certainly we need no reminders that our superiors may say certain things to us that we may not reciprocate to them, or that class variations in usage exist.[1] However, language is such a central aspect of social interaction, and so broad, that manipulations of power involving it take many subtle forms—forms that aren't covered by what we usually study in language. These subtle aspects are what we will look at here. One of the most important of these aspects, and perhaps the best studied, has to do with what we call one another when speaking together.

Terms of Address. One form of address—for example, "Joe" or "Mr. Daniels"—can serve both as status-marker and as solidarity marker, at different times, or even at the same time. Roger Brown and his colleagues have provided us with an excellent example of this dual use, in their explanation of the norms of personal address.[2] In English, as in a variety of other languages analyzed, forms of address are governed by two underlying dimensions, *status* and *solidarity* (i.e., amount of closeness between equals).

On the solidarity dimension, closeness between two persons is indicated

[1] Many books on the relation between language and social structure now exist, for example, Joshua A. Fishman, ed., *Readings in the Sociology of Language* (The Hague: Mouton, 1968); or Frederick Williams, ed., *Language and Poverty* (Chicago: Markham, 1970). For a popular examination of some upper-class usage, see Nancy Mitford (ed.), *Noblesse Oblige: An Enquiry into the Identifiable Characteristics of the English Aristocracy* (New York: Harper, 1956).

[2] R. Brown and A. Gilman, "The Pronouns of Power and Solidarity," in T. A. Sebeok (ed.), *Style in Language* (Cambridge, Mass.: Massachusetts Institute of Technology Press, 1960). R. Brown and M. Ford, "Address in American English," *Journal of Abnormal and Social Psychology*, 1961, 62, 375–85. Roger Brown, *Social Psychology* (New York: Free Press, 1965).

by a mutual use of "informal," or "familiar," address, such as the first name or nickname. In countries that have retained the distinction in their pronouns (English dropped its familiar form, *thou* after the 16th century), such forms as the French *tu,* the German *du,* and the Spanish *tú* are used reciprocally between friends. Distance, on the other hand, is indicated by the mutual use of "polite" or formal address. In English, this means a title and last name (Ms. Brown, Dr. Smith), and in other languages, the pronouns of "respect," such as *vous, Sie,* and *usted.*

Along the status dimension, status difference is indicated by nonreciprocal usage: the lower-status speaker uses terms of respect, such as titles and the formal pronouns. The higher-status speaker addresses the lower-status one informally, for example, by first name or by familiar pronouns (in languages with these informal pronouns, children, animals, and servants are specifically so addressed). Thus, the employer is Mr. Gordon, and the employees, Frank and Mary; the teacher is Professor Black, and the students, Joan and Bob. This pattern of nonreciprocal usage is seen in the family, where the more formal terms of relationship (and respect) are generally mandatory for children addressing adults (e.g., Mother, Dad, Aunt Jane), but rarely used by adults addressing children, in favor of first names, or, frequently, diminutives. This pattern is more than the respect of age, shown in address patterns outside the family also, for it persists past maturity. In the South in years past (and perhaps in some areas today), every white person of any age had the privilege of addressing any black, of any age, by first name, and receiving a polite form in return.

As we learned from Goffman in the first chapter, this pattern of symmetry between equals, and asymmetry between unequals, is not limited to terms of address, but characterizes many facets of such relationships. Brown too has called attention to a number of aspects of solidarity and status which are marked by this pattern, for instance, spatial differences and sentiments. In spatial differences, solidarity and nonsolidarity are shown in proximity or remoteness; status, in being above or below, in front or behind. In sentiments, solidarity relations are marked by mutual liking and sympathy, or mutual indifference and dislike; status relations are marked by pleasant sentiments of superiority and unpleasant sentiments of inferiority.[3] We will see this dual pattern occurring again and again in our discussion of nonverbal behavior and power, and will use it at our conclusion to organize our findings.

Verbal Bullying and Verbal Submissiveness. Form of address is an issue raised, with others, by an observer of the relations of the Watergate

[3] Brown, *Social Psychology,* Chap. 2, especially pp. 71–73.

principals. TRB of *The New Republic* notes several verbal dominance signs in his reading of the transcripts:

> Haldeman and Ehrlichman treat the President barely as an equal; they do not say "sir"; they interrupt him, contradict him, bully him as he vacillates.[4]

Not saying "sir," interrupting, contradicting, and bullying are all privileges of the superior, not the subordinate, and rightly elicit TRB's surprise when seeming to reverse the situation. Interruption is a less-studied phenomenon than address, but it is also clearly reflective of relative status. Underlings may not interrupt a boss, but must immediately cede the floor when the boss interrupts. I believe a hierarchy of power in a group could be plotted by ordering people according to the number of successful interruptions they achieve (and maybe subtracting the number of times they're successfully interrupted).

Eakins and Eakins analyzed faculty department meetings through an academic year and computed individuals' proportion of interruptions to total number of speaking turns. Not only were women interrupted much more (proportionately) than men, but "interruption patterns within the sex group followed a hierarchy of status within the department."[5]

The speech style of the subordinate is stereotypically flooded with hesitancy and self-doubt, qualifying phrases, and self-disparagement: "*I may not know anything* about this and *probably shouldn't say anything,* but I *think* the solution *may* be to . . . [X]." Instead of "We should [X]." The extraneous words serve many functions (as hedging to protect from attack; to give time to think and a chance to withdraw; to impress others with sheer volume, etc.), but at the core they advertise the powerlessness of those who must constantly acknowledge their subordinate status and must approach initiative gingerly, lest they be reminded it's not their prerogative.

Words are not the only way to dominate in conversation, of course. The disdain of an inferior can be well demonstrated by the manipulation of *silence* (an aspect of language, when language is expected). Silence is imposed on subordinates ("Don't speak unless spoken to"), but is a matter of free choice for superiors. Speech can, in fact, be imposed on subordinates also ("Answer me when I speak to you!")—either way is painful. Silence can be either an indication of uninvolvement, as when the service

[4] TRB (R. Strout), "The Plot Sickens," in the Boston *Globe,* May 14, 1974, p. 23.
[5] Barbara Eakins and Gene Eakins, "Verbal Turn-Taking and Exchanges in Faculty Dialogue," paper presented to the Conference on the Sociology of the Languages of American Women, 1976.

worker ignores the queries of a client, or it may suggest that the listener is withholding approval, even concealing disapproval or withholding information of heavy significance.

An example of this is found in a description by Nina Totenberg of an illustrative tape from the Watergate trials, in which then-President Nixon has called his aide H. R. Haldeman at home. Haldeman, she writes,

> . . . sounds as if he has more important things to do than talk to the President of the United States. His answers are monosyllabic, and there are long pauses where Nixon runs out of gas and Haldeman says nothing. Finally Nixon hangs up.[6]

Nixon is, in psychological terms, being *extinguished*. That is, his speaking behavior, in the absence of positive reinforcement in the form of interest or even minimal response, is dying out like a flame in the absence of oxygen.

LANGUAGE BUT NOT WORDS

Another subtle aspect of language is *paralanguage,* which may be defined as noises made by the vocal tract which carry meaning but aren't ordinarily studied as language.[7] Some examples are such utterances as *tch-tch, mm-hmm,* laughing, or even coughing and clearing the throat (at times). Paralanguage applies not to the "meaning" of the words we say, but to the meaning of *how* we say them: here the rhythm, pitch, intensity, nasality, slurring, and so on come in. Our upper-class paralanguage, according to William Austin, prescribes clear, low, and oral (that is, not nasal) speech for men, and clear, oral and soft speech for women, with a choice of high or low pitch. Young people as a sign of rebellion may reject these "refinements" and affect slurring and nasality.

Paralanguage has its political uses and interpretations. Austin points out, for example, that

> The dominant middle-class white culture in the United States has certain

[6] Nina Totenberg, "Obiter Dicta from the Watergate Press Table," *New York,* 1975 (January 20), 8, no. 3, 38–43.

[7] George L. Trager, "Paralanguage: A First Approximation," *Studies in Linguistics,* 1958, 13, 1–12. Starkey Duncan, "Nonverbal Communication," *Psychological Bulletin,* 1969, 72, 118–37, surveys the work in this field up to 1968.

set views on lower-class Negro speech. It is "loud," "unclear," "slurred," "lazy." The myth of loudness should be exorcised at once. Any minority or "out-group" is characterized as "loud"—Americans in Europe, Englishmen in America, and so on.[8]

He does suggest that Negro speech is characterized by "unevenness in pitch, intensity and tempo (social insecurity)," however. This identification of "unevenness" * in certain aspects of speech with "social insecurity" may be questioned. There is a growing literature on black English, some of which traces its roots in African languages; [9] Austin's differences may arise from cultural differences rather than social insecurity. Nevertheless, it is a provocative observation and one that demands further investigation (in terms of class as well as race).

Laughter is a vocalization with well-known social and political character. Its function in the hierarchy is illuminated by Coser's study of laughter among colleagues at mental hospital staff meetings over several months.[10] There are several points of interest in laughing, with regard to the dominance relation: the maker of a witticism, its target, and who laughs at it. Of the 90 intentional witticisms made by regular staff at these meetings, the senior staff members made an average of 7.5 jokes each, the junior staff, 5.5 each, and the lowest rung of the ladder, the paramedical staff, made only 0.7 jokes per person. Eighty-six of the witticisms were directed at a target, and the target was never higher in the hierarchy than the person making the crack: the most frequent target for senior staff was a member of the junior staff, and the junior staff more frequently directed its jokes against patients, patients' relatives, and themselves; while the paramedicals in turn told jokes exclusively against patients or themselves. The function of tension release in joking, then, is not a neutral affair: tension is released downwards, against the vulnerable. "The status structure," Coser writes, "is supported by downward humor." We will return later to the question of who laughs most at others' witticisms.

8 William M. Austin, "Some Social Aspects of Paralanguage," *Canadian Journal of Linguistics,* 1965, 11, 31–39.

* This term itself suggests some inadequacy rather than simply difference; if *variability* were considered the norm, rather than evenness, white middle-class U.S. speech would then have to be labeled "nonvariable."

9 See William A. Stewart, "Toward a History of American Negro Dialect," in Williams, *Language and Poverty;* Walt Wolfram and Nona Clarke (eds.), *Black–White Speech Relationships* (Washington, D.C.: Center for Applied Linguistics, 1971); J. L. Dillard, *Black English* (New York: Random House, 1972).

10 Rose Laub Coser, "Laughter among Colleagues," *Psychiatry,* 1960, 23, 81–95.

OPENING UP . . . WARDS

Self-disclosure is a content area of language that is little noticed as a status correlate. In Chapter 1 Goffman's observation was quoted, that "the boss may thoughtfully ask the elevator man how his children are, but this entrance into another's life may be blocked to the elevator man. . . ." The psychiatrist–patient relation is cited as the clearest form of this non-reciprocity: nothing may be withheld on the patient's side, though doctors need not reveal anything of themselves.

A study of address and social relations in a business organization confirms both these observations about self-disclosure made by Goffman, as well as the basic analysis of forms of address made by Brown and his associates.[11] Male and female employees at four organizational levels in a large state insurance company were interviewed by these researchers about the forms of address used to other company personnel, and about their self-disclosure to them. In such an organization we might expect respectful address to be directed to older personnel, or to those who had been with the company (or job) longer, regardless of hierarchical position, but this wasn't so. The research found that age and time with the firm weren't related to the address patterns. Status was. Forms of address were found to reveal aspects of organizational structure: First Name was used between equals and directed toward subordinates; when status was unequal, the typical address pattern prevailed, superior receiving Title and Last Name and subordinate, First Name.

The self-disclosure part of the interview asked the employees if they had ever confided to other personnel of varying ranks about such things as aspects of their work, cultural tastes, opinions on controversial issues, or personal problems.[12] They reported being most self-disclosing, naturally, to fellow workers of the same rank. But also, they were more self-disclosing to their immediate superiors than to their immediate subordinates.

Self-disclosures were offered upward even when First Name was not, suggesting to the researchers an exception to Brown and Ford's observation that the higher-status individual of a dyad initiates all acts that increase intimacy. What they say may be true; subordinates probably do

[11] Dan I. Slobin, Stephen H. Miller, and Lyman W. Porter, "Forms of Address and Social Relations in a Business Organization," *Journal of Personality and Social Psychology,* 1968, 8, 289–93.
[12] This technique was originated by Sidney Jourard and Paul Lasakow and reported in their article, "Some Factors in Self-Disclosure," *Journal of Abnormal and Social Psychology,* 1958, 56, 91–98. Also see Jourard's book *The Transparent Self* (Princeton, N.J.: Van Nostrand, 1964).

seek a (false) sense of intimacy through disclosing personal information to superiors. But there is another interpretation of this informational relationship. It is that personal information flows opposite to the flow of authority; just as tactual, visual, and emotional information of subordinates is more available to those in power, so is personal history. Or, in the spatial metaphor of our language of disclosure, you can "get closer to," "intrude in the life of," "encroach on the privacy of," "touch on personal aspects of," someone of lower status or less power.

It may be hard to see the political importance of such a fact: personal data seem trivial, and we think of individual relationships and their characteristics (such as disclosure) as unique. But the contrary is true: as we have seen, personal disclosure follows a pattern in relations between unequals, a pattern that fits into and supports institutionalized inequalities. In the incessant grindings of the machinery of our society, *all* knowledge, *all* information, is fodder. Information provides the potential to act which someone without information cannot have. And even when the information itself does not convey power, the act of giving-it-up has come to connote surrender, conveying symbolic power to the receiver. People in positions of power do not have to reveal information about themselves; the ultimate exemplars of this principle of power through mystery have been Howard Hughes and Big Brother.

WOMANSPEAK AND MANSPEAK

A woman begins to speak but shuts up when a man begins to speak at the same time; two men find a simple conversation always escalates into a full-scale competition; a junior high girl finds it hard to relate to her schoolbooks, which are phrased in the terminology of a male culture, and refer to people as "men." What is happening? Males and females speak differently and are spoken about differently, and these differences have consequences in the power relationships of our linguistic community. In this brief survey we can only touch on a broad and complex area; there are now many papers and books examining sex differences and sexism in language.[13] Let's look at these two effects of gender on language separately.

13 This survey is based on research done with Barrie Thorne, which may be found reported in greater detail in "Womanspeak and Manspeak: Sex Differences and Sexism in Communication, Verbal and Nonverbal," in Alice Sargent, ed., *Beyond Sex Roles* (St. Paul, Minn.: West Publishing, 1976); in B. Thorne and N. Henley, eds., *Language and Sex: Difference and Dominance* (Rowley, Mass.: Newbury House Publishers, 1975), and in N. Henley and B. Thorne, *She Said/He Said: An Annotated Bibliography of Language, Speech, and Nonverbal Communication* (Pittsburgh: KNOW, Inc., 1975). All research mentioned here is given full description and citation in this bibliography.

74   BODY POLITICS

How the Sexes Use Language Differently. Sex differences in the use
of language are so pervasive that even pre-kindergarten children are aware
of them. Before we talk about vocabulary and sentence structure differences, however, it would be good to confront two particularly widespread
myths about sex differences in language.

Myth 1—Do Women Talk Too Much? The first myth is that women
speak more and longer than men. This is simply not so. In study after
study, men have been found to speak more often and at greater length than
women, and to interrupt other speakers more than women do. This finding
applies to all kinds of social situations—alone, in single-sex or mixed-sex
pairs, and in groups; it has been found at all occupational levels; and it
applies to "real-life" couples (e.g., husbands and wives) as well as to
experimentally-created dyads and groups.[14]

Sociologist Jessie Bernard has observed that on TV panel discussions
males out-talked females by a considerable margin, and that as a general
conversational pattern, women have a harder time getting the floor in
groups and are more often interrupted than men.[15] The obvious power advantages of monopolizing and controlling conversation can be seen, but
there is the additional advantage that studies of leadership have consistently
found that those who talk more are perceived as leaders.[16] Thus sheer
volume gives power to influence.

As Bernard indicates, women find it difficult to be able to say anything
even if they wish to, because they are eminently interruptible. Add to this
that they themselves are extremely unlikely to interrupt others (or if they
do, are unlikely to be successful at it). Several studies have found that
males interrupt more than females; the best research in this area is
based on conversations of same-sex and mixed-sex pairs taped unobtru-
sively in natural settings. Here it was found that 96% of the interruptions,
and 100% of the overlaps, in conversation were made by male speakers.[17]

[14] See F. L. Strodtbeck, "Husband–Wife Interaction Over Revealed Differences."
American Sociological Review, 1951, 16, 468–73; F. L. Strodtbeck and R. D. Mann,
"Sex Role Differentiation in Jury Deliberations," *Sociometry,* 1956, 19, 3–11; F. L.
Strodtbeck, R. M. James, and C. Hawkins, "Social Status in Jury Deliberations,"
American Sociological Review, 1957, 22, 713–19; W. F. Kenkel, "Observational
Studies of Husband–Wife Interaction in Family Decision-Making," in M. Sussman,
ed., *Sourcebook in Marriage and the Family* (Boston: Houghton Mifflin, 1963), pp.
144–56; F. Hilpert, C. Kramer, and R. A. Clark, "Participants' Perceptions of Self
and Partner in Mixed-Sex Dyads," *Central States Speech Journal,* 1975 (Spring), 26,
52–56.

[15] Jessie Bernard, *The Sex Game* (New York: Atheneum, 1972).

[16] See A. Bavelas, et al., "Experiments on the Alteration of Group Structure,"
Journal of Experimental Social Psychology, 1965, 1, 55–70.

[17] D. H. Zimmerman and C. West, "Sex Roles, Interruptions and Silences in Conversation," in Thorne and Henley, eds., *Language and Sex.*

The authors of this last study give us an interesting example of the murder of attempts at assertiveness, in their analysis of silences. They found that overwhelmingly the greatest amount of conversational lapses was exhibited by females in female–male conversations. Silences were both more frequent and of longer duration following three types of male response: interruption, overlap, and delayed minimal response (giving an *mm-hmm* type response after a long delay instead of within the speaker's utterance, the supportive way). In an example they present, the female speaker's silences seem to grow longer with succeeding delayed minimal responses. If this pattern is true, we can see another example of extinction, behavior being killed off this time by (it seems) negative reinforcement as well as an absence of positive response.

Myth 2—Beast and Bird; How Males and Females Sound. The second myth attributes the high pitch of women's speech to anatomical differences alone. While it is true that there are anatomical differences between females and males that produce slightly higher pitch in females, the anatomical difference is nowhere near so great as to produce the difference that is heard.[18] Recent investigators have concluded that at least some of this difference is learned and constitutes a linguistic convention. *Males and females talk at greatly different pitches because that is the requirement of their social roles,* a requirement so strong that the differences in pitch exceed the expectation from the anatomical differences even in children, before the male voice change of puberty.[19]

The prescription that male voices should be low and female voices high is so strong, also, that any deviation from this expectation produces a powerful effect on other people's impressions of one's personality. Males with high-pitched voices may be reacted to as female in phone conversations and treated accordingly, disregarded in group conversations, and ridiculed behind their backs. But female announcers and newscasters with lower pitch are preferred and hired over other females: since lower pitch is associated with males, who have more authority in our society, it carries more authority when used by females also.

Other differences in speech sounds exist between the sexes. For boys in our culture, masculinity and toughness are carried in a slightly nasal speech; girls and "gentlemanly" boys have non-nasal, or oral, speech. Males also speak with greater intensity than females; their voices carry further and

---

[18] Ignatius M. Mattingly, "Speaker Variation and Vocal-Tract Size," *Journal of the Acoustical Society of America,* 1966, 39, 1219 (abstract).

[19] See J. Sachs, "Cues to the Identification of Sex in Children's Speech," in Thorne and Henley, eds., *Language and Sex.*

sound more forceful. In 1848 the suffragist Susan B. Anthony remarked on this disadvantage for women:

> Taught that a low [soft] voice is an excellent thing in woman, she has been trained to a subjugation of the vocal organs, and thus lost the benefit of loud tones and their well-known invigoration of the system.

Interestingly, Anthony very clearly does not refer to the soft voice as a result of woman's anatomy or "nature," but as a consequence of teaching and training.[20]

Women who do not fit society's behavioral prescriptions may find themselves characterized as loud, whether their actual decibel level exceeds the norm or not. We saw earlier that any out-group is subject to such labeling. A common example of recent years is the frequent reference to feminists as "shrill," i.e., both loud and high-pitched.

There are even differences in the intonation patterns used by each sex. Women have more variable intonations, or more contrastive levels, than men do. This greater variability in women's speech sounds is said to produce unsure intonation patterns, ones of whining, questioning, and helplessness—certainly not patterns to add authority to one's voice. In fact, the attribution is reminiscent of the remarks on the "unevenness" of the speech of blacks ("social insecurity"). The variability may also indicate greater emotional expressiveness of a more positive sort, though as we have seen, emotional expressiveness has worked most often to put women in a vulnerable rather than powerful position.

The building blocks of language and how to throw them (words and sentences). In the area of vocabulary and sentence structure, many descriptions of sex differences have tended to follow stereotypic conceptions of male and female roles: women are said to be people-oriented, concerned with internal states and integrating others into their world, while men are described as self-oriented, concerned with action and the projection of themselves into the environment. Women have been said to be euphemistic, to "prefer" refined, veiled and indirect expressions; of course, language taboos have made such usage more a necessity than a preference. We must be extremely wary of these descriptions: even when they do have some basis in empirical research, the research has often been biased in its assumptions, execution, or interpretation.

Robin Lakoff associates two forms of sentence structure with the un-

[20] Susan B. Anthony, "Woman: The Great Unpaid Laborer of the World" (c. 1848), originally in *The History of Woman Suffrage,* excerpted in Leslie B. Tanner, *Voices from Women's Liberation* (New York: New American Library, 1971), p. 42.

certainty described in women's speech: the use of the tag question and of requests.[21] A tag question takes the form, "This is the place, isn't it?" rather than an affirmative statement alone or a direct question, "Is this the place?" It is neither a flat claim nor a yes–no question, but allows the speaker to avoid full commitment to the statement. In addition to using fewer tag questions, men are said to use *commands* for wishes that women use *requests* for, and are presumably more likely to get their wish.

Differences in language associated with sex interact with those associated with socioeconomic status. The prestigious or "proper" form of speech, that associated with high-status persons, involves such niceties as pronouncing the "g" in running, or saying *th* "correctly," rather than as *d, t,* or *f,* in *with.* A number of detailed studies of how people choose among these patterns have found that females tend to use the "proper" form more than males do. Women's use of more prestige patterns seems to contradict an analysis based on their social subordination, but this is not necessarily so. This pattern has been attributed to women's insecure social position, which has made them more status-conscious, and to men's valuing of "non-standard" speech, on the other hand, because of its association with masculinity.[22]

Grouptalk: Conversational Patterns. There are differences in the conversational patterns of males and females, in addition to the tendency of males to talk more and to interrupt. However, most of the differences noted are again impressionistic. Bernard describes the flavor of the differences in these conversational styles: "Traditionally, the cultural norms for femininity and womanliness have prescribed appreciatively expressive talk or stroking for women . . . they were to raise the status of the other, relieve tension, agree, concur, comply, understand, accept." "Instrumental" talk, more associated with males, orients, conveys information, and may be argumentative and competitive.[23]

The analysis of joking well illuminates women's function in "stroking" males of a group, and Coser's remarks on the structure of joking in hospital staff meetings are relevant to our understanding of this function:

> In this culture women are expected to be passive and receptive, rather than active and initiating. A woman who has a good sense of humor is one who

[21] Robin Lakoff, "Language and Woman's Place," *Language in Society,* 1973, 2, 45–79; also see her book by the same title (New York: Harper and Row, 1975).

[22] See Peter Trudgill, "Sex, Covert Prestige, and Linguistic Change in the Urban British English of Norwich," in *Language in Society,* 1972, 1, 179–95; in Thorne and Henley, eds., *Language and Sex.*

[23] Jessie Bernard, *The Sex Game,* p. 137.

laughs (but not too loudly!) when a man makes a witticism or tells a good
joke. A man who has a good sense of humor is one who is witty in his
remarks and tells good jokes. The man provides; the woman receives. Thus
at the meetings, men made by far the more frequent witticisms—99 out of
103—but women often laughed harder.[24]

Coser makes clear that the women's fewer witticisms were not due to
their smaller number on the staff, and that these women were witty
enough outside of staff meetings.

Grotjahn too has observed that women who adhere to traditional social
demands are "supposed to be incapable of even retelling a joke," though
women have the necessary ingredients for humor ("natural intelligence,
hostility, and tendency to enjoy wit"). They avoid humor because of its
aggressive connotations:

> The women of our contemporary scene have to be careful, because any
> show of aggression, open or disguised, is taken by every man in our com-
> petitive culture as a challenge . . . to which he has to rise.[25]

This observation may give us some insight into the occasional claim that
feminists have no sense of humor.

The tendency to hesitate, to apologize, and to disparage one's own
statements, all patterns associated with subordinates, are also associated
with females. Terms of address, too, as well as reflecting status differences,
may reflect sex status; several linguists and psychologists have observed
that women are more frequently and readily addressed by their first names
than are men, but there are no hard data to support this speculation
(other than women's generally more subordinate occupational positions,
which of themselves receive subordinate address).

Control of a conversation's direction reflects status and power. Partly
because of male patterns of interruption and of female patterns of support
and agreement, control of conversational topics generally rests with the
males, and women may find it difficult or impossible to initiate a topic
when conversing with men. That control need not come solely from men's
own initiation of topics, but may well flow from their failure to respond
to many female-initiated topics. Phyllis Chesler has written,

> Even control of a simple—but serious—conversation is usually impossible
> for most wives when several men, including their husbands, are present. . . .
> Very rarely, if ever, do men listen silently to a group of women talking.

[24] Coser, "Laughter among Colleagues," p. 85.
[25] Martin Grotjahn, *Beyond Laughter* (New York: McGraw-Hiill, 1957), p. 37.

Even if there are a number of women talking, and only one man present, he will question the women . . . always in order to ultimately control the conversation, and always from a "superior" position.[26]

The issue of conversational control goes beyond living room conversations. Mary Jean Tully, writing in the Boston *Globe,* notes the difficult position of women and minority members appointed to Presidential "blue-ribbon" commissions, often forerunners of official policy. "The final problem," she writes,

> has to do with the dynamics of the meetings themselves. The experience of this commission [on Private Philanthropy and Public Needs] as well as some of its predecessors indicates that the non-Establishment voices are either not raised or, if raised, are not listened to. Partly, this is a result of their small relative numbers. It is probably also due in part to the influence of the formal physical set-up that tends to be one in which those members such as corporation heads, who are used to dominating large groups, can make their voices and their views prevail.[27]

Self-Disclosure. Self-disclosure is another aspect of conversation that varies with gender. A number of research studies have found that women disclose more personal information to others than men do, just as subordinates in general are more self-revealing.[28] Women who obtain authoritative positions presumably are less self-disclosing than the rest of us, and like powerful men, keep their cool in ruffling circumstances. Most women, however, have been socialized to display their emotions, their thoughts and ideas. Giving out this information about themselves, especially in the context of inequality, is giving others power over them. Self-disclosure (including emotional display) is not itself a weakness or negative behavior trait: like other gestures of intimacy, it has positive aspects, such as sharing of oneself and allowing others to open up, *when the self-disclosure is voluntary and reciprocal.*

Men's self-disclosure often seems very exclusive: many women will testify about a man, that they alone see his emotional and tender side. They feel privileged at being allowed this intimate peek, and seem to

[26] In Phyllis Chesler, "Marriage and Psychotherapy," in Radical Therapist Collective, eds., *The Radical Therapist* (produced by J. Agel; New York: Ballantine, 1971), p. 177.

[27] Mary Jean Tully, "Open up Those Elite Commissions," *Boston Evening Globe,* December 19, 1975.

[28] Paul C. Cozby, "Self-Disclosure: A Literature Review," *Psychologica! Bulletin,* 1973, 79, 73–91. Though some studies have failed to find a sex difference, none has reported greater male disclosure than female.

suggest the man's negative public self should be forgiven on the basis of this vulnerable alter-ego. This is a dangerous tradition, however: the more women make it possible for men to dichotomize themselves this way, the less will men free their emotionality, to be shown before others and accepted as an integral part of themselves; and the more entrenched will become the hard side they show to other males, and their deprecation of women, as weak and emotional.

Women function as this kind of emotional service station to men (and their families and to a lesser extent, other women) in other ways relevant in an analysis of power.[29] In particular, they take part in cooling-out anger in men,[30] assisting them to accept inferior status, injustice, and all the daily inequities they are subject to. In this capacity they function to perpetuate the hierarchical system between men as well as to preserve sex roles.

The 3 D's: Dismissing, Defining, and Deprecating.   The other sex difference aspect of language (after usage) is the language's treatment of women. Much conversation between the sexes takes place in the context of an underlying power struggle. But for women in that struggle, the language used is itself ammunition for the adversary. They are in the position of the dueler who faces an opponent with a gun which points backwards—the English language, like other languages, is loaded against women. This remains so at a time when heightened consciousness over race, and egalitarian conscience, have effected liberal changes in the language. The forms that sexism takes in English are mainly three: (1) it dismisses (ignores) women; (2) it defines them; and (3) it deprecates them. Again, we cannot examine this aspect of communication in detail, but we can note some of the main points made by those who have critically examined the language.

The paramount example of the ways in which the language dismisses females is the generic use of the male. Such common terms as *spokesman* and *chairman,* such phrases as "the man for the job," "the man in the street," "the working man," "men of good will," illustrate the way in which the female is supposed to be "included in" the male, but is rather "excluded from" the human race.

There is evidence that when the male is used generically, its interpretation is not necessarily generic, but is biased toward the male. Students asked to bring in pictures illustrating categories of social life more often

29 See Phyllis Chesler, *Women and Madness* (New York: Doubleday, 1972).
30 See Erving Goffman's classic analysis, "On Cooling the Mark Out," *Psychiatry,* 1952, 15, 451–63.

chose pictures of males only, when the categories were described in supposedly generic male terms (e.g., "economic man"), than when they were neutrally designated (e.g., "economic behavior"). And studies show that most references to the male *are* to male beings, not the generic. One study of children's schoolbooks, for example, found that of 940 uses of the word *he,* 97 percent referred to male human beings, male animals, or male-linked occupations.

Language reflects and helps maintain women's secondary status in our society by defining her and her "place." While men are often referred to in terms of their occupations—"the Florida banker"—women are more often referred to in relational terms—"the 29-year-old doctor's wife and mother of three." Women are also defined by the groupings they are put in: "women and children" veritably rolls off the tongue, and women are frequently classified with the infirm and the incompetent.[31]

The deprecation of women in the language is seen in the differing connotations and meanings of words applied to male and female things. Women are not only defined on the basis of their sex; it is the basis for their derogation too. One investigator researching terms for sexual promiscuity found 220 referring to women, and only 22 referring to men. Words such as *king, prince, lord, master,* and *father* have all maintained their stately meanings, while the similar words *queen, madam, mistress,* and *dame* have acquired debased meanings (this is a general pattern, not limited to these words). And many terms for females are constructed with feminine/diminutive endings tacked onto words that are not male in the first place: e.g., *poetess, authoress, usherette.*

The end result of this trivialization, derogation, definition and dismissal is hard to assess. There are very few studies that have looked at how male-oriented language disadvantages females, such as the one described on responses to the generic male. An especially provocative study found that young girls did more poorly on math problems traditionally worded in male-related terms, but did as well as the boys on problems worded in female terms.[32] But no amount of laboratory studies can measure the day-by-day effects of millions of females being daily surrounded and bombarded by a language that suggests they are trivial, secondary, sex objects, or just not there.

[31] See M. R. Key, "Linguistic Behavior of Male and Female," *Linguistics,* 1972, 88 (Aug. 15), 15–31; and her *Male/Female Language* (Metuchen, N.J.: Scarecrow Press, 1975).

[32] G. A. Milton, "Sex Differences in Problem Solving as a Function of Role Appropriateness of the Problem Content," *Psychological Reports,* 1959, 5, 705–08.

chapter six

ADVERTISEMENTS FOR THE SELF:

Demeanor

Certain behaviors oriented to one's own body are considered so gross that they regularly elicit expressions of disgust, even though we all engage in most or all of them at times. Yawning, scratching, spitting, picking one's nose or scabs, belching, hiccuping, and passing gas are not countenanced in "polite" company, but do have a certain degree of acceptance among intimates and in extremely informal settings. (Coughing and blowing one's nose are at a lesser level of ceremonial breach.) "Polite" company, that is, the social elite and those who would imitate them, are so removed from their bodies (undoubtedly a sign of spirituality and near-divinity) that they are expected not to feel the need to itch, belch, or fart. Generally, pictures of respected public figures caught in this type of activities are suppressed. In fact, people of some power (often political figures) may demand that no pictures be taken showing them even with tobacco or alcohol, which would convey a certain physical indulgence they don't want to be associated with.

These outcaste behaviors have an interesting position in social interaction, since many of them are seen as unavoidable physical impulses—e.g., yawning, belching, itching, hiccuping, farting—and, though disfavored, may be excused on petition of the offender. They are under a certain amount of willful control, however (probably the reason for their less-than-full excusability), especially by some expert practitioners. Goffman has noted a class of offenses called acts of malice or spite: "These often imply arrogance, disdain, and deep hostility, as when a middle-class person yawns directly before others in a slow and elaborate manner. . . .

When an individual wishes to show hostility to someone before whom he would ordinarily conduct himself tightly, extreme expressions of looseness become an available means." [1] Anyone who has seen young boys deliver soulful belches one after another at a family gathering's elaborate meal, or seen the angry looks directed at them for uncontrolled flatulence, has seen this phenomenon in action. Goffman cites an illustration from T. E. Lawrence, on life in an RAF training depot in which the surest source of humor was an occasional "loud spirtle of wind," which caused wild laughter with impunity since "farts are not punishable like any other retort." [2]

This power of disruption is the ultimate power of the powerless. It can be a potent one; at the other extreme from unstuffing shirts, but on the same continuum, is the strength of a strike—when workers interrupt the steady flow of goods and services. Even deflating the pompous and disrupting authoritative situations have their place in the onslaught against unjust privilege. In the face-to-face situations described above, the object is to ruffle the composed demeanor of authority. (It is often played as a game to push the offense to the limit, with the least punishment.) Authority is supposed to "keep its cool," to show little emotion and to be unaffected by events in the world around. The same uninvolvement is used as a status cue in interaction between status unequals: to ignore another, to disdain the other's concern, is to show you are much more important to the other than vice versa. (This is again the Principle of Least Interest, acting on the general demeanor of two participants in a situation.) To ruffle that cool, then, is to bring down, if only momentarily, that authority.

It is tempting to romanticize disruptions by belch, yawn, and fart, as some authors have, as jolly shows of power against authority. However, this form of "power" is as much a sign of powerlessness as bowing and scraping; only the powerless must exercise their power in covert ways. And the powerless, lest we forget, are those who have little food or money, dress or shelter, comfort and mental peace. Justice speaks better to smiting one's oppressor with a weapon than with a fart.

HANG LOOSE

We tend to think of demeanor, the way one presents and conducts oneself, as a product of something termed "breeding" (which in usage has tended to include both genetic endowment *and* upbringing) and/or

[1] Erving Goffman, *Behavior in Public Places: Notes on the Social Organization of Gatherings* (New York: Free Press, 1963), pp. 218, 228.
[2] Goffman, *Behavior in Public Places*, pp. 228–29.

some mysterious quality of "class." Whatever we think its sources to be, we generally attribute demeanor to an individual, not to a situation or group identification. And yet, those things demeanor encompasses—deportment, dress, bearing—have distinctive class-determined characteristics. There are upper- and lower-class rules of deportment and modes of dress and carriage. Closely related, there are rules and modes that go with power and with powerlessness. For example, the forms of bodily laxness described above are extreme examples of "loose" demeanor. Less dramatic versions of tightness and looseness, however, are part of our everyday interaction and, like other forms of nonverbal communication, have much to indicate about our status and authority.

Demeanor, like deference, can be exhibited to others under either symmetrical or asymmetrical rules. As Goffman has written, symmetry in demeanor seems generally the case between social equals, but not between unequals. Here, those in higher positions are allowed more latitude in behavior, while underlings must be more circumspect: *

> . . . at staff meetings on the psychiatric units of the hospital, medical doctors had the privilege of swearing, changing the topic of conversation, and sitting in undignified position; attendants, on the other hand, had the right to attend staff meetings and to ask questions during them . . . but were implicitly expected to conduct themselves with greater circumspection than was required of doctors. . . . Similarly, doctors had the right to saunter into the nurses' station, lounge on the station's dispensing counter, and engage in joking with the nurses; other ranks participated in this informal interaction with doctors, but only after doctors had initiated it.[3]

These behaviors fall into the complex that Goffman has organized into the idea of "tightness and looseness," that is, "how disciplined the individual is obliged to be in connection with the several ways in which respect for the gathering and its social occasion can be expressed." [4] How disciplined a person must be relates closely to the degree of involvement the occasion requires. The discipline (or lack of it) is shown in such factors as the ceremonial rank and neatness of one's dress; engagement in side activities such as reading, studying the environment, daydreaming;

* I think the use of taboo behaviors as protest does not necessarily contradict the general picture of dominants' greater looseness in demeanor. These body functions are supposedly beyond that realm of manipulated self-presentation. Put another way, the realm in which looseness may be used to convey superiority has lower limits.

[3] Erving Goffman, *Interaction Ritual* (Garden City, N.Y.: Doubleday, 1967), pp. 78–79.

[4] Goffman, *Behavior in Public Places*, Chap. 13.

and engaging in such personal physical caretaking as spitting, picking one's nose, belching, yawning.

Circumspection and tightness are the signals we offer up to superiors, or exhibit in public, to indicate our subordinate position. Mehrabian has presented experimental evidence for actual body tension as a correlate of status. Asymmetrical placement of the limbs, a sideways lean and/or reclining position when seated, and specific relaxations of the hands or neck are all indicators of postural relaxation, associated with a high status communicator. Communicators relax more when paired with an addressee of lower status than with one of higher status.[5]

The Watergate conspiracy trial again gives an example of the relaxed demeanor of self-importance and unconcern, contrasted with the tension and thrust of intense involvement. Here former Attorney General John Mitchell relaxes on the witness stand, being questioned by government prosecutor James O. Neal; the reporter gives us a graphic picture of the contrast in their styles: "Neal leaned forward on the podium, pushed his

[5] Albert Mehrabian, *Nonverbal Communication* (Chicago: Aldine-Atherton, 1972), pp. 25–30.

glasses onto his forehead and unleashed a staccato of questions. Mitchell leaned back in his chair and offered terse, laconic replies." [6]

Of course, relaxation is also the form of demeanor used among intimates. The invitation to "Relax!" or "Loosen up," offered by the high status person, can be seen as another instance in which the higher status has the privilege of initiating greater intimacy. (Under the circumstances, however, it is easier said than done.) Such a suggestion can be compared, in fact, with the military command "At ease." "At ease" is not, in reality, an invitation to relax but a command to shift to a slightly more stable posture, while remaining as restrained and alert as before.

It may be observed that we have here another example of the norm in which that behavior exhibited by superiors to subordinates (looseness) is exhibited symmetrically among members of the lower social strata (when apart from those in power).

Goffman suggests that a pervasive difference exists between middle- and lower-class American males in their degree of public looseness.[7] He claims that lower-class males, not having to worry about keeping their clothes unrumpled or unsoiled, and having a social role that requires less orientation to public gatherings as such, are afforded much more looseness than their middle-class counterparts. These latter must keep relatively neat and clean, erect and stiff, alert to and involved in the gathering.

This picture, though, doesn't jibe with the earlier evidence of subordinates being required to conduct themselves with greater circumspection than superiors. One explanation for greater middle-class circumspection has been its hope for upward mobility, and therefore greater attention (than in either upper or lower classes) to the rules of conduct by which it must prove itself. Moreover, the situations described are different. The lower-class looseness is for public places, and isn't detailed for the presence of superiors, as in the staff meeting. We may well imagine that that looseness would evaporate in the presence of a recognized authority or superior, such as one's father, a police officer, or the boss. A distinction that might be made, then, is that subordinates' circumspection is exhibited only (or mainly) in the presence of dominants, not as a general marker of class. Working class men perhaps spend more time in the presence of their peers than middle-class men (and than women of both classes), who work more often in proximity to superiors.

[6] Jane Denison, "Mitchell Testifies He Kept Silent to Ensure Nixon Win," Boston *Globe*, November 28, 1974, p. 32.
[7] Goffman, *Behavior in Public Places*, Chap. 13.

CLOTHES MAKE THE MAN NOT RESPONSIBLE

We all know that the rich and powerful dress more expensively and exclusively, both because they can afford to and because dress is a primary indicator of their class status. And that the super-rich have more freedom to dress in ratty old clothes if they wish, being under no compulsion to indicate wealth that is everywhere self-evident. The ill fit of mass-produced clothes, the shabbiness of clothes one can't afford to replace, and the inappropriateness of clothes for some occasions because of limited wardrobe all proclaim low social status. What else is to be said about clothing? Are there clothes that dominate, that influence, that diminish?

A clothing consultant who "has spent more than a decade dressing men to succeed" would say so. His comments on clothing for the principals in the Watergate trials illustrate some aspects of influencing people through clothing, as well as aspects of class and race.[8] When Haldeman, Ehrlichman, and Mitchell appeared before the Senate hearings, their need, according to the expert, John Molloy, was to appear credible to the public. Pinstripe suits were the prescription. "The pinstriped suit has been traditionally the most credible appeal for a man to wear when selling something important," he comments.

However, Molloy didn't think this was the proper tack when they went on trial. For one thing, ". . . during the Watergate hearings the credibility of the pinstriped suit shrank." * Moreover, the purpose in a trial is different. Proper dress for defendants is that which, first, does not offend, and second, tries to relate to the jury and judge. The earlier traditional garb that appealed to primarily white middle-class TV hearing-watchers could not be expected to garner much identification from a predominantly black Washington jury.

Molloy suggested they should "borrow Jerry Ford's neckties": "A lot of the President's neckties are non-authoritarian and sporty. His light-colored suits are too. If you're trying to visually communicate to a jury that you weren't the man in charge, wearing non-authoritarian clothes

---

[8] Marji Kunz, "Clothes Make the Defendant," Boston *Globe*, October 12, 1974.
* This is in accord with the "principle of congruity" introduced in 1955 by Osgood and Tannenbaum, which states (loosely put) that when a positively valued thing (pinstriped suit) and a negatively valued thing (untrustworthy government official) are linked, the values given each shift closer toward the other. Charles E. Osgood and Percy H. Tannenbaum, "The Principle of Congruity in the Prediction of Attitude Change," *Psychological Review*, 1955, 62, 42–55.

could be a plus." He thought they should wear nonflashy shirts, suits in medium tones, and neckties that were neither flamboyant nor ultra-upper-class. He added, though, that these men's appearances were so well known that it would be hard to change their image.

However, even without his advice (for the trial), two of the defendants did make some change in image. Haldeman exchanged his famed crew-cut for longer, average-length hair. Molloy comments that the crew-cut, a '50s hair style, had connoted '50s thinking styles to blacks; longer hair made Haldeman look less prejudiced. Ehrlichman showed up at the trial suntanned, in lighter blue suits, eyeglass frames of fine gold wire (less foreboding than his old dark-rimmed half-glasses), and copious smiles. Perhaps these image changes had something to do with the relatively light sentences they received for their crimes; at the least, the new images must have helped to separate these men from their former boss and their former selves. These illustrations remind us that when they *did* wish to appear powerful and responsible, these men dressed in ways that pro-claimed them as such. This is how intimidation may get the jump on any of us, and how the typical superior-subordinate relations are strengthened.

WALKING TALL

The bearing with which one presents oneself also proclaims one's posi-tion in life. We are all familiar with the contrast between what is called "the bearing of a gentleman" and the shuffle of the servant, or the slump of a "nobody." Disease, fatigue, and occupational hazards of the poor and working classes have played a great part in stoop-shoulders, shuffles, limps, and other unpleasant "personal" characteristics, including ugliness. The "beautiful people" retain beauty and exhibit their class through not having to risk life or limb in work, and having the wealth to purchase many of the concomitants of beauty.

But there are postures of deference and dominance beyond those de-termined by class and occupation, of course. Scheflen describes, for ex-ample, habitual submissive behavior exhibited by hunched-down posture and avoiding the gaze of others.[9] Military bearing is, on the other hand, an obvious example of the appearance of command. Drawing oneself up to one's full height, ramrod-straight and impassive of face, the aspect of

[9] Albert E. Scheflen, *Communicational Structure: Analysis of a Psychotherapy Transaction* (Bloomington, Ind.: Indiana University Press, 1973), p. 194.

the withdrawn and wooden, personality-absent commander, is certainly dominating. There is an apparent paradox, however: restriction of expression and movement (hands at the side) are characteristics usually imposed on subordinates, not superiors; one is puzzled to find them prescribed for officers. However, the military is a hierarchy in which every officer must be prepared to be a soldier too: obedience is much more emphasized and obvious in this than in other hierarchical structures, hence the mixture of nonverbal command and obedience in one body.

Standing tall is in itself a good way of achieving dominance; being tall is even better. It is well known now that tall men are more likely to be hired, to receive higher salaries, to be elected president, and to gain many other advantages than are short ones, as demonstrated by research and experience.[10] And it works the other way around: important people seem bigger to us. When nursing students were asked to estimate heights of known faculty and student members (female) of their school, the heights of the two faculty members were overestimated, and of the two students, underestimated.* Similarly, when other undergraduates (presumably both male and female) were asked to estimate the height of a man introduced to them as any one of five different academic ranks, the estimated height increased as the ascribed status increased.[11] We are so used to according privileges and rank to tall people (usually men) that when we see persons of rank, we automatically assume that they're tall.

COMING ON FEMININE

Demeanor has played a major part in the definition of femininity, and in the prescriptions for women's behavior. Clothing, one factor in demeanor, has been long a focus of attention on women, and in our culture

---

[10] See Saul Feldman, "The Presentation of Shortness in Everyday Life—Height and Heightism in American Society: Toward a Sociology of Stature," paper presented at meetings of the American Sociological Association, 1971.

* Despite this finding that women of higher status were perceived as taller, it should be noted that it is *not* so clear that tall women are ascribed greater value and receive the advantages that tall men do. However, Phyllis Chesler and Emily Jane Goodman report that women randomly chosen from *Current Biography* were significantly taller than the average American female (*Women, Money and Power,* [New York: Morrow, 1976, p. 72]).

[11] W. D. Dannenmaier and F. J. Thumin, "Authority Status as a Factor in Perceptual Distortion of Size," *Journal of Social Psychology,* 1964, 63, 361–65. Paul R. Wilson, "Perceptual Distortion of Height as a Function of Ascribed Academic Status," *Journal of Social Psychology,* 1968, 74, 97–102.

has been particularly designed to emphasize their bodily contours.* It has also been a showcase for the display of the frail materials (like lace and chiffon) associated with the female world, so it has been a major point of emphasis for women's weakness. The frailty of the material, its fineness and therefore difficulty of cleaning (compelling one to avoid getting it dirty), and the design of the clothing have combined to restrict women's movements in many ways. Skirts, for example, have kept many girls and women from engaging in certain physical activities and sitting in certain positions. In particular, straight skirts make it impossible to run; but some fashionable shoes make it almost impossible to walk, let alone run. Restrictive underwear—tight corsets, girdles, and the like—has also curtailed women's physical activities.

The design of women's clothing to stick to body contours has precluded the incorporation of pockets into women's clothing,[12] a convenience that men's looser clothing has. Women are forced to carry pocketbooks, which further restricts their physical possibilities—it is awkward to carry other parcels, to deal with doors and children, or to run, with a purse. The function of the purse as women's albatross makes it a symbol of ridicule; many caricatures of women (by both females and males) utilize a purse as a comic focus, and impersonations of male homosexuals likewise use a purse as a sort of badge of shame. (Obviously, its psychoanalytic implications as a "vessel," a treasure chest that may be opened or closed, are not lost in these interpretations.)

Women's restrictive clothing is only part of the armament that keeps women in "dignified, ladylike" demeanor. Their schooling in proper posture for "ladies" is another. Young girls' training in posture is less likely to emphasize upright healthy ("military") bearing than is boys'. In fact, much of the example they see in magazine fashion models clearly glorifies the stylish slump of inactivity. Girls' postural training instead emphasizes propriety—keeping the legs properly closed when sitting, not leaning over so as to reveal breasts, keeping the skirt down to whatever is its current accepted leg coverage. The condensing described by the character Wanda in Piercy's novel (Chapter 2) is part and parcel of women's required demeanor. Women of all classes and status levels may not sit in

---

* Una Stannard, in "Clothing and Sexuality" (*Sexual Behavior*, 1971 (May), 1, 2) shows, however, that female sexuality and male neutrality in dress have not always been the case. Until Victorian times, males as well as females paid great attention to dress, and men's clothing was often scandalously revealing. Females and males through the ages and across cultures have more often dressed alike than differently. For, as Stannard makes clear, traditions like women's skirts and men's trousers have nothing to do with sexuality or anatomical structure: they are mere custom. (Part of Stannard's discussion is found on pp. 24–33 and 64 of *Sexual Behavior*.)

[12] I am indebted to Nancy Lawler for this observation.

undignified positions, swear, lounge on counters, or otherwise show the freedom in demeanor that Goffman describes as the privilege of those of higher status. Circumspection is required of them over and above their inferior work situations in life. As we saw earlier, there appears to be more class variation in demeanor among men.

This circumspection, the tightness of demeanor of the status inferior, is in the tension of their bodies too. Mehrabian's studies of body tension and relaxation found that females are generally less relaxed than are males, and he suggests that females convey more submissive attitudes by these tenser postures.[13] In addition, in his communication studies, other communicators (of both sexes) assumed more relaxed positions when addressing females than males, as they are more relaxed with lower-status addressees than with higher-status ones.

A "loose woman" is one of bad reputation, and her attributed looseness comes from a lack of accepted control over her sexuality. But her portrayal in fiction and drama often carries other displays of looseness, e.g., in clothing, posture and language as well. (The Italian actress Anna Magnani has often created such a character, for example, in *Open City* or *The Rose Tattoo*.) It is furthermore interesting to note that a "tight" woman, one who doesn't relax enough, is also often condemned, from the opposite end of the spectrum. These opposing demands are not as contradictory as they seem, however. They fit into the traditional view that a woman must restrict her sexuality (and its symbols) to all but the one (man) with whom she has a sanctified relationship: and to him she must be an endless fountain of sexuality.

Because of these restrictions on women's demeanor, the extreme looseness of body-focused functions (belching, nose-picking, and so on) is generally not open to women of our culture as an avenue of revolt. In fact, this controlled expression of "uncontrollable" functions may be a peculiarly male type of aggressiveness and hostility toward authority. If it should ever come into women's repertoire, however, it will carry great power, since it directly undermines the sacredness of women's bodies, a cornerstone of their suppression; and it will consequently command greater retaliation.

Height is another factor of demeanor that affects reactions by and to women. Since women in general are shorter than men in general, women are already in a position of deference by having to look up to men. The psychological effects of going through life shorter than most other males has been sympathetically noted as an injustice and burden for short males. But when will we know the dimensions of what may be a devastating toll

---

[13] Mehrabian, *Nonverbal Communication*, pp. 27–30.

LOOSE WOMAN

on women—the psychological burden upon one whole sex going through life shorter than the other? Added to the additional struggle for esteem that shortness creates, is the role prescription, accompanied by myriad rewards and punishments, for women to be small (as it is for men to be tall). Much of the early training of some tall girls is in how to hide, rather than take advantage of, their height. Many of them adopt slumping as a way of avoiding their height and the punishments it brings.*

The different aspects of demeanor contribute to what is known as "first impressions." But what is the first judgment you make about people on initially seeing them? Is your first impression centered on dress, height, face, race, a certain look of the eyes? No, I believe a person's *sex* is the first thing you note about them, though reading the voluminous psycho-

---

* Though there has been a premium on height for women in certain ultra-feminine roles, e.g., fashion models or show "girls," it has not served to make tallness a desirable image for women in general. These people exist as freaks, in a manner. Miss Americas, though often the tall side have not been exceedingly tall. And tall fashion models are often photographed in a fashionable slump. Chesler and Goodman write, " 'Tall' women, especially . . . successful entertainers, tend to earn more . . . than most women . . . ." They make the point that the tall-and-thin standard of ultimate beauty in our society is a form of male impersonation in women—our culture is a male homosexual one, its values favor the look of beautiful male adolescents in women (*Women, Money and Power*, p. 47–48).

logical literature on impression formation will never let you in on that.[14] I began to realize the priority of sex impression after a few experiences in confusing the sex of strangers (including being alone with one in a women's restroom). Trends in youth and counterculture in recent years have provided an excellent natural laboratory for the study of this phenomenon. "Unisex" hair and dress styles caused many outsiders to complain with bitterness and vehemence that they could no longer distinguish the sexes. It was as if their children had taken some carefully-wrought gift their parents gave them, and thrown it in the trash (as indeed they had). Even those of us who thought we welcomed androgyny found ourselves unwittingly searching strangers for breasts, the sole distinguishing characteristic that remained.

Why do we want so badly to "tell the girls from the boys"? The need is felt with such urgency that it must be assumed to be preliminary to action: we intend to behave differently to people, depending on their sex.* Indeed, it is the first thing most people ask or tell about newborn babies; when infants go public, many people won't interact with them without first asking their sex. Anyone who has been mistaken for someone of the other sex—for example, women with masculine-sounding names or men with high-pitched voices (when speaking on the telephone)—can well testify to the different treatment they get according to their ascribed gender.

Author Jan Morris in *Conundrum* describes life from both sides of the gender fence, and writes:

> We are told that the social gap between the sexes is narrowing, but I can only report that having, in the second half of the twentieth century, experienced life in both roles, there seems to me no aspect of existence, no moment of the day, no contact, no arrangement, no response, which is not different for men and for women. The very tone of voice in which I was now addressed [after becoming a woman], the very posture of the person next in the queue, the very feel in the air when I entered a room or sat at a restaurant table, constantly emphasized my change of status.[15]

Gender is the first judgment we make on initiating contact because, sadly enough, it is a prime determinant of the nature of that contact.

---

* A computer analysis of the traits given characters in Theodore Dreiser's novels found that the female/male distinction was a central dimension in his assignment of character. Females were likely to be attractive, charming, defiant, intelligent, cold, clever; males, to have sincerity, genius, greatness. Seymour Rosenberg and Russell Jones, "A Method for Investigating and Representing a Person's Implicit Theory of Personality: Theodore Dreiser's View of People," *Journal of Personality and Social Psychology*, 1972, 22, 372–86.

[14] See Chris L. Kleinke, *First Impressions: The Psychology of Encountering Others* (Englewood Cliffs, N.J.: Prentice-Hall, 1975), for a good review of this literature.

[15] Jan Morris, *Conundrum* (New York: Harcourt Brace Jovanovich, 1974), p. 165.

chapter seven

TACTUAL POLITICS:

Touch

When Michelangelo painted the scene of creation in the Sistine Chapel, he chose to portray the giving of life as a *touch* from God to Adam, rather than what is described in Genesis, that God "breathed into his nostrils the breath of life." And few observers have noted this difference: the magic of touch is seen as so natural one almost senses the spark of life jumping the gap between the outstretched hands. Forgetting a moment the question of whether modern viewers could relate reverently to what could only look like a mouth-to-mouth resuscitation scene, Michelangelo's use of touch reminds us of the special place this gesture has had in human history, particularly as an act of divine and magical connotation. Its background and salience make it the perfect gesture to study in order to illustrate certain points about the social context of nonverbal communication.

Human touch is as old as human beings and as new as encounter groups, as varied as a mother's lint-picking, a hearty slap-on-the-back, and a gynecological examination. That this important sense is now getting the attention from social observers that it has long deserved testifies to

Some of the material in this chapter has been reported in "Status and Sex: Some Touching Observations," *Bulletin of the Psychonomic Society*, 1973, 2, 91–93. It was also partially reported in "The Politics of Touch," a paper at the 1970 meeting of the American Psychological Association, printed in Phil Brown (ed.), *Radical Psychology* (New York: Harper & Row, 1973), pp. 421–33, from which some of the matter is taken. Other research has been described in "Preliminary Report to Participants in Touch Study" (Harvard University), December, 1972. This research was supported by Special Research Fellowship 1 FO3 MH 35977-0 MTLH from the National Institute of Mental Health.

its vast importance in everyday life, as well as to the emphasis that the "human potential" movement has put on it. But most of the writers who have been quick to publish on the subject, whether renowned anthropologist or encounter-group participant, have focused on its use in the communication of intimacy (particularly sexual intimacy), and have overlooked an important aspect of touch in a hierarchy-ridden society: *the use of touch (especially between the sexes) to maintain the social hierarchy.*

Touch is as friendly as peanut butter; how can I be so unfeeling as to put its use in another context, the nasty domain of power? Let me give a few examples that illustrate what I'm talking about. If you work in an office, or store, or factory, are you more likely to go over to the boss and put a hand on his or her shoulder when discussing the job, or is the boss more likely to do that to you? Think of interactions between these pairs of persons of differing status and picture who would be more likely to touch the other—put an arm around the shoulder, a hand on the back, tap the chest, hold the wrist, and so on: teacher/student; master/servant; police officer/accused person; doctor/patient; minister/parishioner; adviser/advisee; foreman/worker; businessman/secretary. If you have had the usual enculturation, I think you will find the typical picture to be that of the superior-status person touching the inferior-status one.

An illustrative incident involves myself and the Vice Chancellor and Chancellor of the university I taught at at the time. After a large meeting one spring, the Vice Chancellor came over to me and took my upper arms in his two hands, saying he wanted to tell me something; he continued holding me in this restrictive fashion as he proceeded to talk with me. After he finished, and he had finally let go, I grabbed him back, then remarked that I would have to tell him sometime about my thesis which is the subject of this chapter. He expressed interest, so I began telling him about it, and he found it plausible; at this moment the Chancellor approached, the only man on campus in higher authority, laid his hand on the arm of the Vice Chancellor, and urged him to accompany him to their next meeting. The Vice Chancellor and I were both struck by the aptness of this action, and I think I made my point.

It is, in fact, often considered an affront, an insubordination, for a person of lower status to touch one of higher status. Goffman's description of the "touch system" in a hospital, in which doctors could touch nurses but nurses could not touch doctors, illustrates the workings of this touch privilege in an institutional hierarchy. The "untouchable" castes of India, it should be noted, are not necessarily ones whom higher castes are forbidden to touch (though few would wish to), but rather ones whose members are forbidden to touch those of higher caste, their touch being considered a defilement. We will look at the hierarchical implication of touching, but first it will help to examine some of our knowledge about touch in a broader sense.

THE POWER OF TOUCH

Both in the past and present, touch has been surrounded by an aura of magic and taboo. The touch of the English king was supposed in years past to cure scrofula, the disease known as "king's evil." The touch of "holy men" throughout the ages, including Jesus and the apostles down through the popes, and "faith healers" everywhere, has been believed to cast out devils and disease.* But then the devil's touch was embued with magical qualities too: it was believed to confer anesthesia to the spot where Satan entered the body of one possessed. Indeed, the search for anesthetic spots was one of the tests used in witchcraft trials during the Spanish Inquisition.

The magic of touch is seen in various religious rites which involve a "laying on of hands" for purposes of consecration. In the Christian church, certain branches proudly claim an unbroken succession of hands laid on their priesthood, from St. Peter down to the present. This "apostolic succession" illustrates an important psychological fact about touching implied in its magical properties, but true too in its ordinary uses: subjectively, touch is no short-lived event, finished when a hand is removed from the person, but rather is perceived as part of one's history, an event of real magnitude, effecting some permanent change. Fans of sports heroes and rock stars often pass on to their friends the touch received from their idol.

Though we still thirst for the healing touch of the super-great, "objective" reporting and our anti-superstitious times sometimes obscure the fact. The same media that report seriously on faith healers and the consecration of bishops, on the masses scrambling to kiss the pope's ring or to shake the president's hand, seldom fail to ridicule the fans of rock stars or of movie and sports stars, who scramble to touch or be touched by their idols, or to gain a magic relic from their person. Clearly, we

---

* In the New Testament, for instance, of 25 miracles of healing attributed to Jesus, 19 occur within touching range and tell the method of healing. Fourteen of these are accomplished through touch, in all but one case Jesus' touch to the afflicted rather than vice versa.

have not left the magic of touch in our past—"She touched me!" is as personally dramatic a realization today as yesterday.

It's not just contact with the magical and great that we desire, however; much evidence suggests that the desire for physical contact *per se* stems from deeply-rooted, perhaps physical, need. The psychologists Bowlby and Harlow, among others, have demonstrated the importance of physical contact to infant development, and there is evidence that this need continues through adult life.[1] Sidney Jourard suggests that "body contact has the function of confirming one's bodily being," in this age of disembodiment.[2]

It shouldn't surprise us that touch is a vital experience to us: as a sensory capacity, touch is the most basic of the senses, the one against

---

[1] See, for example, J. Bowlby, *Attachment and Loss* (New York: Basic Books, 1969); Harry F. Harlow, "The Nature of Love," *American Psychologist*, 1958, 13, 673–85; Ashley Montagu, *Touching: The Human Significance of the Skin* (New York: Columbia University Press, 1971); and Desmond Morris, *Intimate Behaviour* (New York: Random House, 1971).

[2] Sidney M. Jourard, "An Exploratory Study of Body-Accessibility," *British Journal of Social and Clinical Psychology*, 1966, 5, 221–31.

which the others are tested. The skin, which contains receptors for pressure, pain, hot and cold, can be considered a sense organ of giant proportion (compared to the other sense organs, which would together barely
cover one's palm), turned in all directions, operating in dark and in still-
ness, in all conditions but the most extreme, making the finest individual
and pattern discriminations. It is the most primitive sensitivity, develop-
ing out of the same embryonic layer (the ectoderm) as the other sense
organs and the nervous system. "The skin is the mother sense and out
of it, all the other senses have been derived." [3]

As further testimony to its fundamental character and salience in human
experience, the language of touch permeates our speech, probably as
much as that of sight. Montagu remarks that the entry for "touch" in the
Oxford English Dictionary is 14 columns, by far the longest.[4] We use
this metaphor to speak of understanding—for example, words such as
perceive, conceive, grasp, accept, catch on all come from roots meaning
"to take hold of." In speaking of emotion, we have many words from
sources that refer to physical contact: *attraction, affection, attachment,
sentiment, feeling,* for some.[5] And there is another category harder to
classify: we are "touched" by a sad story, "touched" for ten dollars,
"touched" in the head, "touched" to the quick by an insult. All these
latter usages convey the idea of accessibility to privileged areas: to our
emotions, to our purse, to our mind, to our pride. Our language in this
sense illustrates that the act of touching is one of importance to our
person, not to be taken lightly; that touch is a privilege, perhaps, one to
be sought and shared with those closest to us, but to be carefully
guarded from strangers.

Middle-class American norms reflect this notion, remaining opposed
to wholesale touching, despite the influence of the counterculture. This
fact is borne out by the extreme lengths to which we sometimes go to
avoid touching others in public. A person who accidentally touches another generally takes pains to apologize; persons forced into close proximity, as in a crowded elevator, uncomfortably constrict their bodies
and movements to avoid touching. It becomes ludicrous when close
friends are squeezed into close situations, like a small kitchen, and one
apologizes for brushing the other's body, when it cannot be avoided.

[3] F. B. Dresslar, "Studies in the Psychology of Touch," *American Journal of Psychology,* 1894, 6, 313–68.
[4] Montagu, *Touching,* p. 125.
[5] Dresslar, "Studies in Touch," has cited a number of these words and gives further
examples from Chipeway (sic) and Aztec, in which the root words for "love" have
the meaning "to attach, to fasten" (pp. 317, 323). Montagu, *Touching,* also offers a
brief discussion of touch-derived words related to emotional expression (pp. 125–26).

The zoologist Desmond Morris attributes modern society's avoidance of physical contact to its crowded living conditions and to the confusion of tactual contact with sexual contact, which therefore necessitates avoidance of *non*sexual contact as well.[6]

Concomitant with the proscriptions on touching are strong social *prescriptions* about touch, so that people can also be observed to go through strange contortions to touch when the occasion demands it (usually a handshake), moving awkward bundles from one arm to another, or apologizing if they cannot juggle things enough to shake the other's hand. Furthermore, despite extremes of touch-avoidance, it is probably true that people fervently wish, even need, to be touched, and satisfy this desire in whatever way they can. Morris cites ritualized encounters, such as those with encounter groups, as one source of physical contact, and substitutes such as children, pets, objects, and persons with "license to touch" (e.g., doctors and nurses, beauticians and barbers, masseurs and masseuses) as others.[7]

Presumably prostitutes would also fall into this last category, as persons whose touch may be purchased, by men; but the purchase of paid sexual partnership is not as readily available to women, who must have as great a need to be touched. There is evidence that women deprived of human touch do seek it through sex: Hollender describes female psychiatric patients (21 of 39 he studied) who, in their desire to be *held,* resorted to sexual enticement.[8] The same tactic is noted in 8 of 20 unmarried mothers, in the report of Malmquist, Kiresuk and Spano.[9] Hollender believes that for some women this need to be held is a major factor in "promiscuity." Of course, this may also be true for men, to whom the term promiscuity is seldom applied.

These don'ts and do's are, of course, very culture-determined rules, as are nearly all patterns of nonverbal interaction. Hall's classic book *The Silent Language* is familiar to many as an exposition of the ways different cultures approach the universal dimensional systems of time and space. In writing of the different distances we deem appropriate for various types of communication, Hall draws a contrast between (U.S.) Americans

[6] Morris, *Intimate Behaviour,* Chap. 4, especially pp. 104–5.

[7] Morris, *Intimate Behaviour,* Chap. 5.

[8] M. H. Hollender, "Prostitution, the Body, and Human Relatedness," *International Journal of Psychoanalysis,* 1961, 42, 404–13; and "The Wish to be Held," *Archives of General Psychiatry,* 1970, 22, 445–53.

[9] Carl P. Malmquist, T. J. Kiresuk, and R. M. Spano, "Personality Characteristics of Women with Repeated Illegitimacies: Descriptive Aspects," *American Journal of Orthopsychiatry,* 1966, 36, 476–84. These investigators seem to have come to their conclusion independently of Hollender's work, though publishing after him.

and people of other cultures, particularly of Latin extraction. Americans use greater distances for all types of interaction.[10] Since touching is in a sense an invasion of one's personal space, we see the parallel in the amount of touching deemed appropriate in different cultures; Americans (like the English from whom many of us are descended) are very untouching people.

An anecdote by Jourard illustrates the point very well:

> I watched pairs of people engaged in conversation in coffee shops in San Juan (Puerto Rico), London, Paris, and Gainesville (Florida), counting the number of times that one person touched another at one table during a one-hour sitting. The "scores" were, for San Juan, 180; for Paris, 110; for London, 0; and for Gainesville, 2.[11]

Within a country like the United States, with numerous ethnic minorities, we expect and find also cultural variation: persons of Jewish and Italian descent, or from Spanish-speaking backgrounds such as Puerto Rican and Chicano, are believed to use more tactual expression than those of the dominant Anglo-Saxon-derived culture.[12]

One such cultural contrast was found by Thomas Cannon in an observational study made with the purpose of finding out whether Americans' touch frequency decreases as they become more Americanized. To this end he observed persons congregating prior to, and immediately following, church services, in a predominantly Italian section of Boston and in a middle-class suburb (Newton) of northern European derivation.[13] Both churches were Roman Catholic. He observed subjects for two-minute time periods (or to the end of the interaction, if less than two minutes), counting the number of times touches were exchanged during the two minutes (and attempting to observe only extra-familial conversations, to eliminate inflation of his measure by husband–wife hand-holding). He found that the Italian-Americans touched, on the average, every 27 seconds; the more assimilated suburbanites, every 40 seconds. He also noted that qualitatively "the Italians' touches seemed more sincere and

---

[10] Edward T. Hall, *The Silent Language* (New York: Doubleday, 1959). See also Montagu, *Touching*, p. 299; and *A Handbook of Gestures: Colombia and the United States*, by Robert L. Saitz and E. J. Cervenka (The Hague: Mouton, 1972).

[11] Jourard, "Body-Accessibility," p. 222.

[12] See, for example, David Efron, *Gesture, Race and Culture* (The Hague: Mouton, 1972; originally published 1941), subtitled "A Tentative Study of Some of the Spatio-Temporal and 'Linguistic' Aspects of the Gestural Behavior of Eastern Jews and Southern Italians in New York City, Living Under Similar as Well as Different Environmental Conditions."

[13] Thomas Cannon, unpublished paper, Boston University, 1971.

giving; more of their touches were kisses and their hand touches were longer compared to little kissing and short-traditional handshakes of the subjects in Newton."

We have seen then the power of touch to convey great meaning to people—for good, for evil, for information, for individual and ethnic identity, perhaps for sustaining life itself. Let us look now at other distinctions it conveys and systems it sustains.

THE TOUCH OF POWER

A few years ago I became interested in the social patterns in touching, particularly the network of touch privileges by which the social order is maintained, and particularly its expression in the control of women. It had been pointed out to me in high school that people who touch others a lot use it as a form of control (or at least that's how I remember it), and I naively believed that the dominance aspect of touching was generally understood in our society. Surely the annals of psychology would uncover the documentation I needed to understand this phenomenon. Unfortunately, I was wrong; though there were a few oblique references to the power side of the phenomenon, there seemed to be a determined conspiracy to convince us that touching exists only as the ultimate gesture of friendship and sexuality: "Certain categories of personnel had the privilege of *expressing their affection and closeness to others* by the ritual of bodily contact with them. . . . The doctors touched other ranks as a means of *conveying friendly support and comfort* . . ." "Cheek patting, hair patting, and chucking under the chin are, in the Western world, forms of behavior *indicating affection,* and all are tactile." "In general, for men in our culture, proximity (touching) is restricted to the opposite sex and its function is *primarily sexual in nature."* "The author's view is that touching is *equated with sexual intent,* either consciously, or at a less-conscious level" (all italics added).[14]

These printed assurances did not convince me that touching indicated only friendship and sexuality. It was in fact the confusion of power with

[14] The quotes are, respectively, from Goffman, "The Nature of Deference and Demeanor," *Interaction Ritual* (Garden City, N.Y.: Doubleday, 1967), p. 74; Montagu, *Touching,* p. 238; Michael Lewis, "Parents and Children: Sex-Role Development" (*School Review,* 1972, 80, 229–40), p. 237; and Sidney Jourard and Jane Rubin, "Self-Disclosure and Touching: A Study of Two Modes of Interpersonal Encounter and Their Inter-Relation" (*Journal of Humanistic Psychology,* 1968, 8, 39–48), p. 47.

sexuality that became obvious to me as I grew more aware of tactile contact in the world around me (but more on that later).

There did exist some nods of recognition to the use of touch as a symbol of status or dominance, Goffman's "touch system" being one clear example. Similarly, Morris recognized the principle when he wrote, apropos our nontactile society, "It can be argued that our untouchability has to

Beetle Bailey © King Features Syndicate, Inc. 1970.
(*First box*) Superior officer makes condescending overture to non-com.
(*Middle box*) Non-com uses words to accept overture but simultaneously uses touch to express his own superiority as a white man.
(*Last box*) Black officer immediately restores status difference. [This interpretation spoils the joke, which was based upon assumption that black officer arbitrarily reversed himself.]
Comments by Jane Torrey.

do with status, with not wishing to be touched by our inferiors and not daring to touch our superiors. . . ." Others were less direct, such as Dresslar's exposition on the use of touch to make an arrest, and Frank's remark that "It may be safe to say that much of a kinship system, as well as rank, caste, role, age, is learned and maintained in terms of touch." [15] But by and large, references to touching were generally to its affiliative uses.

My own observational study of touching in public, to investigate the connection between status and touching, was designed to look at several status variables: socio-economic status, age, race, and sex. I hypothesized that greater touching would be associated with higher status along these status dimensions (assuming male sex, white race, and greater age to be

[15] The Morris quote is from *Intimate Behaviour*, p. 143. For Dresslar, see *Studies in Psychology of Touch*, pp. 320–22. Lawrence K. Frank, "Tactile Communication," *Genetic Psychology Monographs*, 1957, 56, 209–55; reprinted in Edmund Carpenter and Marshall McLuhan (eds.), *Explorations in Communication* (Boston: Beacon, 1960); the quotation is from p. 11 of this edition.

of higher status). For the study, a research assistant (young, white, male, middle-class) who was unaware of these hypotheses observed people in a variety of public settings, and when one was seen to touch another, the above variables were recorded, along with the setting, who touched whom, and whether the touch was reciprocated.[16] Touch was defined as intentional contact with the hand, and gave no problems of observation. Instances of mutual touching, where initiation of touch was not observed, were not included in the analysis. There were unfortunately not enough cases of interracial interaction observed to examine race as a status variable, so this dimension was dropped from the analysis.

However, other dimensions supported the hypothesis: males were found to touch females much more frequently (42 observations) than vice versa (25 observations); there were overwhelmingly more cases of older touching younger than vice versa (36 to 7). For socioeconomic status, there were fewer cases in which the judgment of status could be confidently made, and in which there were status differences; but in 14 of 19 such cases, the toucher was of higher status. All these findings are statistically significant.

Since this study, another observational study of touching has been reported, by Richard Heslin and Diane Boss of Purdue University.[17] These investigators watched people arriving and departing at a nearby airport, recording their "boundary behavior" of greeting and leave-taking. In the 30 pairs in which initiation of touch was observed, males and older people initiated contact with others more than females and younger people did, giving further support to the status connotation of touching.

Relationships, Situations, and Personality. Though observational studies tell us much about what actually happens between people (as opposed to what they *think* happens), observation cannot tell us everything. We might want to know what people *believe* about touching, what they think are the touch rules for relationships and situations, what their motives and intentions are when they touch, what they think and feel when another touches them, what persons are like who do more or less touching than is usual. My next research attempted to answer some of these questions. While at Harvard University, I conducted a questionnaire survey which asked people to rate their likelihood of touching and being

[16] My thanks to Martin Katzenstein for collecting the data, and to the University of Maryland, Baltimore County, for supportive facilities.

[17] Richard Heslin and Diane Boss, "Nonverbal Boundary Behavior at the Airport," 1975, paper available from Richard Heslin, Purdue University.

touched by others (1) in various relationships to them and (2) in different situations; it asked (3) for people's opinions and self-reports about touching; and it included (4) a measure of dominance as a personality trait. The participants in this survey were 24 women and 24 men from the Boston area, ranging in age from 17 to 70 (median age, 23), and from a variety of occupations. Three-fifths claimed an ethnic identity, generally Jewish (38%); only two were black. The rating system they used had four points, from "Not at all" likely to "Very" likely.

In the area of *relationship,* the respondents were asked, in the questionnaire, how likely they were to touch or be touched by persons in 29 different relationships named, such as "Policeman," "Stranger-Female," "Co-Worker–Male," "Sister." The relationships were based on categories of Closeness, Family relation, Age relation, Work relation, and Authority, and were presented in both male and female forms.

In the "closeness" relationships, people overwhelmingly said they were more likely to touch and be touched by their friends than by acquaintances, and more by acquaintances than by strangers. This is not an earth-shaking finding, but it wasn't supposed to be: this question both gives us a check on the validity of the other questions (it shows people were responding to the scale logically and responsibly) and serves as a comparison level for other findings. For members of the family and for spouse or steady, all probabilities were rated in the top ranks of likelihood.

Within the stratified categories, people reported more likelihood of their touching subordinates and coworkers than bosses; of touching younger or same-age people than older ones; and of touching sales clerks than police officers. Likewise, their expectations of others' touching them also reflected their hierarchical relationship: for example, they reported more probability of boss and co-worker touching them than of a subordinate doing so. People do seem to have expectations of touching based on status.

Another study by Thomas Cannon at Boston University gives further support for a connection between touching and status. Using a slightly modified version of a body chart devised by Jourard (see page 112), Cannon administered a questionnaire on touching to 34 female and 29 male students. Respondents were asked to indicate whether they had touched or had been touched by people in several status categories: "a person of higher professional or social status," "a peer, e.g., a fellow worker or student," and "a person of lower professional or social status." [18]

[18] I'm grateful to Thomas Cannon for sharing with me his unpublished data (1973).

Status did make a difference: touch exchange was reported as highest for lower status targets, next highest for peers, and least for persons of higher status. Women also reported higher amounts both of being touched and of touching others (a finding repeated throughout Cannon's data).

What about the relative likelihood of touching vs. being touched by a particular target person? Again, as we would predict, the mean for *touching* someone of higher status was smaller than that for *being touched* by such a person; the mean for touching someone of lower status was greater than that for being touched by one; and the means for touching and receiving touch from peers were about the same.

In another section of my own questionnaire, respondents were asked whether they thought people were likely to touch them in any of 20 specified *situations*. Eighteen of the situations consisted of two sides of nine types of situation (see Table 1), such as asking or giving information,

TABLE 1
COMPARISON OF RESPONSES TO LIKELIHOOD OF BEING TOUCHED
IN SPECIFIED SITUATIONS

	Others More Likely to Touch When	Others Less Likely to Touch When
Information	GIVING	ASKING
Advice	GIVING	ASKING
Order	THEY'RE GIVING	YOU'RE GIVING
Favor	ASKING	AGREEING TO DO
Persuade	THEY'RE TRYING	YOU'RE TRYING
Worried	YOU'RE	THEY'RE
Excited	THEY'RE	YOU'RE
Conversation	DEEP	CASUAL
Place	PARTY	WORK

asking or giving advice. It was hypothesized that someone in the position of giving information, advice, or an order is in a dominant position (however brief the state) in an interaction;[19] that people asking a favor or trying to persuade someone to do something are attempting dominance in the interaction, i.e., trying to force their will on another; and that dominance in all these situations would be associated with greater likelihood of touching. It was likewise hypothesized that someone in a worried or excited state is in a subordinate position, i.e., "losing cool" and/or

[19] For the reasoning behind this hypothesis, see Homans' discussion of esteem in *Social Behavior: Its Elementary Forms* (New York: Harcourt Brace Jovanovich, 1974); also, John Thibaut and Harold Kelley, *The Social Psychology of Groups* (New York: Wiley, 1959).

acknowledging the need for help, and is therefore more likely to be touched than to touch. The two other situations asked about the likelihood of others touching "in affectionate circumstances" and "when they've been drinking."

People were thought to be more likely to touch when affectionate, in deep conversation, and at a party, because all are affiliative situations. The question on drinking was prompted by the findings of McClelland and his colleagues about the purpose and effects of drinking in men, that it enhances their feelings of personal power.[20]

The results of the paired situations questions, shown in Table 1, support all the hypotheses but one, that of greater touching of an excited person. Also as predicted, people rated the likelihood of receiving touch from an affectionate person and from someone who has been drinking as extremely high. We see then that *situations* in which people are in a dominant position, as well as *relationships* involving dominance, affect their probability of using touch, just as affectionate situations and relationships do.

Finally, in the questionnaire a short scale of *dominance* was incorporated, using 20 questions from the dominance section of a general personality scale, the California Psychological Inventory [21] (in this set, scores for males and females were approximately equal). Those who scored low in dominance were more likely than high scorers to answer, in another part of the questionnaire, that they thought they touch others less than most people do.

Furthermore, females scoring low on dominance were more likely than high-dominance ones to answer that they have felt hesitant to touch another person, even though that person had touched them, or the occasion seemed to call for it. High-scoring males tended to reply that they had never felt this hesitancy; other respondents (high females, low males) were about evenly split on their answers. Thus dominance as a personality trait is also related to touching.

Dual Symbolism: Solidarity and Status. What have we found out with this questionnaire study? First, people do have expectations about touching and being touched by others in particular role relationships to them. Generally, they report they're more likely to exchange touch with those close to them than with more distant others, and they expect to touch subordinates more than superiors, and be touched more by superiors than subordinates.

[20] David M. McClelland, et al., *The Drinking Man* (New York: Free Press, 1972), p. 334.

[21] I gratefully acknowledge the permission granted by Consulting Psychologists Press, Inc., to use the CPI in this research.

Second, touching is affected by situational context. Specifically, the situations (of those examined here) in which one person is more likely to touch another are those in which one person has some dominance over the other, or is attempting or feeling dominance.

Finally, we found some evidence for a link between touching and dominance as a personality trait. Dominance invades our lives in various ways—in relationships in which it inheres, in situations that involve this imbalance, and in our own personal tendencies to seek or exert it. The fact that we find touching associated with dominance in all these spheres speaks strongly for the conclusion that touching expresses dominance.

This does not mean that touching is an expression of power *rather than* of intimacy. The one doesn't exclude the other. As we saw with terms of address, a single gesture can indicate either status or solidarity. In touch, we can observe mutual privileges of touch between equals, with intimates exhibiting a great amount of touching and wide distribution of touchable areas (and more meanings to a touch), and mere acquaintances having, generally, no touch rights except perhaps task-oriented ones (e.g., in gaining attention). When there's a disparity of status, we observe the higher-status person to have more touch privilege than the lower-status person, who is often covertly forbidden to touch at all. These patterns, of course, vary in specifics from situation to situation, but they validly characterize our touch interaction as a whole.

Moreover, the patterns of touching interaction reflect deeper patterns of social structure that Brown has pointed out for terms of address. They illustrate his universal norm for these terms, expressed in the general formula, "If form X is used to inferiors it is used between intimates, and if form Y is used to superiors it is used between strangers." [22] There is also a rule that when there is a clear difference of status between two persons, the right to initiate a change to more intimate forms of relationship, such as mutual first name or familiar address, belongs to the superior ("Why don't you just call me Charley?"). We can see that this privilege of moving toward greater intimacy operates in touching, in the area of dating relations in heterosexual couples: usually the male is the first to place his arm around the female or initiate hand-holding in the course of dating, and as intimacy progresses, the first to attempt more overtly sexual intimacy, such as touching sexually-associated body areas.

Historically, the polite form of address has been the norm of mutual address within the upper classes of a society, and the familiar form, the mutual norm within the lower classes. Another example of this pattern is evident in the study of physical spacing among different racial/ethnic

[22] Roger Brown, *Social Psychology* (New York: Free Press, 1965), p. 92.

groups in New York (Chap. 2): people of the six cultures (all poor) stood closer than middle-class Eastern Americans do.[23] There is also evidence that the pattern is repeated in the area of touching, i.e., that the form used toward subordinates or members of a lower class is found in reciprocal use among the members of that class. Goffman has written,

> . . . apparently, the higher the class the more extensive and elaborate are the taboos against contact. For example, in a study of a Shetlandic community the writer found that as one moves from middle-class urban centers in Britain to the rural lower-class islands, the distance between chairs at table decreases, so that in the outermost Shetland Islands actual bodily contact during meals and similar social occasions is not considered an invasion of separateness and no effort need be made to excuse it.[24]

Although there are no class-differentiated studies of touching frequency among adults, there are three of mother-child interaction which report greater physical contact among mothers and children in lower socioeconomic classes than in higher.[25]

We see now that not only can one gesture be used to indicate different facts about particular interpersonal relationships, but it can reflect deeper aspects of social organization. Social scientists are interested in studying such *unobtrusive measures* because they provide information on relationships and patterns that can't always be obtained by asking the participants directly. Touch may in fact prove to be an excellent unobtrusive measure of relationships, because of its subtlety, and because it probably reveals closer discriminations than would another indicator such as, for example, first naming, which is rather ritualized.

POWER, TOUCH, AND SEX

Related to my ideas about the status aspect of touching was its particular application to women. From my own experience and observations of people around me, it seemed clear to me that women were touched more

---

[23] Stanley E. Jones, "A Comparative Proxemics Analysis of Dyadic Interaction in Selected Subcultures of New York City," *Journal of Social Psychology,* 1971, 84, 35–44.

[24] Erving Goffman, "The Nature of Deference and Demeanor," *Interaction Ritual* (Garden City, N.Y.: Doubleday, 1967), p. 63.

[25] See, for example, Vidal S. Clay, "The Effect of Culture on Mother-Child Tactile Communication," *Family Coordinator,* 1968, 17, 204–10; Susan Goldberg and Michael Lewis, "Play Behavior in the Year-Old Infant: Early Sex Differences," *Child Development,* 1969, 40, 21–31; Terry Hore, "Social Class Differences in Some Aspects of the Nonverbal Communication Between Mother and Preschool Child," *Australian Journal of Psychology,* 1970, 22, 21–27.

than men, and not necessarily for sexual purposes. I spoke with other women about their reactions to touching, and found my hunches corroborated. For example, a woman student who waited on table told me that where she worked she was being touched all the time by men customers; these men did not touch the male waiters, nor did women customers. Female secretaries and factory workers are also used to having such liberties taken with their bodies; they too felt there was something more than sex, the unwanted part that was perhaps power, perhaps threat. But I was also interested in the more subtle everyday touching we may be less aware of, the touch in passing, in giving orders, or simple conversation.

What happens when women do touch men, if, as I say, they are not supposed to? Another woman told me the following incident: At a party one evening, a male friend of hers and her husband sat often with his arm around her in what she took to be a friendly gesture. When she reciprocated the gesture, with only friendly intent, he soon got her alone and suggested sleeping together. She showed surprise at the suggestion, but he said, "Wasn't that what you were trying to tell me all evening?" In other words, women do not interpret a man's touch as necessarily implying sexual intent, but men interpret a woman's touch in that way. I will consider later the hypothesis that touching is a sexual gesture, and my own analysis of the difference in the implications of touching for men and women.

Despite women's experience of being touched, there is a strong belief abroad that women **are** much *less* restricted than men in their freedom to touch, and that they touch more. The belief is so strong that it is voiced by psychologists and other academics as fact:

> Perhaps because women are sex objects themselves—or perhaps because society considers them an inferior class and therefore allows them certain licenses—they are permitted to touch other people, both women and men.[26]

The rare suggestions that women may receive more touching treat the matter in a rather cavalier way. They refer to the daughters of a family being "the favored ones" for physical contact, to females' having "less discrimination than the males in accepting or spurning the extended hand of others," and to "the American female being so much less uptight about tactuality than the American male." These writers on sex differences in touching tend to recognize only the affectionate uses of touching, emphasizing the heterosexual, and almost universally cite women's "greater freedom" to touch others. My own research and observation lead me to

[26] John Holt, "The Cuteness Syndrome," *Ms.*, March 1974, 2, 9, p. 78.

recognize the status use of touch equally with the affectionate, to de-emphasize the sexual, and to cite men's greater privileges of touch. Sex differences in touching are many and complex; let us begin our exploration of them with that most homely gesture, the handshake.

The Handshake. The handshake is a specialized form of touch with quite specific rules and rituals surrounding it. Everyone would agree that men shake hands more frequently than women—it is a clearly masculine gesture, and often an obligatory act in the male subculture. As a masculine ritual of recognition and affirmation, it serves to perpetuate male clubbi-ness and to exclude women from the club. The handshake is a gesture rare between two women, and optional between a man and a woman.* When women do shake hands, it is likely to be on their introduction, rather than on greeting someone already known (as men do). And, in my experience, handshaking between women, or between women and men, is more likely to take place in a group containing men (who are likely to shake hands).

Schiffrin has analyzed the handshake as a ritual bracketing of a coming-together of some sort; an initiation of a shake is simultaneously a request for access to another and an offering of access to oneself.[27] This ritual imputes a certain sacredness and worth to the participants, but the implied value is not the same for a female shaking hands with a male. Schiffrin writes that when two men shake hands, their equally active participation in the ritual celebrates the worth of both. But women's participation is optional and often passive, implying an unequal status. Emily Post even codified this, telling women they may clasp an old (male) friend's hand firmly, but should still shake less than he does, and with an acquaintance, allow him to do all the shaking.†

In recent years alternative handshakes have replaced the traditional handshake among countercultural and left-political people who wished to

---

* According to Morris, from his observations two-thirds of the handshakes made are between males; of the remaining one-third, male–female handshakes have three times the frequency of female–female ones. (*Intimate Behaviour*)

[27] Deborah Schiffrin, "Handwork as Ceremony: The Case of the Handshake," *Semiotica*, 1974, 12, 189–202.

† It may seem that a woman's choice to initiate a handshake with a man contradicts the notion of men's greater freedom to touch. However, this privilege comes from the tradition of chivalry; while this is not the place for a full analysis of chivalry (see Chap. 4), we may observe that (1) chivalry has numerous such contradictory ges-tures which ceremonially reverse the true order of things; (2) men who temporarily role-play at subservience by, e.g., opening a door, kissing a woman's hand, giving up a seat, do not, like real servants, fade into the woodwork but instead gain attention as a primary focus of the ritual; and (3) present-day chivalrous attitudes have been shown to be correlated with attitudes advocating the open subordination of women.

express solidarity but not with such an establishment symbol as a regular handclasp. The "black" or "soul" handshake (one palm slapping the other's upturned palm) and the "solidarity" handshake (shifting 90° from the usual grasping right hands to a thumbs-linked, fingers-over-side position) became much more popular—among males. Women in counter-cultural and political groups found themselves largely excluded from this expression of solidarity. Of course, secret handshakes have long been a form of identification for male clubs and secret societies, and this latter version is little different; much of the counterculture and left organizations have been "male clubs." *

TOUCHING QUESTIONNAIRES AND OBSERVATIONS

What exactly has been known about the frequency patterns of touching between the sexes? Very little. We start with the studies of Sidney Jourard, who in 1966 first reported the questionnaire study of body-accessibility.[28] Young unmarried students of both sexes filled out a questionnaire he devised, in which they indicated on which of a number of different body regions they had touched, or been touched by, various designated persons. The body regions in his study were demarcated as in the figure; the persons for whom the subjects were to describe their touch exchanges were Mother, Father, Same-Sex Best Friend, and Opposite-Sex Best Friend.

Touching was greatest between opposite-sex friends, about twice as much as with any other target person, followed by same-sex friends and parents. † Males reported touching their opposite-sex friend in more regions

* Barrie Thorne has noted that the sexes have single-sex subcultures (or "semiotics") —ways of talk, gesture, description. When the sexes mix, the male semiotic dominates, so that to take part, women are pressed to adopt the male form (personal communication, April, 1976). The male semiotic, having more power, is seen as the "neutral" form; for example, male speech forms are often described as *the* language for a speech community, while women's forms, if they are described at all, are labeled "women's language." Men may have more (single-sex) group rituals than women do, like the handshake, making men's groups more strongly bounded and impenetrable.

28 Jourard, "Body-Accessibility," 221–31.

† The scores for exchange of physical contact with parents showed a pattern which Jourard claimed made the daughters "the favoured ones": females reported being touched by their fathers—and touching them in return—on more body areas than did the males. Males and females were reportedly touched by their mothers on about the same amount of regions, though in the first study males did not reciprocate to the extent that females did (in the later study they did).

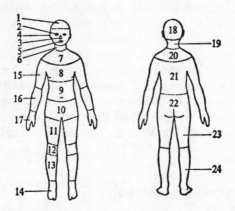

Diagram of the front and rear view of the body as demarcated for the Body-Accessibility Questionnaire. Sidney M. Jourard, "An Exploratory Study of Body-Accessibility," *British Journal of Social and Clinical Psychology*, no. 5 (1966), 223.

than did females; and, in a second study,[29] females reported more regions touched by their opposite-sex friend than males reported.

Women's mean total "being touched" score was the greater, though of marginal statistical significance (its probability lying between one in 20 and one in 10). Out of the six comparisons that were significant in the second study, in four of them females are being touched more widely than males; and in none are males being touched more.

The later questionnaire study by Cannon, which was based on Jourard's studies, not only supported the existence of status differences in touching, but also found sex differences. Women respondents reported higher amounts of being touched by others than did men (and they also reported higher levels of touching others themselves).

In my own questionnaire study, when asked about touching others in various relationships to them, people of both sexes overwhelmingly reported greater likelihood of their touching females than males. However, on *receiving* touch from females and males, they were not so consistent.

[29] Sidney M. Jourard and Jane E. Rubin, "Self-Disclosure and Touching," 39–40. Jourard and Rubin are apparently mistaken in their report that "Among the men, it is the mother who does the most touching, followed in rank order by same-sex friend and father." In fact, the reported male mean for being touched by Opposite-Sex Friend is about 2½ times that for being touched by Mother. Jourard made no statistical comparisons between the sexes on body-region touchability; the conclusions I have drawn on these are my own, from sign tests of significance.

Each sex rated specified others of the *other* sex as being more likely to touch them.

People who responded to my questionnaire also answered the question, "Do you think you touch others more or less than most people do?" Almost all the women who believed they touched others more than usual identified themselves as having an ethnic background. There was also a significant relationship between female subjects' answers here (though not males') and their mean ratings for touching others in designated relationships: the higher their ratings, the more likely they were to say they touch people more than is usual.

There were large and significant differences between males and females in their responses to a question about inappropriate or excessive touching. Females reported being made mad or resentful by that more often than males.

Respondents were asked which sex they thought does more touching of their own sex and which touches the opposite sex more. Here we find again the prevailing impression that women do more touching, especially of their own sex. Both males and females agreed that females do more touching of their own sex. They were in less agreement, however, about the second part of the question. Females tended to answer that men do more touching of women than vice versa, but males were split on the question.

Why did these people believe women touch women more than men touch men? They may be right. Although my own observational studies have not supported this hypothesis, the airport study by Heslin and Boss did. Or, such beliefs may be based on what seems to be popular myth. As the unsupported claims by social scientists (quoted earlier) demonstrate, the notion of greater touching among women than among men is a strong one. Whether it is based on "intuition" that grows from years of informal, even unconscious, observation, or whether it is a convenient myth that helps to disguise the power aspect of touch, we can't know at this time. On the second part of the question, why did men and women both think that the opposite sex touched them more than vice versa? First, women are reporting their experience accurately. Perhaps men are subscribing to the folk myth of women's greater touching tendencies. Men could be more susceptible to this belief because the evidence contradicting it is less salient to them and believing the myth may be more satisfying.

There is empirical evidence, then, of sex difference as well as status difference in touch exchange, but the data are from self-reports. What people do and what they recall that they do may be different things. Actual observations of touching behavior would be helpful.

An analysis of photos by Morris, a kind of observational study, seems to support the notion of men's more frequent touching. He reports a number of sex comparisons for various forms of body contact, "based on personal observations backed up by a detailed analysis of 10,000 photographs taken at random from a wide variety of recent news magazines and newspapers." [30] * According to Morris, the commonest form of embrace, the shoulder embrace (bodies make contact side to side, heads usually apart, one arm wrapped around another's body) is five times as likely to be performed by a male as a female. It is in fact such a male gesture that males do it to each other—one quarter of all shoulder embraces are male–male, he says. Of three other interpersonal contact gestures for which Morris gives sex breakdowns, two are also "male" gestures: the hand-to-shoulder contact and the handshake. The arm link, Morris says, is a female gesture, one women do to men.

There have also been observational studies of touching of and by children, which found girls to receive more touching than boys (from mothers), at least from the age of six months on; [31] but there were no parallel studies of adults before my own observational study, previously described. In that study, males touched females much more often than vice versa; Table 2 shows the frequencies.

TABLE 2
INSTANCES OF TOUCHING CATEGORIZED BY
SEX OF TOUCHER AND TOUCHED

Sex of Toucher	Sex of Person Touched	Total
Male	Female	42
Female	Female	17
Male	Male	17
Female	Male	25
All Categories		101

[30] Morris, *Intimate Behaviour*, p. 122. The observations following come essentially from pages 122–41.

* Unfortunately, no other information on the sample, the analysis, or numerical results are reported, only some relative frequencies for selected comparisons. His observations are nevertheless of interest, though they may represent more impression than science, and we should interpret them with caution.

[31] Clay, "Mother-Child Tactile Communication," and Hore, "Class Differences in Nonverbal Communication Between Mother and Child." M. Lewis and C. D. Wilson, "Infant Development in Lower Class American Families," paper at the 1971 meeting of the Society for Research in Child Development.

Moreover, considering only those cases in which all the other recorded data were equal except sex, the predominance of males touching females was even greater: 23 cases, compared with five in each of the three other categories. In other words, when all else is equal, men touch women at an even greater rate than when other things are *un*equal, as (for instance) when women have other status advantages, such as being older or of higher social class.

The study of arrivals and departures at the airport previously described found similar sex differences: males touched females in 10 of the 30 cases of touch initiation observed, but females touched males in only 4 of those instances.[32] *

Flix and Comix. Another "observational study" was made by me, in 1972, of touching in comics and films. Popular culture is a good arena for studying norms. We can assume, following other psychologists, that cultural material gains some of its importance and popularity from the fact that it expresses certain cultural values that are important to a people. In this small pop culture study, I surveyed nine television movies; the only discrimination applied was that foreign-made films were not observed, since they would not be expected to illuminate American culture. (Primarily because their time of showing was convenient to another observer and me, the nine were mostly evening mystery-type movies.) I also surveyed 11 comic books of the adventure type.[33]

In both the films and the comics, the frequency of males touching females was far greater than vice versa: for films, males were seen to touch females 74 times, though females touched males only 35 times; for comics, the score was 34 vs. 13.[34]

A detailed analysis of an individual movie can illustrate in more depth just how hierarchical touch relations work, especially the interplay of social status and sex status. In the 1946 movie, "The Face of Marble," a young doctor comes to work with an older doctor, living with the older

---

[32] Heslin and Boss, "Nonverbal Boundary Behavior at the Airport."

* The 16 other cases had a high incidence of female-female touching (13) and the usual low frequency of males touching males (3). This difference may be partly explained by the authors' note that there was an overrepresentation of women in their sample, for various reasons.

[33] I wish to thank Craig Jackson and Henry Pearson for their assistance with scoring films and comic books, respectively.

[34] In both these media also, males' touching of males far exceeded females' same-sex touching (by about 20 to 1), contrary to popular belief. But this is probably due to the far greater number of major male roles, compared with those for females in the 1970s—in films, males have been estimated to have 12 times the speaking roles of females.

doctor and his wife in a house with a male and female servant, both black; later his fiancée joins them, and at one point a policeman briefly appears on the scene. The younger doctor treats the older one with great respect, calling him "sir" and rising as he leaves the room; the older doctor repeatedly addresses the younger one as "my boy."

Of the 52 instances of touching in this movie among the four male and three female characters, 36 are by the two doctors, and nine are by the highest-status female character, the older doctor's wife. Table 3 summar-

TABLE 3
TOUCHING BY STATUS AND SEX RELATIONSHIPS IN
"THE FACE OF MARBLE"

Superior touches Subordinate		25
Male:Female	1	
Female:Female	3	
Male:Male	16	
Female:Male	5	
Subordinate touches Superior		14
Male:Female	9	
Female:Female	1	
Male:Male	4	
Female:Male	0	
"Equal" touches "Equal"		13
Male:Female	11	
Female:Male	2	

izes the touching by both status and sex. It shows there is more touching of subordinates by superiors than vice versa, and of women by men than vice versa. The greatest incidence of female touching male comes when the female is in a superior position, from the highest-status female; and the greatest incidence of subordinate touching superior comes when the subordinate is a male touching a female.

Even more detailed analysis would show that three of the four instances of the older doctor's wife touching the younger doctor occur in one highly emotional scene, in which the woman shows great fear and tries to warn the young man to stop his course of action. Or, that one of the three instances of the younger doctor's touching the older one occurs when the former grabs the other's arm to warn him of danger (the touch is immediately reciprocated); another, when the older doctor is crying over the loss of his wife; and the third, in gaining the older doctor's attention, also at a dramatic moment. The superior–subordinate touching, and male–female touching, on the other hand, come as a matter of course in the ongoing interaction of the film—usually a hand laid on the arm, shoulder or back, while conversation and other action continue.

SEXUALITY AND TOUCHING

As we have seen, (male) social scientists who have written on touch emphasize its sexual connotations. So do non-social scientists. A male physicist said to me, arguing against my power interpretation of touching, that he touches women all the time because "I just can't keep my hands off them."

We are so used to thinking of men as sexually active (and women as sexually passive) that sexuality is the first explanation that leaps to mind to account for men's greater tendency to touch. There is generally also a greater frequency of touching reported between the sexes (in both directions) than within, further support for the sexuality hypothesis. Of course, homosexual inhibition can account for this fact as well as heterosexual attraction can, and seems to be especially marked between males. However, sexual attraction is not sufficient to explain men's greater touching of women, since it cannot account for women's lesser use of touch, unless we postulate a weaker sex drive in women. In the face of evidence accumulating in the past 20 years, especially from the sex research projects of Kinsey and of Masters and Johnson, it seems impossible today to claim less sexual motivation in women than in men. Of course, overt forms of sexual *expression* have been suppressed in women, but that fact could as well be an argument that female sexual touching should increase, as a more subtle outlet for strong sexual needs.

Taken with the evidence of greater touching by the dominant figure in other situations and relations in which inequality exists, inequality of touching between the sexes can most parsimoniously be attributed to sex inequality.

In fact, for students in a study interpreting the meaning of different types of touch, "sexual desire" was the *least* likely of five possible interpretations for the different touches, except when it was explicitly applied to areas of the body that (males and females agreed) were associated with sexual desire. In this questionnaire study carried out by Nguyen, Heslin, and Nguyen,[35] subjects rated their agreement or disagreement that certain meanings could be attributed to various types of touch on certain areas of the body. The possible meanings assigned were (1) playfulness, (2) warmth/love, (3) friendship/fellowship, (4) sexual desire, and

[35] Tuan Nguyen, Richard Heslin, and Michele L. Nguyen, "The Meanings of Touch: Sex Differences," *Journal of Communication*, 1975, 25, 92–103.

(5) pleasantness. The touch modalities were pat, stroke, squeeze, or brush, and the body areas rated were modified from those of Jourard. The subjects, male and female unmarried undergraduates, were asked, "What does it mean when a (close) person of the opposite sex [not a relative] touches a certain area of my body in a certain manner?" They indicated the extent of their agreement with the statements, for example, that playfulness is conveyed when someone of the opposite sex pats your area 1.

Touch conveys warmth/love, and is pleasant, according to the responses, but there was some disagreement between the sexes about the meanings of touch to different areas, as indicated by significant interactions of the sex variable with body area and touch modality. Females discriminated between their body areas to a greater extent than males did, perhaps a function of their general greater nonverbal sensitivity. And they felt that love and friendliness were shown by touch on the hands (preferably squeezing), or strokes or pats on the head, face, arms, or back, but not touches on the breasts or genital areas. In fact, touch that signified sexual desire to females was *opposed* to pleasantness, love/warmth, friendliness, and playfulness (as determined by a computer process called factor analysis). For males, on the other hand, pleasantness, sexual desire, and warmth/love formed a cluster. Do these findings suggest that it is women, not men, who distinguish sex from love?

Males were less discriminating about body areas, but they were more attuned to the various touch modalities. Interestingly, they tended to ignore (accidental) brushes, giving more attention to stroking and patting (perhaps women cannot afford to ignore brushes, since their experience has shown them that brushes are not so likely to be accidental). Not only is touch not likely to suggest sex to people unless in a sexual area, but the sexual areas themselves are not so sensitive to touch as folklore would have it, these authors point out: sexually associated areas (buttocks, thighs, breasts) have poor point localization ability, and a proportionately smaller area of the sensory cortex is devoted to them (though, of course, these factors are not necessarily the determinants of sensitivity, or of the sensation of touching).

These results are consistent with the view of touch as an expression of dominance, along with women's greater likelihood of being touched. There is, unfortunately, no way to judge the extent to which a meaning of dominance would be assigned to certain sex-body area-modality combinations, since nothing like it was given as a possible meaning for touch. We may note that this is not only another example of social scientists' assuming only solidarity interpretations for touching, but that the assumptions, being built into the research, therefore predetermine a finding such as the above, that "touch conveys warmth/love, and is pleasant"; it was either that, or playfulness, friendship, or sex.* Even asking about the dominance connotation of touching, of course, wouldn't guarantee that people would attribute it to any touches, even if it is indeed a factor in tactual expression.

The question of the sexuality explanation is not simply one of academic interest. While in the other status areas the inequality is generally overt and mutually acknowledged, in sex inequality it is not. We may be hard put to separate threads of sentiment and dominance in our minds, whether we're male or female. If dominance is indeed a factor in touching, but social science continues to insist or assume that it is not, females will continue to be socialized to receive touch and, receiving it, fail to understand its subtle influence on them.

This socialization to be touched, documented in the studies of children described earlier, plays a part in the socialization of the passive female. Michael Lewis, who has done much study of sex differences and sex stereotypic behavior in infants and young children, has described this process. Lewis has put forward the thesis that "the major socialization process" for children in our society,

> in terms of attachment or social behavior, is to move the infant from a proximal mode of social interaction [i.e., involving physical contact—touching, rocking, holding] to a distal mode [i.e., one which can be performed at a distance—looking at, smiling, vocalizing to]; the former is an infant mode, while the latter is an adult mode of interaction.[36]

He has found in his studies that for the first few months of life, boys receive more proximal behavior than do girls, but by six months of age, it's the other way around, girls getting more than boys, and it continues that way. His data also suggest that boys are moved faster from the proximal to the distal form of social relation than girls are, indeed, that girls are never socialized as thoroughly in this sense (to the distal relation) as are boys.[37]

And female children become the passive and dependent types their training makes of them, to grow up to be the passive and dependent—and exploited—women society demands. Florence Rush, a social worker who has worked for the Society for the Prevention of Cruelty to Children, has

---

* It's unfortunate also that in their brief interpretation of their results, the authors, after describing how males *and* females view sexual desire with regard to other touch meanings, refer to "this female attitude" and go on to try to account for it, while taking the male attitude for granted. This falls in the longstanding tradition of psychological research that males are the norm and females, the deviants.

36 Lewis, "Parents and Children," p. 234.
37 Lewis, "Parents and Children," p. 235.

been concerned with the sexual abuse of children, and has written several papers on this topic. In one, presenting a survey of studies covering 2,152 cases of sexual offenses against children, she observes that the overwhelming majority of sexual offenses involving children (about 90%) are those committed by older males on young girls, and that about 75 percent of these offenses are committed not by strangers, but by persons known to the victims—by fathers and other relatives, or by visitors and family friends. The pattern of such abuses, she concludes, shows "an early manifestation of male power and oppression of the female." She argues that

> sexual abuse of children is permitted because it is an unspoken but prominent factor in socializing and preparing the female to accept a subordinate role; to feel guilty, ashamed, and to tolerate, through fear, the power exercised over her by men. . . . the sexual abuse of female children is a process of education which prepares them to become the sweethearts and wives of America.[38]

The implications that women perceive, that they are supposed to accept touch, are well expressed by a woman interviewed by Phyllis Chesler for her book *Women and Madness*. Frances, a lesbian, had been urged by her (male) psychiatrist to let men touch her. She told Chesler,

> I was getting very uptight, y'know, at being touched by men. A lot of men come up to you in a very familiar way, touch you like you're a piece of equipment, or, I don't know, like you don't belong to yourself. Y'know, they come and touch you as if you owe them this kind of thing, to be soft for them, and to be responsive to them. And it got me really uptight.[39]

It's not in terms of sexual attraction that much touch is promoted but in terms of sexual obligation and sexual coercion. Although sex is the medium here, the message is dominance.

TACTILE HOSTILITY AND TACTILE WARMTH

Every woman knows what is meant by a man who is "all hands," and most have a category for it, into which some of their acquaintances, including professional men (doctors, dentists, lawyers) fall. There seems to be no parallel category by which men classify "handsy" women as sexually

---

[38] Florence Rush, "The Sexual Abuse of Children: A Feminist Point of View," *Radical Therapist*, December 1971, 2, no. 4, 9–10.
[39] Phyllis Chesler, *Women and Madness* (New York: Doubleday, 1972), p. 196.

aggressive, but they do have the "clinging vine"—a female whose socialization to dependence succeeded all too well. There is also the "touchy" person, usually female and older, who is always picking invisible lint from your clothes. She is resented by men, and probably by women, perhaps because of the suspicion that one's grooming is not all that bad, but the excuses of lint, or crooked scarves and ties, are coverups for a suppressed urge to touch. Whether the touch is resented because it's not open, or because it's presumptuous (on either the solidarity or status dimension), or because it signifies an ill-concealed urge to dominate, can't be known.

Lint-picking may in fact be a sign of repressed hostility. It seems likely that touch gains its association with dominance as a remnant of earlier days when physical force was the means of establishing and maintaining power. A touch is, in a way, shorthand for coercive force. Children seem particularly aware of the aggressive implications of even the slightest brush from another child (which was perhaps intentional). It will often be met with a pat or slap of slightly greater intensity, which will in turn be called and raised, until the escalation (barring submission or intervention) reaches the level of an all-out fight.

Other reminders of physical combat persist in tactile gestures of hostility disguised as love. Montagu reminds us that in the nineteenth century, and well into the twentieth (and probably also in earlier centuries),

> males in the Western world often indulged in the peculiar custom of greeting children with noxious manipulations of their skin. . . . It is of interest to note that males exclusively were guilty of such sadistic practices, and then usually only towards male children, although girls with braids did not entirely escape their attentions.

He describes such tricks as cheek-tweaking, ear-pulling, hair mussing, pinching, a spank on the bottom, or a push, as "among the other engaging indignities to which children, all in the guise of affection, were subjected." (Montagu is the one, by the way, who was earlier noted to claim that cheek patting, hair patting, and chucking under the chin are all "forms of behavior indicating affection.") Adolescent boys and males up to middle age might receive a too-hearty slap on the back, crushing handshake, or punch in the chest or abdomen as a "mark of affection." [40]

We might note here how many of these hostile and painful gestures are perpetrated on women also, in the cloth of affection. I have seen women swung painfully dizzy at square dances, chased by playful gangs of men and thrown in water, carried, spanked, or dunked at a beach, all clearly against their will. The cheek- and hair-patting, chin-chucking, and bottom

[40] Montagu, *Touching*, pp. 315–16.

patting and pinching continue as part of many women's daily experience.

Goffman too writes of the aggressive overtones of such teasing, or "playful profanation," that in our society "is directed by adults to those of lesser ceremonial breed—to children, old people, servants, and so forth— as when an attendant affectionately ruffles a patient's hair or indulges in more drastic types of teasing."[41] One cannot get mad at such hostility, because of its outward guise of affection, just as one cannot get mad at coercive touching for the same reason.

Does touch actually convey a meaning of affection, or promote warmth? The study of Nguyen, Heslin, and Nguyen seems to indicate that it does (though, as pointed out, the choices precluded its being given any nonaffiliative meaning). Other studies have mixed findings about the effect of touch on our sentiments. Fisher, Rytting, and Heslin set up a situation in a university library in which users who checked out books were either touched or not touched by the clerk who returned their cards. Asked then to take part in an evaluation of the library, they rated their own feelings (essentially, positive–negative), the library clerk, and the library environment. Subjects who were touched reported a more positive affective state and evaluated the clerk more positively than those who weren't. Touched females tended to evaluate the library more positively also, though males in the *no*-touch condition tended to evaluate the library more positively than touched males. The authors concluded that the response to touch was uniformly positive for females, but ambivalent in males.[42]

Another team of investigators has looked at the evaluation of a toucher, testing the hypothesis of many encounter groups that touching increases interpersonal attractiveness. Among their subjects, female college students, those who were touched rated the accomplice who touched them more favorably than did subjects who were not touched.[43] But perhaps the accomplice acted more warmly toward those touched; other researchers repeated the experiment and added another element: the accomplice acted either warm or cold when touching. They found the only significant effects to be due to the new factor, and not whether one was touched or not.[44]

After such a discussion of the negative power, or indifference, of touch, it may be hard to recall that touch does indeed communicate warmth and

[41] Goffman, "The Nature of Deference and Demeanor," p. 87.

[42] Jeffrey D. Fisher, Marvin Rytting, and Richard Heslin, "Hands Touching Hands: Affective and Evaluative Effects of an Interpersonal Touch," *Sociometry* (1976), in press.

[43] A. Boderman, D. W. Freed, and M. T. Kinnucan, " 'Touch me, like me': Testing an encounter group assumption," *Journal of Applied Behavioral Science*, 1972, 8, 527–33.

[44] George Breed and Joseph S. Ricci, " 'Touch me, like me': Artifact?" *Proceedings* of the American Psychological Association, 1973, 8, 153–54.

affection, that it is recognized as a basic human need. In fact, the with-holding of touch, for example, between lovers or family members, may serve in as hostile a way as its application. It is difficult to imagine that doctors who would undoubtedly agree that a human being is a "social animal" would prescribe an *absence* of human contact for beneficial effect, especially for a mental patient, but "No P.C." (No Physical Contact) is such a medical order in some hospitals. This seems to be another act of anti-tactile hostility.

The evidence we have accumulated relating touching to power and to gender illustrates the action of a subtle gesture in maintaining the social order. In this male-dominated society, touching is one more tool used to keep women in their place, another reminder that women's bodies are free property for everyone's use. We can further project a picture of the way touch, in combination with other nonverbal behavior, must work to perpetuate the social structure in other status areas, though we have fewer data showing the details of this function.

One is appalled to consider that something so human, so natural, as touching should be perverted into a symbol of status and power. But a moment's thought reminds us that this is the story of other simple facts of our being, unrelated to status: clothing, shelter, and food have all been turned into status symbols in the competitive struggle. A movement to freer tactual exchange ought to liberate touch from these perversions, but even that has its cautions. Greater social touching might simply in-crease the handling of women, just as similar exercises have proceeded along sexist, rather than liberated, lines, in many encounter groups.

What can be done? Acceptance of my thesis has certain implications for men and women who wish to change the male-dominant nature of our society. Men should become conscious of their tactual interactions with women especially, and guard against using touch to assert authority; they should be careful not to teach their sons to do so. At the same time, men should monitor their reactions to being touched by women, correcting and reversing negative feelings based purely on receiving touch. Women simi-larly have a responsibility to themselves to refuse to accept tactual asser-tion of authority—they should remove their hands from the grasp of men who hold them too long, and remove men's hands from their person when such a touch is unsolicited and unwanted. They should train themselves, at the same time, not to submit to another's will because of the subtle implication of his touch (although the touch may have backup coercion one is less able to resist, such as economic control), and—why not?—start touching men, if the situation is appropriate, in order to break through the sexist pattern of tactual interaction. I happen to favor forcefully ap-plied tactual interaction when the situation calls for it.

chapter eight

THE DANCE OF LIFE:

Posture, Gesture, and Body Movement

Excerpt from the First Venusian Anthropological Expedition to Earth·

. . . As we have written, the Earthlings' major communication is by means of the movements of their body parts, in a veritable continuing dance, essentially symbolizing their hierarchical relations. Explorer Glk, in an experiment, sped up his body rhythm to the point where Earthlings' movements were relatively slower, and he could examine them in careful detail. He has found, and the rest of us have verified, an amazing synchrony of motion *detectable only from that body setting*: they carefully coordinate movements with their own speech and different body motions, and with each others' speech and motions. They mimic each other and adopt mirror-image reflections of each other when they are in harmony; or show great discoordination with themselves and others when they disagree and wish to protest. These motions are often very quick in passing, and this is the crux of our problem: they occur at a speed that human perceptions are not set to function at. How can they plan, act out and interpret these coordinations, if they cannot perceive them (much less intentionally send them)?

Gestures, like other clues to power we have mentioned, are well known to politicians. In January of 1975, a few months after assuming office as an unelected President following the near-complete discrediting of that office, Gerald Ford made a State of the Union address on TV. It was known that TV consultants were hired and that President Ford had an image to project as a decisive, honest and effective head of state. Columnist Joseph Kraft's account took note of Ford's attempt to convey this image, through gesture and environment:

Mr. Ford appeared on television Monday night with two aides serving up documents—the perfect picture of a working President. He gestured to show forcefulness and walked about to demonstrate energy. The setting for the production was the White House library—the one place in the world most calculated to unsay the widespread public impression that Mr. Ford is not very bright.[1]

However, it was Kraft's opinion that all the hand-waving and jumping around (and direct-camera staring, to convey sincerity) failed because of Ford's verbal, not nonverbal, inadequacy. The preponderance of gesture wasn't lost on the public, however, and Kraft wasn't the only viewer to observe this background attempt to make an impression. It became so notorious that about six weeks later a cartoon showed two poll-takers conferring, and one of them is saying: "That's 38 percent who approve of the President's speech, 29 percent who disapprove, and 33 percent who were watching his hands and didn't hear what he said." [2] Nonverbal gestures carry the most influence when they are natural and not affected, when they enhance and harmonize with the verbal message. Ford gave himself away by trying to graft on gestures not his own, to present a "self" other than his own self, and it didn't take. This is a lesson to be kept in mind as we study the body movements related to power, status, and influence.

We have previously discussed some aspects of posture—the effects of nonimmediacy in the interracial interview, the status difference in the tension/relaxation dimension of demeanor. There are many such subtle aspects of posture and its related body behaviors, gesture and body movement, that affect our relationships. Researchers in nonverbal behavior are in the process of mapping out this elaborate dance of life whose study we call kinesics, and what is being uncovered is fascinating. Though there is not yet a great body of data relating to status, power, or influence, we will examine what there is.

THE WHOLE (BODY) IS MORE THAN THE SUM OF ITS PARTS

In *Body Language and the Social Order,* Scheflen illustrates a number of encounters involving dominance. One, between two young men of apparently equal status, involves mainly gestures of threat and preparedness for battle. One hooks his thumb in his belt, the other puts his hands on his

---

[1] Joseph Kraft, "Looking 'Tough,' " Boston *Globe,* January 17, 1975, p. 23.
[2] "Dunagin's People," Boston *Globe,* March 4, 1975, p. 2.

hips; one clenches his fist; the other steps forward, raises his head, makes a verbal threat, and points his finger in the other's face; they push each other around a little. But an occasional smile or laugh characterizes this encounter as a playful, not serious one; without that nonverbal qualifier, the encounter would probably escalate into physical combat, with one emerging the winner (dominant). De-escalation occurs in this instance as one tilts his head (and makes a conciliatory statement), the other drops his head, slumps, and backs down.[3] We have all seen versions, either miniature or intensified, of this kind of encounter between men, even among genteel business or professor types. Male competitive encounter seems typically to involve remnants of physical threat in attempts to dominate.

Scheflen also points out a gesture by a speaker of status in a group: this person may lean back in the chair to speak, putting the palms on the back of the neck or head (and perhaps taking the floor from another speaker). Nierenberg and Calero cite the same gesture as one of superiority, or more specifically, "relaxed aggressiveness." In addition, they claim it is a particularly American gesture, even particularly a Southwestern (male) gesture.[4] These two authors base their interpretation of a wide range of gestures, with special reference to negotiation, on having held hundreds of seminars with thousands of participants and having recorded 2,500 negotiating situations. By involving their audiences in their research, asking the observers to decode video-taped scenes and to separate meaningful from meaningless body movements, they have provided an approach to the problem of whether there exists a "nonverbal community," a consensus of interpretation. However, since they do not report any carefully controlled data-gathering, we have to view their claims with a certain amount of caution.

Nierenberg and Calero describe numerous postures and gestures indicating dominance or superiority. Sitting with one's leg over the arm of the chair, straddling a chair turned backwards, sitting with one's feet on one's desk, and leaving the jacket unbuttoned, hand in pocket (thumb out)— said to indicate superiority—can all be seen as examples of relaxation gestures, which we already know to be correlated with status. Conversely, the "closed" position of subordinates—coats buttoned, faces grim, contracted bodies—are examples of the tightness required of them.

Competition and disagreement are also associated with some of these

---

[3] Albert Scheflen, *Body Language and the Social Order* (Englewood Cliffs, N.J.: Prentice-Hall, 1972), pp. 23–25.

[4] Gerald I. Nierenberg and Henry H. Calero, *How to Read a Person Like a Book* (New York: Hawthorn, 1971; Pocket Books, 1973). All quotations are from Pocket Books edition.

same gestures, these authors say, for example, the chair and desk straddling positions. In this context, arms folded and jacket buttoned indicate defensiveness, unwillingness to be open or change one's mind. Leg-crossing, another closed-body gesture, can indicate competitiveness, particularly where it is ankle-to-knee crossing ("figure 4"); uncrossing the legs may indicate that agreement has been reached.

Spiegel and Machotka report a series of experiments in which subjects made judgments about drawn figures, female and male, shown alone and in groups, in various minimally different postures.[5] People responded to the drawings by rating the figures on descriptive scales, such as "superior . . . subordinate," "important . . . insignificant," "active . . . passive." * The results of this research on people's perceptions of body communication confirm a number of our folk conceptions, for example, that hands on hips (akimbo) is a "bossy" position. When shown drawings of a (nude) male figure in which only the arm positions differed, subjects judged the arms akimbo position as the most imperious (also as cold, strong, and unyielding). When both the figure's arms were extended forward, the drawing with palms exposed was judged more cold, weak and yielding (also "effeminate") than a similar one without palms showing.

In a set of drawings of males in a group (clothed), hands were again seen as a primary influence on judgments of dominance. A man portrayed gesticulating was rated the most superordinate and important (as well as expressive and initiating action); and another man, standing with hands on hips, was seen as the second most dominant, superordinate, important, etc. (and haughty). The one judged as most subordinate, insignificant, and humble was off to the side, his hands behind his back.

Other gestures assert territorial rights, such as putting a foot or leg on a desk drawer, desk top or chair, touching or leaning against property, distributing personal articles to mark territory, crowding what is ostensibly someone else's space or property (as in another's office). Only a superior may stand relaxed in another's territory, as well as crowd it. Rights of possession of another person are indicated much as territorial rights are, as Nierenberg and Calero point out, by putting an arm around the other's waist, holding the other's hand, or otherwise touching the other's body or property.

[5] John Spiegel and Pavel Machotka, *Messages of the Body* (New York: Free Press, 1974), Chaps. 12 and 14.

* Such a set of scales is known as a Semantic Differential; respondents do not have to choose one or the other pole, but may rate the stimulus as anywhere in between. The Semantic Differential is explained in *The Measurement of Meaning*, by Charles E. Osgood, George J. Suci, and Percy H. Tannenbaum (Urbana: University of Illinois Press, 1957).

Participants in an interaction often show synchronized nonverbal behavior with such postures as legs crossed in the same manner, similar standing positions, hand to chin or hip, or arms similarly folded (and maybe mirror-image style). Several researchers have studied this interactional synchrony,[6] and have noted that even fast-passing motions which most of us are unaware of exhibit synchrony. Persons in agreement will show high synchrony, and those in disagreement, dissynchrony. The effect of power may be seen in a group by considering whose motions the other interactants are in harmony with—it is the high-power person whose behaviors will be unconsciously reflected by others.

Dominant individuals and those in positions of authority may use cues related to height as a symbol of superiority. They may elevate their bodies in some way (as we noted previously), such as standing up to emphasize a point, or standing close to or towering over seated persons while lecturing them. The chin-up position, particularly seen in the military style, hands clasped behind the back, may be a form of elevation, a way to appear to look down on others when one doesn't have the elevation from height alone.

Spiegel and Machotka also had people make judgments about drawn figures (male dyads) in different height relations to each other, with heads facing either toward the other or straight out, or bowed.[7] As we would expect, the higher male was seen as the more dominant of the dyad, in several ways: except when with bowed head, he was judged more superordinate and important; when looking at the other, he was also judged as more initiating; when looking straight ahead, he was seen as haughty, hostile, and distant. The lower man, with bowed head, was of course judged to be subordinate, insignificant and humble.

Authority is also shown in controlling others from a distance: a dominant person may summon others by a beckon, direct them by gesture, and point at them in a way that will shut them up, stop other action, or evoke attention and submissiveness. Dominant persons can assert their authority by leaning towards the other to express negative opinion; subordinate persons had better lean forward only in ingratiating circumstances, to express positive evaluation. This is probably because leaning forward is an invasion of personal space, associated with situations either of intimacy or aggression. Gesturing toward a person with the fist is another such incursion, allowed to dominants but not to subordinates.

Gestures exuding confidence also belong to the dominant person in an

---

[6] See especially W. S. Condon and W. D. Ogston, "Sound-Film Analysis of Normal and Pathological Behavior Patterns," *Journal of Nervous and Mental Disease*, 1966, 143, 338–47; and Adam Kendon, "Movement Coordination in Social Interaction: Some Examples Described," *Acta Psychologica*, 1970, 32, 101–25.

[7] Spiegel and Machotka, *Messages of the Body*, Chap. 15.

encounter. "Steepling" (Birdwhistell's term), the gesture of touching the fingertips together in a raised position, is one of these. Nierenberg and Calero describe it as "the confident and sometimes smug, pontifical, egotistic, or proud gesture" used by Sherlock Holmes and Nero Wolfe when educating their ignorant sidekicks. Steepling may be done either high or low, subtly or openly, according to one's status. "Our research data indicates," they write, "that the more important the executive feels he is, the higher he will hold his hands while steepling." [8] A prevalent gesture in superior-subordinate relationships, they say, is that of steepling at eye level, staring at the other through the hands.

Steepling is a gesture frequently used by professionals. Another such gesture, which helps emphasize the professional vs. client relationship, is the hand-to-face (perhaps chin- or beard-stroking) gesture indicating thoughtfulness and evaluation. Other elements of the situation, such as taking notes and distancing oneself with a desk barrier (perhaps intensified by leaning backward in an unconcerned manner) keep the professional perspective dominant.

The handshake, a peculiarly male gesture, may be used to establish or convey dominance. The aggressive, even hurtful handshake is an example of this, again probably a remnant of physical aggression. Nierenberg and Calero claim that turning the handshake over so that one's palm is on top is a type of physical domination. Offering a hand palm-up, correspondingly, is the gesture of a subordinate. There is a type of shake used between intimates, where one or both grab the other's arm simultaneously with the handshake. When a non-intimate attempts this, it is seen as false and an attempt at ingratiation, such as an insincere politician might make. Here is another example of touch being used in an outward gesture of friendship, but in fact to attempt influence.

CROSS-CULTURAL DOUBLES, OR DOUBLE-CROSSING CULTURE?

With so little known about nonverbal dominance even in our widely-studied U.S. white middle-class culture, we can't expect to have much cross-cultural knowledge of it. However, there is a tradition of cultural comparison here, particularly in gestural research, some of which we have already noted in Chapter 7. In addition, recent interest in ethnic and class differences within our own society has spurred new research in kinesic (body movement) cultural differences.

[8] Nierenberg and Calero, *How to Read a Person*, p. 96.

A study in Japan by Bond and Shiraishi applied kinesic measures developed in the United States to the study of interaction among Japanese subjects.[9] Male and female undergraduates were interviewed by male graduate students who had been trained to present a forward or backward body lean, with constant distance from the interviewee. The interviewers were introduced as either of equal or of somewhat higher status than the subject, and dressed accordingly. The researchers were interested in how these variables of posture and status (as well as the subject's sex) would affect subjects' nonverbal behavior.

They found that the status variable did affect subjects' responses. For male and female subjects combined, higher status interviewers provoked shorter pauses, more eye contacts, more head and hand gestures, and greater speech totals. However, females were much more responsive to the status manipulation than were males. The forward lean by the interviewers was also shown to produce in the subjects more head and hand gestures (and gestures in which one part of the body was in contact with another), most speech output, and quicker responses to questions. However, most of the response difference was again contributed by female responses, and there were other such sex differences. Bond and Shiraishi interpret these results as being generally consistent with U.S. findings except that greater tension was not seen in persons interacting with high status interviewers; head and hand gestures are considered relaxation measures, but they increased when with high status persons.

Another pair of investigators, Michael and Willis, looked at cultural differences between classes and sexes in the U.S., in the development of nonverbal interpretation and transmission skills in children. They chose a dozen gestures for which there is good agreement as to meaning,[10] and presented them as encoding or decoding problems to children either with no schooling or with one year of school. For example, one encoding problem was "If you had to be quiet and you were over there (pointing away) and you wanted me to come to you, what would you do?" (The children were told to use their hands, arms, or fingers.) A decoding problem was presented by the interviewer's making a gesture and asking the child "What does this mean?" Low and middle socioeconomic groups were compared, and all groups were racially mixed.

[9] Michael H. Bond and Daisuke Shiraishi, "The Effect of Body Lean and Status of an Interviewer on the Non-Verbal Behavior of Japanese Interviewees," *International Journal of Psychology*, 1974, 9, 117–28.

[10] Geraldine Michael and Frank N. Willis, Jr., "The Development of Gestures as a Function of Social Class, Education, and Sex," *Psychological Record*, 1968, 18, 515–19. The gestures used were those for: go away, come here, yes, no, be quiet, how many, how big, shape, I don't know, good-bye, hi, and raised hand for attention.

Middle-class children were found to be "superior" to lower-class ones, in both transmission and interpretation; children with one year in school were found to be superior to children with none, in both transmission and interpretation; and boys were found to be superior to girls in interpreting gestures. In addition, in interpretation there was an interaction between schooling and class: though lower-class nursery children started out at a great disadvantage, one year of schooling virtually wiped out the class difference, so that there was almost no difference between the lower and middle socioeconomic groups (both were now performing at a near-"perfect" level). The authors write:

> The often observed superiority in verbal development of middle-class children as compared to lower-class children is apparently accompanied by a superiority in both the interpretation and transmission of gestures. . . . The significant interaction between social class and education indicates that for the interpretation of gestures this first year in school is more important for the lower-class children.[11]

This latter finding, in fact, illuminates some questions that may be raised about this experiment. If one year in school has meant so much in lower-class children's development of gestural understanding compared to middle-class children's, might it not be because there is something they have encountered there for the first time, namely middle-class cultural habits? The explanation the authors offer, which is also feasible, is that many of the middle-class children were achieving perfect scores without schooling, which limited their ability to improve. Nevertheless, the arguments developed here still apply.

This is an example of research based on the behavior of the dominant middle-class, scoring "correctness" on an absolute scale of agreement with those middle-class behaviors, and interpreting the findings on an implicit assumption of middle-class superiority.

It is quite possible, of course, that a different set of gestures might have been presented that would have been well-known to lower-class children and not to middle-class children, but we have no way of knowing whether this is true or not. It is possible that gestural knowledge might be related to ethnicity, and that though both class groups were reported to be racially mixed, the lower-class and middle-class children came from or were influenced by different ethnic groups. It is also possible, as has been shown to be the case in linguistic investigation, that nonverbal responsiveness is inhibited in the face of cultural/class differences between interviewer and

11 Michael and Willis, "Gestures as Function of Social Class," p. 518.

subject. It is even possible that the lower-class children develop a nonverbal *superiority* because of having to become "bilingual" nonverbally, as black children are forced to become verbally bi-dialectical (learning both white middle-class and "black" English). All of these alternatives must be kept in mind and, in fact, considered more carefully than that of middle-class superiority, because the latter explanation is status-quo-preserving and self-serving for academicians, and reflects the habitual stance of social science as apologist for the social order.

COLOR, CULTURE, CLASS, AND GENDER

An interesting study by Kenneth Johnson begins to remedy the situation of lilywhiteness in U.S. kinesic investigation, with a detailed analysis of black nonverbal communication patterns.[12] In the tradition of much linguistic investigation, it is descriptive and does not report "controlled" investigation, but it gives a good account of patterns to be observed within black culture. Of special interest to us, Johnson has given particular attention to gestures of insubordination. He puts forward the hypothesis that black–white kinesic differences result from different cultural backgrounds, the black patterns having some distant relation to African body movement (as Black English has been shown to be influenced by African languages originally spoken by slaves). Cultural isolation of whites and blacks in this country, of course, is assumed to have played a part in creating and maintaining their kinesic diversity.

Young blacks, particularly males, according to Johnson show defiance to authority by adopting a limp stance which develops gradually during a conflict encounter: the head is lowered, the body extremely relaxed and motionless. Young white males, he notes, assume the opposite stance in such a situation: body rigid, legs spread, arms still at their sides, hands in fists. (This is also recognized as a form of the tightness seen in subordinates.) The young black's limp stance communicates that the authority is talking to thin air and might as well give up, because the message is not being received.

The "Black walk" ("pimp strut," "soulful strut") is also employed to show defiance to authority, if it is displayed after a reprimand, Johnson writes. This male walk is described as more of a stroll, with slow, casual and rhythmic gait, almost a dance; the head is perhaps slightly elevated, casually tipped to the side; one arm swings at the side, with hand slightly

[12] Kenneth R. Johnson, "Black Kinesics—Some Non-Verbal Communication Patterns in the Black Culture," *Florida FL Reporter*, 1971 (Spring/Fall), pp. 17–20, 57.

cupped, while the other hangs limply or is tucked in the pocket (thumb out). Young white males' walk, on the other hand, is generally brisk, on the balls of their feet "with strides of presumed authority," both arms swinging. The message of both black and white youths is, according to Johnson,

> "I am a strong man, possessing all the qualities of masculinity, and I stride through the world with masculine authority." . . . In addition, the Black walk communicates that the young Black male is beautiful, and it beckons female attention to the sexual prowess possessed by the walker. Finally, the Black walk communicates that the walker is "cool"; in other words, he is not upset or bothered by the cares of the world and is, in fact, somewhat disdainful and insolent towards the world.[13]

This walk in its stationary form becomes the "rapping (courting) stance" for black males. We will return to the use of "cool" and of masculinity to assert authority in the pages ahead.

The black female postures and movements that communicate rejection of authority are somewhat different from those of males: females pivot quickly on both feet (in an "about face"), sometimes with a raising of the head and twitching of the nose, and walk briskly away. Their most aggressive stance is nonchalant, with hand on hip: feet are placed firmly in a stationary step, weight on the rear heel, buttocks protruded, one hand on the extended hip with fingers spread or in a fist. It may be accompanied by a slow rock, rolling the eyes, and twitching of the nose. This is a position indicating intense involvement, Johnson writes, including hostility and negative feelings toward the speaker, but at times it is used in courtship, when attending to the black male's courting rap. Johnson says too that Chicana females have a similar stance for the same communication: they place both hands on hips, with feet spread wide and head slightly raised.

Sex differences have appeared in other kinesic comparisons of varied American cultures. In his study of spacing among black, Puerto Rican, Italian and Chinese ethnic groups (see Chapter 2), Jones found a large sex difference in shoulder orientation (though no sex differences in personal space were noted).[14] Shoulder orientation is the angle at which people orient themselves toward each other in an encounter, and may vary from face-to-face (most direct), through slight twists to a 90° angle, and beyond. Both in his small sample of females in the first study, and in the larger

13 Johnson, "Black Kinesics," p. 19.

14 Stanley E. Jones, "A Comparative Proxemics Analysis of Dyadic Interaction in Selected Subcultures of New York City," *Journal of Social Psychology*, 1971, 84, 35–44.

Black rapping stance.

group of his second study, Jones found that female pairs showed more direct shoulder orientation than did male pairs (male–female pairs showed an angle falling between the single–sex pairs). Moreover, this highly significant sex difference (probability less than .001) so outweighed differences among subcultures that "the effect of cultural membership on these sex differences was negligible," according to Jones. So, sex is seen to be a more influential variable than the highly-vaunted "subcultural" one here, as class was also seen to be more influential than culture in proxemics, in this study.

Jones speculates that the reason for the sex difference perhaps "stems from females having greater affiliational needs, more desire for emotional involvement, a higher degree of interest in nonverbal feedback or a combination of these factors." But, he goes on, "A reverse causal relatiorship could also be posited; *proxemic behaviors may be acquired at a rather early age and serve to structure and reinforce sex roles"* (my emphasis).[15] He suggests that sex differences in shoulder orientation may be basic to the species, across cultures, and makes the certainly valid point that sex differences should be considered in future cross-cultural proxemic research.

WOMEN'S MOVEMENT

Disguised in a dress in a famous incident, Huckleberry Finn gives away his sex by closing his knees to catch a lump of lead, rather than spreading his lap in a feminine way. As the woman who detected him pointed out, he had also tried to thread a needle by bringing the needle to the thread instead of vice versa; and threw the lump of lead (at rats) too well to be a girl.[16] It's rare that we are as astute as this woman in articulating the kinesic features which distinguish females and males.

To start with, what do we know about how males and females differ kinesically? Birdwhistell has described some examples of what he terms "American gender identification signals." [17] He emphasizes that these are not to be taken as solely sexual, or as invitations to intercourse, but rather must be considered in the total context of the ongoing situation in which they are produced. They are, however, "gender signals" which are "sent," or presentations that are made as a reciprocal to gender signals of the other sex. What Birdwhistell seems to mean by gender presentation is kinesic forms that tend to be displayed mainly by one sex or the other (and may be affected by the gender of others present), but which do not belong exclusively to the repertoire of that sex. (Birdwhistell's claims are based on painstaking analysis of filmed interaction by trained observers in his kinesics laboratory.)

One example Birdwhistell gives concerns the angle between the upper legs (intrafemoral angle): American females in gender presentation "bring the legs together, at times to the point that the upper legs cross, either in a full leg cross *with feet still together,* the lateral aspects of the two feet parallel to each other, or in standing knee over knee," whereas American males display an angle up to 10° or 15° (more open).

Or take arm position: female gender presentation arm position similarly

15 Jones, "Comparative Proxemics Analysis," p. 43.

16 Mark Twain, *The Adventures of Huckleberry Finn* (New York: Dodd, Mead, 1953), pp. 63–67.

17 Ray L. Birdwhistell, "Masculinity and Femininity as Display," in *Kinesics and Context* (Philadelphia: University of Pennsylvania Press, 1970). The quotations here and in the next four paragraphs are from p. 44.

keeps the upper arms close to the trunk, while male gender presentation has the arms 5 to 20 degrees away from the body. Pelvic position, and walking movement, give further female/male differences: according to Birdwhistell, "the American male tends to carry his pelvis rolled slightly back as contrasted with the female anterior roll." Though our kinesic ideology, and its expression in theatrical and visual media presentations, claims that females wiggle their hips while males walk more smoothly, Birdwhistell's observations indicate the opposite to be true: the male "may subtly wag his hips with a slight right and left presentation with a movement which involves a twist at the base of the thoracic cage and at the ankles." In moving, the female may present the length of the entire body as a moving whole, while the male does not, moving his arms independently of the trunk.

It is not immediately clear what the connection is between these sex differences and the theme of power in this book. Indeed, when they are presented in the usual apolitical context in which many of them are given, without interpretation, there seems to be no connection. But closer examination suggests more. For example, the leg and arm "gender displays" described by Birdwhistell are recognized as the prescribed leg position for females and echo the condensed arms-to-body, defensive-and-not-intruding-on-the-environment, female arm position described by Piercy (Chapter 2). These "gender displays" are acting out female shrinking and male spatial expansion—in other words, they are power displays as well.

But what of differences which can't so readily be interpreted as relating to power differences and sex role prescriptions? They too play their part in expressing the power differential. For the most part, the very existence of such sex differences seems almost designed to perpetuate sex division and sex inequality. As Birdwhistell notes, anatomy has very little to do with the differences; rather, these "tertiary sex differences," like social class differences (in clothing, kinesics, etc.), exist to emphasize and create distinctiveness. An observation by Birdwhistell further illustrates the universally malleable character of these differences—and the universal belief in their immalleability: informants from seven different societies all reported that young children "matured into" gender-signalling behaviors, and older people gave up or "matured out of" them (they are most prominent in persons of mating age), but still believed the sex-typed behaviors were instinctual.[18]

Sex differences in head movements have been noted by various authors; or rather, certain female gestures have been noted as deviances—we can

[18] The seven societies are: Chinese, middle- and upper-class London British, Kutenai, Shushwap, Hopi, Parisian French, and American.

White male/female interaction.

often only infer the male gestures as what females do *not* do.* Nierenberg and Calero, noting Darwin's observation that both humans and animals cock their heads in attentive listening, go on to say: "From a very early age, women instinctively understand the significance of this gesture. They use it consciously when conversing with a male whom they want to impress—and they do." [19]

Key points out that in magazines and newspapers, females are very often shown with tilted heads. "This head gesture may convey an attitude of coyness or submissiveness," she writes, "but it is so common that one can almost always find such a head position in any group of women." [20]

---

* This is an example of a widespread phenomenon in social science (e.g., anthropology, sociology, psychology, linguistics) whereby male behavior is assumed as the norm and female, as the deviant. Freud's writings on women exemplify it, as do anthropological accounts of "women's languages" in certain cultures (without labeling "men's languages" as such).

[19] Nierenberg and Calero, *How to Read a Person*, p. 60.

[20] Mary Ritchie Key, *Male/Female Language* (Metuchen, N.J.: Scarecrow Press, 1975), p. 112.

Head behavior in greetings was observed by investigators Kendon and
Ferber, who filmed an outdoor birthday party.[21] There were 20 observations in which the head was cocked to one side, and 18 of these gestures
were made by women. On the other hand, of 35 observations of forward-
tilted heads, 27 were made by males. Of the 24 females the researchers
observed, over a third exhibited the headcock at least once; but among the
19 males, only about a tenth did so.

One reason for head cocking by females when with males may be com-
pensation for height (and this does not rule out the other sources or
functions of the gesture); the side-tilted head may be less uncomfortable
than the back-tilted one. Whatever its origin, the cocked head is not as
dominating as the forward and/or chin-up position. Women are not supposed to assume these dominant head positions (and it may be hard to
look down on someone, chin up, when shorter). The traditional head position for women is the modest one of head slightly lowered, eyes looking up
faithfully to superiors. We may laugh at such a description of Victorian-
sounding prissiness, but I believe that though the overt prescriptive words
may be outdated, the positions are much more prevalent than we might
guess. Kendon and Ferber suggest that head position may function as a
kinesic gender marker—head erect or forward for males, cocked for females. This notion is supported further by their impression that females'
tendency to headcock in the final approach (of a greeting sequence) was
more obvious in male/female greetings than in female/female ones.

Many other "feminine" behaviors may similarly show higher density
during male/female encounters than in all-female combinations. Smiling
seems to be one such gesture cited by various authors, often in the context
of submissiveness (more on this in Chapter 10 on Facial Expression).
Rita Mae Brown not only explicitly describes certain female behaviors in
the presence of men, but distinguishes between the kinesics of feminist and
non-feminist women:

> Lowering a shoulder in the presence of a man, pulling the body in (literally,
> to take up less space so he can have more), turning the head upward or
> tilting it to the side, often with persistent eyebrow signals, are motions most
> non-feminists perform automatically. Such gestures elicit favorable male
> response. Muscles tighten around a woman's jaw and upper back in the
> presence of a male. . . .
> When around men, many women cross and uncross their legs incessantly,
> modify their voices, open their eyes dramatically, signifying animated interest
> in the male, and play with their hair. As hair is so important to femininity

[21] Adam Kendon and Andrew Ferber, "A Description of Some Human Greetings,"
in R. P. Michael and J. H. Crook, eds., *Comparative Ecology and Behavior in Primates* (London: Academic Press, 1973), pp. 591–668.

in America, I take this to be some sort of request for sexual affirmation. Another basic pose of non-feminism is casting the hip slightly forward in male company.[22]

Brown's observations are partially confirmed by a controlled-observation study by two students at the University of Lowell. They watched for three preening behaviors among female college students, half in interaction with males and half with other females. These observers (both women) found that 30 out of the 40 hair-stroking gestures observed were made by females with males; similarly, 11 out of 15 clothes-rearranging gestures, and 25 out of 40 gestures of pushing hair from the face, were performed when with males rather than with other females.[23]

Brown suggests feminists have abandoned (or are abandoning) submissive postures and gestures:

> The disappearance of poses resulting from oppression is partly because women in the process of becoming feminists spend more time with other women and those postures look absurd when we're all together. Affecting such postures indicates power relationships and since no woman has the same power over another woman that a man does, the protective gestures are wildly out of place.[24]

The gestures which other authors describe as female-associated, as "feminine," or as gender display, are thus put in a clearer light. If, as Brown claims, feminist women are less likely to perform them, and "male-identified" women more likely, they take on even more the aspect of submissive gestures rather than simply sex-differentiated forms.

There is another set of gestures that further clarify this point, gestures used in everyday situations by males or females which resemble those of courtship, but which are not. These gestures, which Scheflen has described so insightfully as *quasi-courting,* carry some sort of disclaimer so they won't be mistaken for real courting. They signify lively engagement in an interaction, and thus (in systems theory terms) serve a system-maintaining function.[25] Examples of these courtship-like behaviors are high muscle tonus, brightened eyes, preening, direct body orientation (vis-à-vis), soft speech quality, flirtatious glances, gaze-holding, "demure gestures," head-

[22] Rita Mae Brown, "The Good Fairy," *Quest,* 1974, 1, no. 1, 58–64. The quotation is from pp. 61–62.

[23] Karen Barbett and Judy Abbott, "Preening Behavior in Females," unpublished paper, University of Lowell, 1975.

[24] Brown, "The Good Fairy," p. 62.

[25] Albert E. Scheflen, "Quasi-Courtship Behavior in Psychotherapy," *Psychiatry,* 1965, 28, 245–57.

cocking, and pelvis rolling. In addition, Scheflen cites invitational gestures specific to women (though none for men): these are crossing the legs, exposing the thigh, placing a hand on the hip, exhibiting the wrist or palm, protruding the breast, and stroking the thigh or wrist.

Quasi-courting regularly occurs, according to Scheflen, when there is confusion around gender within the interaction.* The gender confusion may arise "when some participant behaves in a way that is inappropriate to his [sic] gender—for instance, when a woman acts very aggressive and domineering or a man behaves passively and femininely." [26] Or gender ambiguity may be felt when someone is in a position usually held by someone of the other sex (e.g., two men are at a nightclub table). Quasi-courting in these situations seems to be used to affirm gender—gender identification signals are heightened—or to determine that a member will fill some sex-identified role in the interaction.

We see then in Scheflen's account an explanation for these observations of "feminine" behavior, heavier gender identification signals by women, in the presence of men. Presumably males are sending "masculine" signals at the same time (indeed, Brown suggests as much). However, the whole truth here goes beyond gender "identification." When the signals of one gender are typically those of submission, and those of the other are typically associated with dominance, power as well as gender is being displayed.

O'Connor takes this difference into account when she comments on just such a situation of "gender confusion" as Scheflen does, but quite differently: "Women who use gestures of dominance are sometimes subjected to heavy taming campaigns on the part of aggressive men." [27] We must look more carefully at the terms we so casually apply to interaction situations; "gender ambiguity" may instead be *dominance* ambiguity. Labeling it as a gender problem tends to settle the issue, unscientifically direct our attention to the wrong variable, and work politically (and subtly) to preserve the status quo.

Birdwhistell too has commented on "inappropriate" gender display, especially that of "feminine" males and "masculine" females. Informants in those seven societies not only distinguished typical male and female nonverbal gender communication but cross-sex deviant display. Although they could identify such deviance, they could not necessarily describe exactly

* The other situation in which quasi-courting is common is when a participant has withdrawn or been excluded.
[26] Scheflen, "Quasi-Courtship Behavior," p. 254.
[27] Lynn O'Connor, "Male Supremacy: A Theoretical Analysis," (1970) available as a reprint from KNOW, Inc., P.O. Box 86031, Pittsburgh, Pa. 15221, p. 6. There is an excellent photo-essay, "Men and Women," by O'Connor, accompanying a portion of the Male Supremacy essay in *It Ain't Me Babe*, July 1, 1970, Vol. 1, no. 8, pp. 10–11.

what it was that made it so.* All these societies had such stereotypes. Bird-whistell emphasizes the importance of interpreting gender display behavior in context: though the message, by either male or female, that says "I wish to be considered homosexual" is easily interpreted by observers, Birdwhistell and his co-workers have not found any single, isolated com-ponent, masculine or feminine, that in itself indicates sexual preference (in practice). Cross-gender messages, of course, are more important to transvestites (usually male) than to homosexuals who are not transvestites; a major problem for new transvestites, beyond the intricacies of feminine clothing, is learning how to pass as female in body movements, especially learning to walk like a woman. (The exaggeration of feminine style prac-ticed by transvestites, of course, serves to perpetuate the feminine stereo-type.)

There are further sex differences in body movement, posing further questions. Various writers have observed that females typically cross their legs knee-over-knee, holding the lower legs parallel and together, whereas American males more often use the ankle-to-knee, "figure-four" cross.† Is this difference due to males' seeking relief from crowded crotches by keeping the legs parted as much as possible? It may be a factor, but if so, how can we explain the fact that European males cross their legs in a manner similar to American females?

---

* This is not uncommon: in many areas—e.g., using grammar, learning pattern concepts—people can identify an example of a concept but can't tell the rules that make it so.

† In addition, various stereotyped sex differences were "found" in the studies by Spiegel and Machotka (*Messages of the Body*). A claim that the important dimen-sions of these figures to subjects were "feminine" passivity and receptiveness, though subjects were not given these dimensions by the researchers, is ridiculous, since the structure of the study allowed for little other than stereotyped findings.

Spiegel and Machotka admit that they gave the male a firmer stance, and greater intrusiveness into space, than the female. In moving from study of the female to the male figure, they changed their set of scales; but I'll let the authors describe these changes and their rationalizations for them: "One dimension not retained was 'affected-ingenuous'; although one can see how a male position may appear affected, one has more difficulty summoning up a body image of male ingenuousness. Another dimension was altered: 'receiving-rejecting' became 'receiving-giving,' in order to give an active scope to the ratings. Three dimensions intended to measure attributes im-portant to male figures were added: 'effeminate-virile,' 'strong-weak,' and 'imperious-humble.' "

Three studies of kinesics in groups—on gaze direction, arm positions and height —all use male groupings; female figures are used again only in the studies of male-female encounter [see footnote 38 below].

When stereotyped preconceptions are put into the design of an experiment, it's little wonder that stereotypes fall out in the results. Computer users have an expres-sion for this phenomenon, GIGO: "Garbage In, Garbage Out." It's only unfortunate that these studies have been praised by two well-known psychologists, Jerome Kagan and Thomas Cottle, both associated with child development and advocacy. With friends like these, young girls don't need enemies.

Aside from the space-consuming qualities of the two positions (which parallel female/male spatial behavior), the difference may be believed to emerge from the proprieties associated with female dress. Perhaps when females wear long pants they too cross an ankle over a knee (Nierenberg and Calero suggest they do). This is not what they are advised, however, by those who pass on rules of dress and posture: Stannard writes that, according to etiquette arbiter Amy Vanderbilt, a woman in a pantsuit "must not walk like a man or sit with her legs apart or put her feet up on her desk. . . . Psychically she must not 'wear the pants' nor even assume the postures of masculine freedom and assertion." [28] Again we see that sex differences in posture are developed not from anatomy or dress, but for the purpose of . . . creating sex differences in posture!

Many of the positions described earlier as "closed," with arms folded, legs crossed, clothing fastened, etc., are those prescribed for females in our society. They are the contracting of oneself and one's space, and protection of the soft tissues, that Piercy describes as characteristic of women. Nierenberg and Calero also note women's protective use of the hand-to-chest gesture, that is, the palm laid flat on the breast. The gesture is used (presumably by men) as a symbol of honesty, but in women serves as "a protective gesture indicating sudden shock or surprise." These authors also point out that women fold their arms lower on the body than men do (because of the difference in chest configuration), and that "Girls entering puberty assume this protective position with a far greater frequency than their older sisters," presumably because of greater breast-consciousness.[29]

Women's movement to protect soft tissues is illustrated in a study by Collett and Marsh, who observed patterns of collision-avoidance at a pedestrian crossing in London. They found that females passed others in a "closed" manner, i.e., with body turned away from the other; males tended to pass with an "open" position, body turned toward the other. Moreover, in both the closed and open pass, women more frequently drew one or both arms across themselves. Collett and Marsh interpret these female behaviors as endeavors to protect the breasts—"whether it be from painful collision or from violation of a body region which, in our culture, is ritually associated with the erotic." [30]

So much of women's interaction style focuses on kinesic prescription that special attention must be given to these restrictions in posture, gesture, and motion. A consciousness-raising cartoon of a few years back, called "Exer-

[28] Una Stannard, "Clothing and Sexuality," *Sexual Behavior,* 1971 (May), 1, 2, 24–33, 64.

[29] Nierenberg and Calero, *How to Read a Person,* pp. 126, 51.

[30] Peter Collett and Peter Marsh, "Patterns of Public Behavior: Collision Avoidance on a Pedestrian Crossing," *Semiotica,* 1974, 12, 281–99; the quotation is from page 298.

Exercises for Men

1. Sit down in a straight chair. Cross your legs at the ankles and keep your knees pressed together. Try to do this while you're having a conversation with someone, but pay attention at all times to keeping your knees pressed tightly together.

2. Bend down to pick up an object from the floor. Each time you bend remember to bend your knees so that your rear end doesn't stick up, and place one hand on your shirtfront to hold it to your chest. This exercise simulates the experience of a woman in a short, low-necked dress bending over.

3. Run a short distance, keeping your knees together. You'll find you have to take short, high steps if you run this way. Women have been taught it is unfeminine to run like a man with long, free strides. See how far you get running this way for 30 seconds.

4. Sit comfortably on the floor. Imagine that you are wearing a dress and that everyone in the room wants to see your underwear. Arrange your legs so that no one can see. Sit like this for a long time without changing your position.

5. Walk down a city street. Pay a lot of attention to your clothing; make sure your pants are zipped, shirt tucked in, buttons done. Look straight ahead. Every time a man walks past you, avert your eyes and make your face expressionless. Most women learn to go through this act each time we leave our houses. It's a way to avoid at least some of the encounters we've all had with strange men who decided we looked available.

6. Walk around with your stomach pulled in tight, your shoulders thrown back, and your chest thrust out. Pay attention to keeping this posture at all times. Notice how it changes your breathing. Try to speak loudly and aggressively in this posture.

Willamette Bridge / LNS

cises for Men," and reprinted in full on pp. 143–44 very well illuminates the absurdity of "ladylike" postures:

1. Sit down in a straight chair. Cross your legs at the ankles and keep your knees pressed together. Try to do this while you're having a conversation with someone, but pay attention at all times to keeping your knees pressed tightly together.

2. Bend down to pick up an object from the floor. Each time you bend remember to bend your knees so that your rear end doesn't stick up, and place one hand on your shirt-front to hold it to your chest. This exercise simulates the experience of a woman in a short, low-necked dress bending over.

3. Run a short distance, keeping your knees together. You'll find you have to take short, high steps if you run this way. Women have been taught it is unfeminine to run like a man with long, free strides. See how far you get running this way for 30 seconds.[31]

As a matter of fact, the kinesics here are not simply absurd. They contribute to feelings of inferiority in the women who must perform them, and to impressions of inferiority in those who observe them. It is most interest-

[31] "Exercises for Men," from *Willamette Bridge* (and Liberation News Service), 1971. Printed in *The Radical Therapist*, Dec.-Jan. 1971, 1, no. 5, p. 15.

ing to note that those "undignified" positions that are denied women—such as sitting with an arm over the chair leg, or feet on desk, or backwards straddling a chair—are precisely those positions that are used among men to convey dominance. Thus prescribed female postures are just those which cannot be used to get power—are ones that must convey impotence, submission.

Of course, the positions of relaxed aggressiveness described in the earlier part of this chapter are most often used by people of status and power, who are least often female. It's unclear whether some of them are characterized as male because of the confounding of sex and status, or if they are gestures that even women in positions of power do not adopt. I believe for the most part the latter is true; or, if women do use such gestures when in dominant positions, that they are toned down (Nierenberg and Calero remark that women typically steeple in the covert, lower position), or qualified with other signals that temper their assertiveness.

Chesler and Goodman, in *Women, Money and Power* (New York: Morrow, 1976), describe this tempering of dominance signals by women in positions of power, for survival, and from fear:"Women communicate deference, inconsequentiality, helplessness, and maternality—visually, ver·bally, and nonverbally. For example, many different "poses," the exaggeration of sexuality or its denial, via clothes, voice tone, and eyes, may help a woman communicate her basic deference—a stance supposed to put others at their ease and men 'on top.'" (p. 22)"Most women are convinced the body language of female deference and/or of a 'beautiful appearance' will save or protect them from 'worse' in a world of male violence and power." (p. 39)

Theeman puts forward a striking illustration of two distinct systems of gestures, one elaborating a male culture and the other a female culture, differentially valued and rewarded in our society. These are the worlds of sports and dance. Sports, the major outlet emphasizing body development —strength and agility—for men, is widely visible and among the highest paid occupations in our society. Dance is the major outlet of this type associated with women, and though it is not exclusive to women, it exemplifies a "female" culture (e.g., in dress and gesture)—men in dance are typically disdained as feminine for their participation. Dancers, in contrast with athletes, are barely visible and greatly underpaid; dance companies must struggle (assisted by grants) to put together enough money to stage their limited season each year.[32] This contrast in popular and economic support dramatically captures the differential rewards for "masculine" (aggressive, competitive) and "feminine" (graceful, cooperative) gesture systems in our society.

[32] Margaret Theeman, "Rhythms of Community: The Sociology of Expressive Body Movement," doctoral dissertation, Harvard University, 1974.

AGGRESSION: FEMALE AND MALE

In recent years many women have wanted to show directly the anger they felt intellectually and emotionally, but found they could not get angry. They learned that their real anger, previously suppressed, had been coming out in the form of tears. Attempts to express anger to its true target sometimes turned into nervous laughter and incoherence; feelings of conditioned guilt almost always followed the expression of anger, even when its owner felt morally/intellectually justified. Like men who could not cry or feel tenderness, their emotional repertoire was stunted. The expression of anger is central to aggressive behavior, about which little is known concerning women, especially in the nonverbal realm.

The type of aggressive encounter between young males illustrated by Scheflen is rare between women, although it must take place. Since females are shown very clearly that they are not to be aggressive and competitive, however, the more likely aggressive displays between women are probably in the form of the approved emotional expression for women, i.e., defeated rather than attacking. Negative emotional displays of hurt, disappointment, fear and self-incrimination, accompanied by crying, may be the only safe form of emotional expression, much of that being expression of disguised anger. Verbal aggression may also take the place of physical attack in women, sometimes subtly disguised in the positive speech forms deemed appropriate for females. The cartoon "Momma" showed a good understanding of this allowed form of female infighting, in a panel showing Momma and her daughter-in-law oozing compliments at each other:

> "Tina, you are the finest daughter-in-law a mother could want!"
> "And you're the best mother-in-law!"
> "You're simply perfect for my Thomas!"
> "I'll never compare to his mother!"
> "And I'm very proud of the way you care for him!"
> "I have you for a model, Mother Hobbs!"

In the last frame, Momma says to the reader, "Would you believe it's a power struggle?" [33]

One problem women face in expressing hostility is the lack of an expressive hostile vocabulary, both verbal and nonverbal. Slang and obscenity are generally taboo to women, and their nonverbal counterparts, such as obscene gestures and what we can call gestural slang, are likewise pre-

[33] Mell Lazarus, "Momma," Boston *Globe*, November 30, 1971, p. 49.

rogatives of male culture. Of course, much of slang and obscene language consist of deprecations of females, references to their physical attributes, and allusions to sexual acts; these cannot be used as hostile expressions by women, as they can by men. An example of what I mean by "gestural slang" is the common street gesture used by men of the two hands in the air moving downwards in parallel, with outward excursions to outline an exaggerated female torso. The best-known obscene gesture is "the finger," the middle finger extended above the fist, indicating hostility with strong sexual overtones ("fuck you" and "up yours"), generally between men. (This ultimate deprecation takes the form of implying the recipient is a woman or should be treated as one.) A well-known semi-obscene gesture performed by women is the rump-presenting institutionalized in the can-can and chorus line. As various authors have pointed out,[34] this gesture mimics the submissive gesture of nonhuman primates, known as "presenting."

While we know little about aggression between females, we should know more about male/female aggression, since encounter between the sexes has at least been studied. Such studies, however, seldom look at (or recognize) inter-sex aggression; and even when they do, we must remember to examine the findings cautiously for limitations unconsciously built in by sex bias and other such failures in scientific method. Spiegel and Machotka present two studies of female/male encounter which illustrate this problem, but from which we still may derive some interesting observations: one study used ratings of drawings, as in the previously reported research, and the other had people arrange artists' manikins in positions to illustrate certain qualities of the encounter.[35]

In the first study, 32 drawings of male/female dyads were constructed by combining each of eight female figures with each of four male figures. The female figures, by the authors' descriptions, were varied in static poses: four arm positions × two leg positions. The male figure variations were in his relationship to the encounter rather than arm and leg posturing: he is shown as either advancing or retreating, and near or far (within or without the female's axial space). Thus the ratings for these figures (e.g., on activeness, feelings/motives) are limited by the incomparability of the stereotyped figures and their variations. However, we can draw some conclusions from the differences in subjects' responses to the drawings (since all saw the same ones). The authors concluded that male subjects were more likely

---

[34] See Nicole Anthony, "Open Letter to Psychiatrists," *Radical Therapist*, 1970 (Aug.–Sept.), 1, 3, 8 (available also from KNOW, Inc., P.O. Box 86031, Pittsburgh, Pa. 15221); O'Connor, "Men and Women," pp. 10–11; and Desmond Morris, *Intimate Behaviour* (New York: Random House, 1971).

[35] Spiegel and Machotka, *Messages of the Body*, Chap. 16.

to connect eroticism and aggression: "men see eroticism as quite aggressive, and warmth as quite erotic, and . . . women distinguish between them somewhat more fully." [36]

The second study, by Paul Williams, provides somewhat solider evidence of this connection. In this investigation, female and male subjects were given a pair of manikins, one with makeshift breasts applied to the chest, and asked to arrange them to represent such encounters as: aggressive/unaggressive; male initiating/female initiating; male receiving/female receiving; erotic/nonerotic; warm/cold; sincere/calculating; good/evil.[37] Again males were seen to confuse the aggressive and the erotic; Williams writes:

> In erotic and (to a lesser degree) warm encounters, men seemed to find it necessary to produce highly initiating males: ones who stood higher, approached the female, and defined their axial space. While the women stressed their equality (in the isotrope [position of equal height]) and the partners' mutuality (shared responsibility for boundary intersection), the men once more confused eroticism and aggression, and accounted for a striking presentational similarity with the aggressive dimension.[38]

In depicting aggressive interactions, 14 of the 20 constructions showed one figure higher than the other; 11 of these figures were males. The withdrawing figures were most often females. The sex of the subjects also affected the focus of responsibility in the scenes depicted: in about half the aggressive encounters, male manikins were shown as responsible, and most of these constructions were by males. In one-quarter of the aggressive scenes, the responsibility was mutual; all of these scenes were created by female subjects.

The use of height to indicate physical superiority was of interest, and differed by sex:

> Men, it would seem, produce what they believe are more powerful male manikins without resorting to superiority in height, but women portray the aggressive male as aggressive partly by virtue of his height—which may represent, here, superior size or brute strength.[39]

[36] Spiegel and Machotka, *Messages of the Body*, p. 302.
[37] Paul Williams, "Male–Female Encounter: Fresh Constructions," Chap. 17 in Spiegel and Machotka, *Messages of the Body*. This experiment, like others in this book, suffers from rampant sex stereotyping and uncontrolled variables. Only the sexual aspects of the encounter are examined, as if all female/male encounters are sexual. And the predetermined situations allowed to the subjects could not show *both* female and male initiating, *both* male and female receiving.
[38] Williams, "Male–Female Encounter," p. 340.
[39] Williams, "Male–Female Encounter," p. 311.

Males do resort to height, it seems, when confronted with female initiative: when creating "female initiating" encounters, men tended to show the male manikins in higher positions, while women subjects showed the female higher. Williams writes,

> From the men's point of view, when the female initiates, she does so from a position of physical inferiority, as if the initiative had to be more seductive or insidious than physically overbearing. For the female to initiate—so men seem to think—she has to take the male's 'natural' physical or positional superiority into account and work from there; either she tackles the physical superiority directly (and risks the male's determined resistance, as in [one construction]), or she attempts seduction (as in the unsubtle production illustrated in [another construction]).[40]

Reading these passages, it is all too easy to miss the fact that when people discuss aggression between males and females, it is almost excluvively male aggression directed against females. We don't notice that female or mutual aggression is not dealt with, because, for one thing, female aggression is not as salient a category in our minds as male aggression. But this tendency also reflects another reality: the overwhelming aspect of male-female gestural relations is one of male physical control over women.

In a way so accepted and so subtle as to be unnoticed even by its practitioners and recipients, males in couples will often literally push a woman everywhere she is to go—the arm from behind, steering around corners, through doorways, into elevators, onto escalators, darting out in front when crossing the street. It is not necessarily heavy and pushy or physical in an ugly way; it is light and gentle but firm, in the way of the most confident equestrians with the best-trained horses.

Physical control by males over females goes beyond this public herding, however, to the point of heavy "man-handling." Thousands of women are still beaten up by "their" men daily, despite the passing of those old wife-beating jokes (why were they funny, one wonders?) and tacit agreement that that sort of thing doesn't happen any more.[41] On a less severe scale, there are the threats conveyed by some men when they wish to slightly punish and to warn a woman attempting to go against the man's will. These threats may be such as a hard squeeze of the upper arm, or of the hand,

[40] Williams, "Male–Female Encounter," p. 316.
[41] "At Boston City Hospital approximately 70 percent of the assault victims received at emergency are women who have been attacked in the home," according to Betsy Warrior, "Battered Lives," in *The Second Wave*, 1975, 4, no. 2, 8–12, 14–19. More attention is being given to this problem, and support groups and refuges are being set up for battered wives.

physical restraint (holding her back), stepping on the toe or kicking the ankle surreptitiously when seated.

There is often mock play between males and females, especially younger ones, which also carries strong physical overtones of dominance. In public places, particularly recreation areas, the play may take the form of the male "pretending" to twist the female's arm, hitting her buttocks hard, punching her a little too hard on the arm, picking her up and carrying her. Groups of males may pick up a female and toss her around from one to another in the air, chase women to lift and spank them, throw them in water, and so on. It's noteworthy that many of these same activities are used to control children, and to maintain a status hierarchy in adolescent same-sex peer groups.

At a country square dance a few years ago I saw an offensive game between two men on opposite sides of a square, to see who could swing the women hardest and highest off the ground. What started out pleasantly enough soon degenerated into a brutal competition that left the women of the square staggering dizzily from place to place, completely unable to keep up with what was going on in the dance, and certainly getting no pleasure from it. The message that comes through to women in such physical displays is: you are so physically inferior that you can be played with like a toy. Males are the movers and the powerful in life, females the puppets.

chapter nine

DON'T LOOK NOW:

Eye Contact

Eye engagement is like touch in its mystic and magnetic qualities. As in touch, a spark seems to pass between two persons whose eyes meet —sometimes a spark of recognition, sometimes one of love, sometimes one of conflict. Though an extremely subtle cue, such contact is reliable enough that auction bids and bets at cockfights are made with eye contact between knowledgeable people. As with touch, many of our expressions use the visual metaphor, for example, "I see your meaning," or "here are my views." We look to the eyes for meaning, and find them so significant that our popular culture would have us believe that masking the eyes alone, while leaving all other personal characteristics—face, hair, clothing, body size, shape and gait—observable, is enough to cloud the identity (and it might be). Cartoon outlaws and comic book super-do-gooders protect their anonymity thus. Censored eyes are used also in books, movies, and TV interviews, for the blamed-but-unblameworthy, such as mental patients, single mothers, homosexuals, and prostitutes.

Our popular culture enshrines the eyes in sentimental composition, proclaiming "Drink to me only with thine eyes, and I will pledge with mine," "Eyes are the mirror of the soul," "Your eyes are the eyes of a woman in love," and various other sentiments, the gist of which may be summed up as: "Some enchanted evening you will see a stranger across a crowded room, your eyes will meet in love at first sight, something magic will pass between you, and you'll never be the same again." We seem to believe this romanticism; an experiment showed that when people viewed video-tapes of "engaged" couples, highly positive ratings were given the couples that gazed at each other the most.[1]

Two major messages emerge from all this: that eyes are important in our evaluation of others, and that eye contact is an invitation to, or indication of, intimacy. Research in visual behavior supports these ideas: eye contact is central in the expression of attraction and intimacy, and has been much studied in this context. Numerous investigators have found that people look more at those they feel positively toward,[2] and at those from whom they expect or desire approval.[3] These two aspects of eye behavior, though obviously related, are at least partially independent; we generally do want approval from those we feel positively toward, though not all those we want approval from are persons we have positive feelings for.

IT'S NOT POLITE TO STARE

But eye contact, like touching, has its negative side too. We don't like to be stared at, and believe it's impolite for us to stare at others ourselves. We engage in seemingly petty competitions of staring down another, across the table or across the room, and feel defeated (or laugh nervously) if we are the first to break our gaze. We are half-frightened by the prospect of being controlled by someone's eyes, in the popular image of a "Svengali" who intones, "Look into my eyes . . . Look *deeeeep* into my eyes!" It is interesting to note that the two heavyweights of nonverbal communication, touch and gaze, are used in the traditional acting-out of the archetypical scene of external control, the hypnotist or mad doctor exerting power over the innocent subject. The Svengali pose has arms outstretched, nearly grasping but not touching, and eyes unwaveringly riveted on the hapless one who will do the bidding.

[1] Chris L. Kleinke, Frederick B. Meeker, and Carl La Fong, "Effects of Gaze, Touch, and Use of Name on Evaluation of 'Engaged' Couples," *Journal of Experimental Research in Personality*, 1973, 7, 368–73.

[2] For example, Ralph V. Exline and Lewis C. Winters, "Affective Relations and Mutual Glances in Dyads," in S. Tomkins and C. Izard (eds.), *Affect, Cognition, and Personality* (New York: Springer, 1965), pp. 319–50; Albert Mehrabian, "Communication Without Words," *Psychology Today*, Sept. 1968, 2, 4, 52–55; Zick Rubin, "Measurement of Romantic Love," *Journal of Personality and Social Psychology*, 1970, 16, 265–73.

[3] For example, Jay S. Efran and Andrew Broughton, "Effect of Expectancies for Social Approval on Visual Behavior," *Journal of Personality and Social Psychology*, 1966, 4, 103–7; Jay S. Efran, "Looking for Approval: Effects on Visual Behavior of Approbation from Persons Differing in Importance," *Journal of Personality and Social Psychology*, 1968, 10, 21–25.

Indeed there are dominance aspects of looking, and the steady gaze plays a major part. (There is a stunning illustration of such visual dominance in the eye behavior of actor Al Pacino in his role as head of a gangster clan throughout the movie "Godfather II.") Findings of empirical investigation of eye contact demonstrate, first, that the stare is an aversive stimulus. A questionnaire study of comfort under different visual and speech conditions found that, among 500 U. S. and British students, the steady stare in silence is one of the least comfortable situations (complete visual *dis*regard from the listener when one is speaking is another).[4] And in both naturalistic and laboratory experiments in which subjects were stared at by a stranger, then asked to help the starer, they were less likely to give help than were people who hadn't been stared at.[5]

In a series of experiments, Ellsworth and her colleagues have demonstrated the aversive nature of staring. In one study, subjects evaluated an unfavorable conversation and an interviewer more negatively when eye contact was high than when it was low. In another, a stare was a stimulus to flight, when the targets were drivers stopped at an intersection—they pulled off faster than drivers who were not stared at. And in a third experiment, subjects believed they were delivering electric shock to victims, but the victims were really confederates only pretending to receive shock. In this situation, for the victim to look at the subject before the "shock" was highly aversive to the subject.[6]

These investigators have interpreted the stare as an aggressive as well as an aversive stimulus, and compared it with similar threat displays among primates. Baboons, rhesus and bonnet macaques, langurs, and mountain gorillas are among nonhuman primates that have been reported to engage in some form of the mutual glance as a form of threat. Exline, who has done extensive research in visual behavior (particularly with relation to power), demonstrated along with Yellin that rhesus monkeys even react to a stare from a male *human* as an aggressive gesture. Monkeys in cages who were stared at by men (not in cages) exhibited all the responses to

[4] Ralph V. Exline, "Visual Interaction: The Glances of Power and Preference," in James K. Cole (ed.), *Nebraska Symposium on Motivation,* 1971 (Lincoln: University of Nebraska Press, 1971).

[5] Harry T. Reis and Ann Werner, "Some Inter- and Intra-personal Consequences of Eye Contact," Eastern Psychological Association, 1974.

[6] Phoebe C. Ellsworth and J. Merrill Carlsmith, "The Effects of Eye Contact and Verbal Content on Affective Response to a Dyadic Interaction," *Journal of Personality and Social Psychology,* 1968, 10, 15–20. P. C. Ellsworth, J. M. Carlsmith, and A. Henson, "The Stare as a Stimulus to Flight in Human Subjects: A Series of Field Experiments," *Journal of Personality and Social Psychology,* 1972, 21, 302–11. P. Ellsworth and J. M. Carlsmith, "Eye Contact and Gaze Aversion in an Aggressive Encounter," *Journal of Personality and Social Psychology,* 1973, 28, 280–92.

such aggression reported in field studies—the "hard stare," threat display, attack, and avoidance.[7]

Ethologists who have observed free animals often report, furthermore, that the attack of another primate is inhibited by the target's lowering of the gaze. This same gaze aversion has been reported in autistic children * and has been interpreted as a phenomenon similar to that in animals: the children were not attacked by other children, despite being easy targets.[8]

On the other hand, nonaggressive eye contact has other uses. Exline, Ellyson, and Long suggest that, in both humans and nonhuman primates, "greater visual attention of subordinates to superiors can function to facilitate less troublesome interaction." In primate hierarchical behavior, they point out, such attention by subordinates to a dominant animal is common. They believe it serves to minimize aggression by helping to adjust the spacing among animals, and it allows humans both to "psych out" a superior and to show acceptance of the superior's power status.[9]

How may aggressive staring, however, be distinguished from non-aggressive "visual attention"? People may get clues from the length and type of eye contact (e.g., eyes wide open or half closed, tracking the other's movements or riveting the other in place), as well as from other body cues (such as head slightly raised or lowered) and external circumstances (relationship, nature of interaction). Much further study is needed, though, to spell out these distinctions satisfactorily. We will return to this question later in a discussion of sex differences in looking. Meanwhile, let us examine some of the information that has come from studies of attentiveness.

There is evidence from human as well as animal behavior of greater attention to superiors, for example, research showing greater looking at persons from whom we hope for approval. Other supporting evidence is seen in the questionnaire survey of American and British students. Though these subjects reported they would be most uncomfortable when receiving a silent stare, they said they would be *less* uncomfortable receiving it from

[7] Ralph V. Exline and A. Yellin, "Eye Contact as a Sign Between Man and Monkeys," Symposium on Non-Verbal Communication, Nineteenth International Congress of Psychology, London, 1969.

* Childhood autism is sometimes called "childhood schizophrenia." Its central characteristic is a failure to form relationships with other people (or to the environment).

[8] C. Hutt and C. Ounsted, "The Biological Significance of Gaze Aversion with Particular Reference to the Syndrome of Infantile Autism," *Behavioral Science,* 1966, 11, 346–56.

[9] Ralph V. Exline, Steve L. Ellyson, and Barbara Long, "Visual Behavior as an Aspect of Power Role Relationships," in P. Pliner, L. Krames, and T. Alloway (eds.), *Nonverbal Communication of Aggression* (New York: Plenum, 1975), pp. 21–52. See also M. R. A. Chance, "Attention Structure as the Basis of Primate Rank Orders," *Man,* 1967, 2, 503–18.

a younger person (subordinate in age) than they would from a peer or older person.

Exline and his co-authors suggest that a norm exists in our society which prescribes different amounts of visual attention (in normal discourse) for persons having different degrees of social power: the higher one's standing, the less looking one has to give to others, and vice versa. This notion is supported by three experiments in which low-power members of dyads gave more visual attention to high-power members than vice versa. The findings are more complex than that, and it is worth our while to look at them more closely.[10]

The Power Eyelite. In the first experiment, dyads were created in which one person had higher power, based on being able to dispense chips which were exchangeable for money. Twenty dyads were "legitimate" power hierarchies: they were composed of ROTC cadets, an officer and a basic, the officer having the higher power in the experiment. Twenty more dyads had no underlying power/status difference, only the one created by the difference in resources. In both types of dyads, low-power subjects were found to spend more time looking at high-power subjects than vice versa, and the effect was stronger in the ROTC dyads than in the "non-legitimate" condition.

The second study took into account the different situations of looking while listening and looking while speaking. When speaking we must organize our thoughts and words; if we looked constantly at the listener we would suffer from information overload, and be distracted from the speaking task. Therefore, a need to inhibit feedback acts on the speaker, and looking away is common. The norm of attention, however, operates in both the speaking and listening roles. These two factors account for the common findings that people tend to look while listening more than they do while speaking.[11] Since power affects the attention norm, it should work to create a difference between low- and high-power interactors in the amount of time spent looking while listening, but not while speaking.

The results confirmed the research hypothesis: low-power subjects looked

[10] The first experiment, by Exline and Long, is reported in more detail in Exline, "Visual Interaction"; the second and third studies were carried out by Ellyson, and reported as his Master's and Ph.D. theses at the University of Delaware (1973, 1974).

[11] See, for example, Ralph V. Exline, "Explorations in the Process of Person Perception: Visual Interaction in Relation to Competition, Sex, and Need for Affiliation," *Journal of Personality*, 1963, 31, 1–20; R. Exline, D. Gray, and D. Schuette, "Visual Behavior in a Dyad as Affected by Interview Content and Sex of Respondent," *Journal of Personality and Social Psychology*, 1965, 1, 201–9; Adam Kendon, "Some Functions of Gaze-Direction in Social Interaction," *Acta Psychologica*, 1967, 26, 22–63; and Exline, Ellyson, and Long, "Visual Behavior," 21–52.

significantly more when listening than when speaking, but the high-power subjects looked no more when listening. Put another way, low-powers have a higher ratio of look–listen to look–speak than high-powers have. In an interesting follow-up, the officers' leadership performance ratings from a previous summer camp were obtained. The *lowest* leadership ratings went to the officers who paid *more* visual attention to the low-power other in the experiment. We might speculate that concern for our subordinates (expressed visually) is not perceived as a sign of command.

These two studies have manipulated the power (control over resources) of an experimentally-created situation; in some cases the real-life power or status was also coordinate with the power in the experimental situation. Power and status connote control over others, and so does personal dominance, that is, a personality trait implying a tendency to exert control over others. A third study by these same researchers explored the effect of this type of interpersonal control orientation on visual attentiveness. The degree of a subject's control orientation was judged with a personality measure for this purpose; *visual dominance behavior* was defined as being inversely proportional to the ratio of look–listen to look–speak behavior. It was found that subjects with high control orientation did indeed exhibit more visual dominance than subjects with low control orientation. In other words, those who wish to control people show the same behavior to peers as a superior shows to a subordinate in a power hierarchy. Thus status, power, and personal dominance are all shown to be related to visual dominance behavior in the same way.

In another experiment by Exline and his colleagues, subjects were implicated in cheating while the experimenter was out of the room. The subjects had previously been tested for "Machiavellianism," another measure of personal manipulativeness.[12] After the experiment, in an interview, the experimenter confronted the subjects with the suspicion of cheating. High "Machs," those with a greater orientation to the manipulation of others, less often confessed to the cheating, and were judged to lie more plausibly by independent judges, than low Machs. Though all subjects looked less at the experimenter than they had in a pre-cheating interview, high Machs did not reduce their eye contact as much as low Machs did, and when denying cheating, high Machs showed a fascinating ability to look the interrogator in the eye. It is as if the urge to control is manifested by adopting the manner of one who actually does control, the person of high power. Credibility, a side benefit of power, is also

[12] Ralph V. Exline, et al., "Visual Interaction in Relation to Machiavellianism and an Unethical Act," in Richard Christie and Florence L. Geis (with others), *Studies in Machiavellianism* (New York: Academic Press, 1970), pp. 53–75.

attempted in the same way. Magic may be all in the hands, but chutzpah is all in the eyes!

Lest you worry that such experimentation has no application in the everyday world, it is reported, in a fascinating translation from the African jungle to the executive jungle, that an American business executive hired a racketeer practiced in the "evil eye" to keep employees at work by glaring at them.[13]

KEEPING A HIGH PROFILE

Visibility is another aspect of eye contact. We especially dislike being stared at when we ourselves can't see the other person: an illustration is our persistent suspicion and resentment that people with sunglasses, espe-

Visibility (being observed).

cially mirrored ones, are staring at us. Visibility is related to both eye contact and self-disclosure, which will be examined later. It is the availability of visual information about oneself to others, with all the power that information conveys.

[13] Reported in Silvan S. Tomkins, *Affect, Imagery, Consciousness: The Negative Affects,* Vol. 2 (New York: Springer, 1963), pp. 164–65.

Argyle and his colleagues have experimented with the effect of varying degrees of visibility in interacting dyads.[14] They found that when one person is visible and the other partly invisible, the one with more visual information tends to dominate the encounter, feel more at ease and become the "observer," while the other person becomes the "observed." This feeling of being observed, however, seems to be not otherwise related to *actual* experimental visibility, since it wasn't greater for persons placed in a brighter light or actually looked at more. People felt observed more when they were being interviewed than when they were doing the interviewing, when they were with an older person than with a younger, when they themselves looked less at the other, and when they were females, especially when with a male.

Argyle and Williams analyze the feeling of being observed as "a cognitive set produced by the nature of the relationship," that is, produced by being subordinate. In an interpretation consistent with our knowledge of submissive gaze aversion, they suggest,

> It is possible that people who feel observed have in the past been stared down by others, and adopted a low level of looking themselves—i.e., their feelings of being observed are based on real experiences of being looked at in the past.[15]

LOOKING ACROSS THE GULF OF RACE

Eye contact is important in the regulation of interaction, most notably as a turn-taking signal for speech: eyeball-watchers have established that a speaker when nearing the end of an utterance looks away from the other briefly, then on ending returns the gaze to the other, in effect transferring the floor.[16] This pattern is superimposed on the one reported earlier, that in general, conversants tend to look at the other more while listening than when speaking. This is a white scenario, however. The pattern of eye contact in conversation between blacks, and in interracial dyads, has been found to be different.

La France and Mayo minutely analyzed films of a black male shown in

[14] Michael Argyle, Mansur Lalljee, and Mark Cook, "The Effects of Visibility on Interaction in a Dyad," *Human Relations*, 1968, 21, 3–17. Michael Argyle and Marylin Williams, "Observer or Observed? A Reversible Perspective in Person Perception," *Sociometry*, 1969, 32, 396–412.

[15] Argyle and Williams, "Observer or Observed?" p. 410.

[16] Kendon, "Some Functions of Gaze-Direction," 22–63; Starkey Duncan, "Some Signals and Rules for Taking Speaking Turns in Conversations," *Journal of Personality and Social Psychology*, 1972, 23, 283–92.

interaction with a white male and with a black male, and of two other black males conversing, and they report a complete reversal from the white pattern of gaze direction, in a black dyad. In a black dyad, the speaker regularly gazed at the other before and during the turn, while the listener looked away both before and during the turn. A naturalistic observation study of 63 black and 63 white dyads (same-sex and mixed-sex) corroborated the finding that black listeners gaze less at the speaker than do white listeners.[17]

These researchers' suggestion that blacks do not look when listening, presumably using other cues to communicate attention, is confirmed by others who have studied black interaction patterns. Scheflen remarks that in black culture eye-to-eye gazing is considered rude, a putdown or confrontation.[18] Johnson, whose study of black kinesics was reported earlier, also cites the

'reluctance' of Black Americans to look another person (particularly, another person in an authority role) directly in the eye. . . . In the Black cultural context, avoiding eye contact is a nonverbal way of communicating a recognition of the authority–subordinate relationship . . .[19]

Johnson notes that this pattern is common in western Africa, and its American usage possibly originates in the former African cultures of black Americans. It is a Japanese cultural pattern as well, he notes; other writers have pointed out that Puerto Ricans and Mexican-Americans show respect by looking down, also.[20] As both Scheflen and Johnson point out, culture clash occurs when these symbols of respect are used in a white Anglo-dominated culture where they may be interpreted as inattention, evasiveness, or dishonesty. In the white middle-class tradition of "look at me when I'm speaking to you" or of showing rapport through eye contact, many U. S. teachers have tried to force black or Puerto Rican children to look them in the eye, and become enraged at what they consider is lack of respect for authority that the children show them.

17 Marianne La France and Clara Mayo, "Racial Differences in Gaze Behavior During Conversations: Two Systematic Observational Studies," *Journal of Personality and Social Psychology*, 1976, 33, 547–52. Marianne La France, "Nonverbal Cues to Conversational Turn Taking Between Black Speakers," American Psychological Association, 1974.

18 Albert Scheflen, *Body Language and the Social Order* (Englewood Cliffs, N.J.: Prentice-Hall, 1972), pp. 95–96.

19 Kenneth R. Johnson, "Black Kinesics—Some Non-Verbal Communication Patterns in the Black Culture," *Florida FL Reporter*, 1971 (Spring/Fall), p. 18.

20 Erving Goffman, *Relations in Public* (New York: Basic Books, 1971), p. 45; Scheflen, *Body Language and the Social Order*, p. 96.

Adult interracial interaction may suffer in a similar way. La France and Mayo report several misunderstandings of turn-taking cues between the black and white conversants. When the black speaker ended a syntactical unit with a pause and a sustained gaze at the other (a white cue that the floor is yielded), the white began to speak, but the black speaker had not stopped, and both were talking at once. And when the white speaker gave the cue that he had ended his utterance, and waited expectantly for the black to take the floor, the cue wasn't received as such; the white speaker resorted to repeating himself and finally, directly asking a question to deliver over the floor.

SEX DIFFERENCES IN LOOKING

Eye contact is probably the most extensively researched area in nonverbal communication, and, according to Duncan, "Perhaps the most powerful single variable [in eye contact] is sex." [21] It is an area, however, that is complex and contradictory. New research, rather than clarifying old ambiguities, seems to create fresh ones. Nowhere is this more evident than in the study of sex differences in eye contact.

Probably the most accepted finding in this area is that women engage in more eye contact than do men, especially with each other. Exline's 1963 experiment was a sort of prototype for this type of study: [22] Groups of three women or three men were formed, and asked to conduct a group discussion around a problem: naming a (hypothetical) "newly developed soap product for automatic washers." Each subject had previously come up with a suggested name privately. While they were discussing the name, their visual interaction was being observed from behind a one-way mirror by observers practiced in scoring visual behavior.

Exline found that women engaged more in both mutual and non-mutual gaze, and held the mutual gaze longer, than men did.

This study, however, was limited to partners of the same sex; would men do less looking when paired with women, as well as with men? Or, when with someone of the other sex, would both sexes gaze equally? Exline two years later published another study (along with colleagues) that answered this question.[23] In this study, male and female students were interviewed individually in a room with a one-way mirror, again with

[21] Starkey Duncan, "Nonverbal Communication," *Psychological Bulletin*, 1969, 72, 118–37.
[22] Exline, "Explorations in the Process of Person Perception," 1–20.
[23] Exline, Gray, and Schuette, "Visual Behavior in a Dyad," 201–9.

their visual behavior under observation, by either a female or a male experimenter. The interviewer–experimenter kept a steady gaze at the subject for the entire period of the interview, so that any eye contact on the subject's part was mutual eye contact with the interviewer. The observers recorded each instance of a person looking at another, along with the duration of the gaze. This information was synchronized with the speaking turns of the individuals. And again, women did more looking than men. Female subjects looked more than males while speaking, while silent, during the interviewer's speaking, and in informal discussion following the interview. Since then, other researchers have come up with similar findings, in experiments that did not involve such artificialities as an interviewer's 100 percent gaze, or even the status distinction of interviewer/interviewee.[24] Exline has remarked, "We have consistently observed this sex difference in visual attentiveness in all studies in which sex has been a variable."[25] Sex differences have been found in other aspects of visual behavior, though they are generally more complex than this one or not well supported by data.*

[24] For example, Zick Rubin, "Measurement of Romantic Love," 265–73; Michael Argyle and Roger Ingham, "Gaze, Mutual Gaze, and Proximity," *Semiotica*, 1972, 6, 32–49; J. R. Aiello, "A Test of Equilibrium Theory: Visual Interaction in Relation to Orientation, Distance and Sex of Interactants," *Psychonomic Science*, 1972, 27, 335–36.

[25] Exline, "Visual Interaction," p. 178.

* Some of them are:

a. Highly affiliative *females* tended to look more at one another than less affiliative ones; but males showed the opposite tendency, looking more when *less* affiliative. In a competitive situation, females high in need for affiliation showed *fewer* mutual glances, and low affiliators showed *more*, than in the noncompetitive one. (Males showed the same pattern, but to a lesser degree.) (Exline, "Explorations in Person Perception," pp. 1–20.)

b. Both men and women who were oriented towards inclusive and affectionate interpersonal relationships engaged in more mutual gaze, and women as a group scored higher in these qualities than men did. (Exline, Gray, and Schuette, "Visual Behavior," pp. 201–9.)

c. Other researchers found less looking in male-female pairs than in all-male or all-female pairs. (Argyle and Ingham, "Gaze and Proximity," pp. 32–49.)

d. In visual behavior over time, in generally *positive* interaction, males had a tendency to decrease eye contact, and females to increase it. In addition, the effect of liking the other was different on the two sexes: it modified females' looking while talking but males' looking while listening. (Exline and Winters, "Affective Relations," pp. 319–50.)

e. In negative interaction, both sexes tended to decrease their eye contact. (Exline, Gray and Schuette, "Visual Behavior," pp. 201–9.) But as dislike grows even greater, contact begins to increase again; and male communicators showed a much *greater* amount of eye contact with extremely disliked males than with extremely disliked females, a finding attributed to heightened vigilance in the face of threat. (Albert Mehrabian, "Nonverbal Betrayal of Feeling," *Journal of Experimental Research in Personality*, 1971, 5, 64–73.)

Why do men engage in less eye contact than women? Exline and other investigators have looked for the answer in personality variables, such as differences in affiliation and field dependence * between the sexes. But rather than looking at (perceptual or) personality variables, we can observe the social context in which visual behavior occurs. Women are more frequently dependent on men—economically, socially, etc.—than vice versa. Information concerning the social environment may be crucial to their economic survival, not to mention social/political and psychological survival. We previously noted that more eye contact is characteristic of those who must seek approval from others. Rubin recognizes this fact when he observes that not only may gazing serve as a vehicle of emotional expression for women, but it may allow women to obtain cues from males concerning the appropriateness of their behavior.[26] Visual information may have more value for women, in addition, because it is less available to them as a result of their exclusion from informative interaction and of men's greater concealment of their feelings.

Then again, men may have reason to avoid eye contact. Webbink has pointed out that male visual behavior patterns may typically be interpreted differently from female ones. If, for example, male gaze has traditionally had an aggressive or sexual connotation, men may avoid eye contact to avoid appearing aggressive or seductive.[27]

There is ample explanation of the sex difference in eye contact, then, in the social environment, without having to postulate basic personality differences between males and females. Such an explanation is certainly preferable to ones which are built on such shaky grounds as "field dependence" variables.[28]

---

f. Female subjects maintained less eye contact with disliked male addressees than with liked ones, or with either liked or disliked female ones. Male subjects' eye contact, however, did not differ by the addressee's sex. (Albert Mehrabian and John T. Friar, "Encoding of Attitude by a Seated Communicator via Posture and Position Cues," *Journal of Consulting and Clinical Psychology*, 1969, 33, 330–36.)

* Field dependence refers to heavier reliance on external, environmental cues than internal (bodily) ones in making certain perceptual judgments, e.g., decisions about body orientation, or identifying hidden geometric figures.

[26] Rubin, "Measurement of Romantic Love," pp. 265–73.

[27] Patricia G. Webbink, "Eye Contact and Intimacy" (module), Morristown, N.J.: General Learning Corporation, in press.

[28] See, for example, Julia A. Sherman, "Problem of Sex Differences in Space Perception and Aspects of Intellectual Functioning," *Psychological Review*, 1967, 74, 290–99; Jeanette Silveira, "The Effect of Sexism on Thought: How Male Bias Hurts Psychology and Some Hopes for a Woman's Psychology," in Jean Ramage Leppaluoto (ed.), *Women on the Move: A Feminist Perspective* (Pittsburgh: KNOW, Inc., 1973); Edward Zigler, "A Measure in Search of a Theory," *Contemporary Psychology*, 1963, 8, 133–35; Mary B. Parlee, "Sex Differences in Perceptual Field Depen-

Can Women Be Subordinate and Superior at the Same Time? What does this consistent finding of sex difference in gazing mean for the role of eye contact in maintaining the power difference between the sexes? There is apparent contradiction in the fact that women do more looking than men, and the earlier data that higher-status, higher-power persons are seen to have the "stare privilege." If women are truly of lower status, how can they do more staring? There are a number of possible answers to this question.

First, women's gazing can be seen in the context of subordinate attentiveness: like all underlings of the animal world, they must watch for cues from the powerful. Second, greater female looking could be due to the fact that women do more listening than men,[29] and people tend to look more while listening than while speaking.[30] Or, gazing in experimental situations may be different from that in real-life interaction, between people who have ongoing relationships and/or who can affect each other's lives in some way.[31]

Most fruitfully, we can ask about the nature of the looking done by women and men. Can subordinate attentiveness be distinguished from dominant staring? Obviously it can by the participants. One way outside observers could distinguish might be to look for gaze aversion, another sign from the subordinate which confirms inferior status. Though females may look more at others, they may also avert the eyes more, indicating submissiveness when looked at themselves.* Two questions are thus raised:

---

dence: A Look at Some Data Embedded in Theory," mimeo, 1974 (Radcliffe Institute); H. L. Pick and A. D. Pick, "Sensory and Perceptual Development," in Paul Mussen, ed., *Carmichael's Manual of Child Psychology,* 3rd ed., Vol. I (New York: Wiley, 1970).

[29] This was taken up in more detail in Chap. 5.

[30] However, preliminary evidence doesn't support this hypothesis. This evidence is from the experiment of Exline, Gray, and Schuette, "Visual Behavior," pp. 201–9, who report subjects' scores for the percentage of time spent looking while speaking (LS) and looking while listening (LL). My own calculation from these data give a "visual dominance score" (ratio of LS:LL) of .614 for males, .694 for females. Though we can't know if this difference is significantly higher for females, it is certainly not lower.

[31] However, Zick Rubin reports that in his research, females looked more at both boyfriends and male strangers. "The Social Psychology of Romantic Love," Ph.D. dissertation, University of Michigan, 1969 (University Microfilms, Ann Arbor, Michigan, No. 70–4179).

* Female children from an early age are less often the targets of aggression than are males, according to Eleanor Maccoby and Carol Jacklin in *The Psychology of Sex Differences* (Stanford: Stanford University Press, 1974, Chapter 7; p. 352). Could it be that girls learn gaze aversion as a means of inhibiting attack, as autistic children apparently do (Hutt and Ounstead, "Biological Significance of Gaze Aversion," 346–56)?

do men do more staring than women, and do women tend to avert their eyes more frequently than men?

Our language has specific words for males' staring at women, such as *ogling* and *leering,* leading us to assume that male staring (at women) exists as a category of behavior found noteworthy in the language. Whether it is noteworthy because it exists in great frequency, or has received its own terms because it is simply improper, we can't tell from linguistic information alone. Women, however, have seldom questioned the fact that they are more frequently stared at than men are, and stared at by men, especially when walking in public and past idle men.

On the question of gaze aversion, a number of writers have assumed that women do avert their eyes more readily than men do. Rita Mae Brown, for example, writes:

> Eye contact is a sure indication of status. Most [female] non-feminists lower the eyes or look to the side, returning a gaze furtively, even more furtively with men. Feminists use more eye level contact than non-feminists and lesbian-feminists sometimes hold their eyes so level in a conversation that it unnerves other non-lesbian women, since this sort of eye contact is considered predatory among heterosexuals.[32]

And one of the "Exercises for Men" (to see what it's like to be a woman) mentioned earlier is to:

> Walk down a city street. . . . Look straight ahead. Every time a man walks past you, avert your eyes and make your face expressionless. Most women learn to go through this act each time we leave our houses. It's a way to avoid at least some of the encounters we've all had with strange men who decided we looked available.[33]

Most likely such gaze aversion is learned even earlier than the age of such encounters with strange men, in the socialization period, when young girls are taught "ladylike" behavior. Etiquette books have certainly prescribed dropping the eyes as proper facial behavior for the "modest" young woman.

Students in my courses have conducted informal studies of gaze behavior in public which are relevant to the questions here. Two students carried out 84 naturalistic observations of eye contact in passing in public. In their study, when female and male passed each other, 71 percent of the males established eye contact with the female, but only 43 percent of the

[32] Rita Mae Brown, "The Good Fairy," *Quest,* 1974, 1, no. 1, 62.
[33] "Exercises for Men," from *Willamette Bridge* (and Liberation News Service), 1971. Printed in *The Radical Therapist,* Dec.-Jan. 1971, 1, no. 5, p. 15.

females established eye contact with the male.[34] Students from several classes have collected observations on gaze return: they looked at someone in public for about three seconds, and noted whether the person returned the gaze. Almost 400 such elicitations have now been made (about 100 in each sex combination), with the results shown in Table 4. The overall pattern is one of non-return: females do tend to avert the eyes, from both

TABLE 4

PERCENTAGE EYE CONTACT RETURNED BY TARGET PERSONS GAZED AT

	Target Persons			
	Male		Female	
Gazers	Return	Avert	Return	Avert
Male	20	80	41	59
Female	60	40	39	61

female and male starers, and males show a striking avoidance of eye contact with other males. But there is one case where gaze is returned: males tend to stare back at female starers.

In another study, a male stared at 60 individual males and females and found a pattern of "repetitive eye contact" in the females: about 40 percent of women he stared at would return but immediately break contact, and then reestablish it. This happened as many as four times in one encounter. Only one male out of 30 made this repetitive eye contact.[35] In these several studies, then, is preliminary evidence that females avert the gaze in real-life situations. (Needless to say, further study of this question would be welcomed.) In the intriguing observation of repetitive eye contact, we may even see the pull of contradictory demands on females—to avert the gaze, and to be alert to what the male is doing.

For many women, in many real-life situations, visual information may be a prize furtively caught in stolen glances when men have turned their gaze momentarily, or when men are occupied with each other or with other matters. The image of the female gossip peeping out windows from behind draperies may suggest something about the dis-ease with which women are expected to intrude visually upon their world.

---

[34] Gail Borges and Debra Rizzeri, "Eye Contact in Passing," unpublished paper, University of Lowell, 1975.

[35] John Considine, "Observation of Reaction to Eye Contact With a Male," unpublished paper, University of Lowell, 1975.

When women do use the direct stare, they may do so in a way different from the way males use it. O'Connor writes,

> [In some species of primates] special coloration of parts of the body used in displays of dominance make the displays more obvious from a distance. Our own species provides a clear example in the large area of white around the dark part of the eyes. This coloration makes a direct stare very clear and threatening, and in fact, the direct stare or glare is a common human gesture of dominance. Women use the gesture as well as men, but often in modified form. While looking directly at a man, a woman usually has her head slightly tilted, implying the beginning of a presenting gesture or enough submission to render the stare ambivalent if not actually submissive.[36]

This author further suggests that women's eye makeup "has the effect of modifying the direct stare and reducing its threatening effect." However, it is often just the opposite, that eye makeup is applied for the purpose of dramatizing the eyes, making them more prominent and forceful, even more staring. In this situation, it would seem we have another instance in which the assumption of a gesture of dominance by a woman is interpreted sexually.

What I think we may conclude from the overall picture of dominance in eye contact is that superiors use two forms to communicate their superiority: staring is used to *assert* dominance—to establish, to maintain, and to regain it. On the other hand, superior position in itself, especially a secure one, is communicated by visually ignoring the other person—*not* looking while listening, but looking into space as if the other isn't there. This is the reciprocal of the visual attentiveness that the insecure subordinate must show. In other words, both looking and not looking may communicate power, and their use is not so hard to figure out. Women's tendencies both to look more at the other, and to avert the gaze, do not contradict each other, but are understandable in the power/status interpretation.

The Transparent Woman

In the experiments on visibility mentioned earlier, how much one partner in interaction was allowed to see the other was varied. The one who could see more became dominant in the interaction. In addition, females (but not males) found communication more difficult when they could not see the other person, and wanted to see even when invisible themselves. While

[36] Lynn O'Connor, "Male Supremacy: A Theoretical Analysis," 1970. Available in reprint form from KNOW, Inc., P.O. Box 86031, Pittsburgh, Pa. 15221.

women when invisible *decreased* their speech by about 40 percent, males when invisible *increased* their amount of speech by 40 percent (in addition to talking more than females in general). A significant interaction between visibility and sex was found in which "males talk more when invisible *and* talking to females." [37] These results suggest sex differences in the effects of invisibility; though invisibility conveys a certain advantage, perhaps women are not as able (because of past experience outside the laboratory) to take advantage of it as are men. They have been more often the watched than the watcher.

Another visibility condition was introduced by Argyle and Ingham: [38] subjects were divided by a one-way screen so that only one could see the other. Those who were able to see their partners looked significantly more at them than partners did in the mutual visibility experiment, suggesting that the possibility of being seen has an inhibitory effect on looking. And females were more inhibited than males by mutual gaze.

In these experiments, in which one may become "observer" and one, "observed," women were more likely to feel observed and subordinate than men, whether they were more observed or not. Argyle and Williams [39] suggest that this difference is due to cultural roles of performer (women) and audience (men)—and therefore "will not be due to differences of security or dominance." But what these authors fail to recognize is that the experience of "being a performer" in one's everyday life may be related to a difference in the underlying security or dominance in one's situation. Indeed, to be a performer is to be at one's most vulnerable.

Argyle and Williams are on the mark when they relate feeling observed to one's past experiences of being observed. In a society in which women's clothing is designed explicitly to reveal the body and its contours; in which women are ogled, whistled at, and pinched while simply going about their business; in which they see advertisements in magazines, on billboards, on TV in their own homes, showing revealingly clad women; in which tactual information about them is freely available, their bodies accessible to touch like community property; in which even their marital status is the first information by which a stranger identifies them—in such a society it is little wonder that women feel "observed." They are.

[37] Argyle, Lalljee, Cook, "Effects of Visibility on Interaction," pp. 3–17.
[38] Argyle and Ingham, "Gaze and Proximity," pp. 32–49.
[39] Argyle and Williams, "Observer or Observed?" pp. 396–412.

chapter ten

SMILE WHEN YOU SAY THAT:

Facial Expression

As we noted in the last chapter, masked eyes are somewhat ludicrously assumed to hide the identity. Since in fact the eyes are allowed an opening in a mask, it is the *area* surrounding the eyes (or sometimes a greater part of the face) which is covered, especially in comic books. It has been the burden of many superheroes of the comics (and a few superheroines) to have to lead a second life as Nondescript Persons (hereafter known as NDPs) whose connection with their colorful and admired alteregos is only supposed to be that of good friend (in whose company the NDP is, strangely enough, never seen). When the NDP disappears, for that split second allowed to assume the more glorious identity, what clever disguise do they adopt so that those who have just been looking at them won't notice the striking similarity? Naturally, they cover the face or the area of the eyes. Never mind that the body is the same in height, weight, proportions, and movement—the dazzling costume supposedly conceals that fact.

In fact, some superpersons don't even wear masks: never mind that Superman's hair is the same as Clark Kent's in color, length and style, or that (the old) Wonder Woman's only hair change was to take out her hairpins; both Lois Lane (Superman's "girlfriend" and Clark Kent's co-worker) and Steve Trevor (Wonder Woman's best admirer and a friend of her NDP alterego, Diana Prince) are easily deceived when their humdrum friends merely take off their eye-glasses! * Never mind that all these

* To be fair, we can suggest that there may be some kinesic changes noted among the males; Clark Kent's awkwardness and Bruce Wayne's effete playboy image have sometimes been unfavorably compared with the vitality and strength of their other selves, Superman and Batman.

characters speak with the same voice. For the Flash, Batman, Daredevil, and Captain America, to name a few, covering the back of the head and the upper part of the face suffice to fool all they come in contact with. (When anyone does suspect the identity of the NDP and the great one, it is never for their physical resemblance.)

That so many of us were and still are willing to suspend this much disbelief for such a silly convention testifies to the powerful influence of the face, and particularly the area of the eyes, in identification and impression formation. Comic book convention seems upheld by a finding that subjects who were required to be deceptive in an experimental interview more often mentioned the face as the focus of deceptive alteration than the body—people apparently do attempt to lie more with the face than with the body.[1] Facial expression has long been the major consideration in the expression of emotions and in detecting deception, and has probably a longer history of scientific study than other nonverbal behaviors. Darwin started it in recent history, with his conjecture in *The Expression of the Emotions in Man and Animals* (1872) that there are evolutionary connections between animal and human facial expression, and human universals in emotional communication with the face. Throughout the history of U.S. psychology, this has continued to be a field of investigation, small but persistent.[2]

What has this to do with dominance? Faces are the means by which we attempt to create an impression, and they will therefore be a major focus for displaying the impression of status, power, or authority. We all have a mental image of "the stern face of authority," the jutting chin, overhanging eyebrows, the frown, the drawn muscles, the unwavering stare. These together make a formidable challenge. It may be in fact that the face is particularly implicated in hierarchical relationships. Nierenberg and Calero claim that in superior/subordinate relations (especially long-term ones), facial expressions predominate over other nonverbal communication. These authors give the example of a boss indicating nonacceptance of a subordinate's idea by raised eyebrows, slight twisting of the head, and a look of doubt.[3] They suggest that facial expression is the first type of signal sent in such a communication; if a message, for example of dismissal, is not

[1] Paul Ekman and Wallace V. Friesen, "Detecting Deception from the Body or Face," *Journal of Personality and Social Psychology*, 1974, 29, 288–98.

[2] For example, see Paul Ekman and Wallace V. Friesen, "Constants across Cultures in the Face and Emotion," *Journal of Personality and Social Psychology*, 1971, 17, 124–29, which also has a **brief** review of this literature.

[3] Gerald I. Nierenberg and Henry H. Calero, *How to Read a Person Like a Book* (New York: Hawthorn, 1971; Pocket Books, 1973), pp. 142–43.

picked up by the target, the sender may next shift to body gesture, escalating to involvement with other objects in the environment, and finally to verbal communication as a last resort.

On the other hand, subordinates have their way of handling dominants, too. Johnson's description of "rolling the eyes" in black kinesics shows it is a gesture of insubordination, whose main message is hostility. This elaborate procedure consists of the following sequence of eyeball movement:

> First, the eyes are moved from one side of the eye-socket to the other, in a low arc (usually the movement of the eyes—that is, the rolling—is preceded by a stare at the other person, but not an eye-to-eye stare). The lids of the eyes are slightly lowered when the eye balls are moved in the low arc. The eye balls always move *away* from the other person. The movement is very quick, and it is often unnoticed by the other person, particularly if the other person is not Black. Sometimes, the eye movement is accompanied by a slight lifting of the head, or a twitching of the nose, or both.[4]

Johnson remarks that the gesture, when made by black children, is often lost on white teachers, which is just as well, since the child can thus release hostility and endure the reprimand with minimal conflict.

Young children begin early to exhibit signs of dominance and submission, as well as insubordination, and they exhibit these relational messages to each other in intriguing ways. One researcher, for example, has reported the existence of a "win face" and "loss face" among preschool children.[5] When in free play situations one child is involved in a competitive encounter with another, the two telegraph their expectation of the outcome (and their grasp of their place in the hierarchy, presumably) by displaying the appropriate face. The win face, displayed by winners in two-thirds of the encounters, consisted of raised brows, wide-open eyes, firmly jutting neck posture, and conspicuously raised chin. This expression is similar to expressions of dominance among nonhuman primates.

The loss face, exhibited in over half the loss situations, was composed of furrowed brow, slightly squinted eyes, retracted neck, and conspicuously lowered chin. All but one of the children displayed both of these faces in the appropriate situations, girls as well as boys, though to a lesser extent. Moreover, the appropriate faces were still displayed when the children could not see each other in a conflict situation, though the frequency of the

---

[4] Kenneth R. Johnson, "Black Kinesics—Some Non-Verbal Communication Patterns in the Black Culture," *Florida FL Reporter*, 1971 (Spring/Fall), p. 18.

[5] Gail Zivin, "Facial Gestures as Status Signals in Preschool Boys," paper presented at Eastern Psychological Association, 1975.

"win" face was somewhat reduced. This suggests that though the faces may serve as communication, they are expressions (of an internal state) also. It appears that by kindergarten we are well equipped to begin asserting facial dominance, and to know when the submissive gesture is appropriate.

Laugh and the World Laughs at You. Subordinate monkeys and apes are said to smile in appeasement to dominant ones, and smiling is a human facial expression also associated with subordinate status. The unctuous Uriah Heep, the shuffling Uncle Tom, anyone seeking to ingratiate is de-

picted with a perpetual grin. The "nervous" smile, like the nervous laugh, conveys tension more than pleasure, and in many people has had to be held so long and so often that it has become a habit and an etched facial expression. Though little research has been done on smiling, it is understood as a gesture offered upwards in the status hierarchy; indeed, a powerful and successful person may be said to be surrounded by a thousand suns!

Laughter is another facial (and vocal) expression exhibited to those higher in status: to laugh long and hard at the boss's jokes is a cliché, but at the same time a painful reality (which was further examined in Chapter 5). Both smiling and laughing are ostensibly expressions of pleasure and relaxation which, when coming from subordinates, belie the true nature of the situation. It is as if they are exhibited for the purpose of maintaining the myth of pleasant relations and equality between superior and subordinate. Those powerful and successful persons surrounded by a thousand suns are likely to see serious faces only on their peers: it's no wonder that they think of their subordinates—be they "contented darkies," "beer-loving workers," "brawling hardhats," or "flighty dames"—as happy-go-lucky and carefree.

Especially in our society, as compared with some others, we are not supposed to show the depth or full range of our emotions. (The admonition to "wipe that smile off your face" illustrates an assumption that smiling is not just an involuntary expression, but is also a facial display under our control for ceremonial purposes—as other expressions must be.) Extremes of expression are out: screaming, crying, hysterical laughter, any intense feelings, are to be released in private if at all. And the more important you are, the more this rule applies—this is called "keeping your dignity." Underlings may show occasional emotional lapses, but in the top dog they are *prima facie* evidence of weakness.

Rosabeth Kanter has described the development of an ideology in business organizations to the effect that successful managers are able to control their emotions, whereas ordinary workers cannot.[6] Writers on organizational behavior made a distinction in their works between "the managerial elite's logic of efficiency" and "the workers' logic of sentiment." Needless to say, this ideology has worked to support the exclusion of women from management, and no doubt many unassimilated men of ethnic background, as "temperamentally unfit."

The wooden countenance, though it shares nothing with friends, also gives away no secrets to enemies. This control of facial expression is one form of overall information control, which in turn is an important factor in authority: "Knowledge is power." Compare the controlled aura of the professional or VIP (doctor, corporation head, judge) with the more variable demeanor of ordinary people, particularly children, working class people, women, and persons of "ethnic" background. Those who are not professionals, who must come to see "important" people in their carefully-

6 "Women and the Structure of Organizations: Explorations in Theory and Behavior," in *Sociological Inquiry*, 1975, 45, no. 2–3, 34–74. Reprinted in Marcia Millman and R. M. Kanter (eds.), *Another Voice* (Garden City, N.Y.: Doubleday, 1975), 34–74.

planned domains that project an image but give no information, are already labeled as losers and information-givers.

In less hierarchical situations too, we often try to keep some of our personal power by not disclosing personal information. "Cool" is nothing more than the withholding of information, that is, refusing to disclose one's thoughts and emotions. The value it gives to street people, poker players, and psychiatrists is of the same sort. Smart ones, those in power, those who manipulate others, always keep their cool, maintain an unruffled exterior. (Of course, the unemotional demeanor associated with Anglo-Saxon cultural style is an asset in a society dominated by persons of Anglo-Saxon descent.) We have long held that knowledge is power; exclusive knowledge is the most powerful, i.e., knowledge withheld from others. But the poet Todd Gitlin has wisely written: "Whoever said 'Knowledge is power'/had power first." [7] We might as well say that power is knowledge.

PUT ON A HAPPY FACE (IF YOU'RE FEMALE)

"Rolling the eyes" among black Americans, as detailed by Johnson, has already been described as a sign of impudence and disapproval of authority, and it too differs by sex: Johnson states that the gesture is more common among black females than among black males.[8] Eyeball motion per se (disregarding contact) is a form of facial expression of low saliency to many people, but as silent movies show us, it is very expressive. There are furtive eyes, shifty eyes, calm and languid eyes, supplication to heaven, significant glances to the side, and so on. We don't have a complete description of female and male eye expressions, though we have some comments from Birdwhistell on some sex differences in eye movement. Birdwhistell writes that informants from various societies will often describe particular lid and eye behavior as masculine or feminine. But only careful observation will reveal that males in our society are prohibited from moving the eyeballs when the lids are closed, or that (except when signaling sleepiness or distress) "males should close and open their lids in a relatively continuous movement." [9] These differences are mentioned here only as spurs to further study. In the absence of further knowledge, including social context, there is little to be gained

[7] Todd Gitlin, "On Power Structure Research," *100 Flowers*, 1 (1971), p. 35.
[8] Johnson, "Black Kinesics," p. 18.
[9] Ray L. Birdwhistell, "Masculinity and Femininity as Display," in *Kinesics and Context* (Philadelphia: University of Pennsylvania Press, 1970), p. 44.

in speculation about the reasons for their existence. We must assume, however, that like other gender signals they are learned at some point in the socialization period, through imitation and teaching. But the socialization of facial expression doesn't stop with the eyes.

Training of children's facial expressions by adults is surely a primary avenue of sex stereotyping. Boys are told it's not manly to cry, and girls are admonished that frowning isn't pretty.* It's probable that girls get more of this: growing up we learned that we don't look pretty when we're crying, pouting, mad, yelling, or sad, either. Looking pretty, the not-so-unspoken goal of all mothers' (and fathers') hearts for their little girls, required showing only smiling or bland, expressionless faces. It was unthinkable that we didn't want to "look pretty."

Facial control is an attempt at emotional control by adults, and it seems to have succeeded to an overwhelming degree, judging by the number of men handicapped by an inability to cry and women, by an inability to get mad. Ekman has suggested that males in our society (middle class, white, adult, and urban) tend to neutralize (not show) sadness and fear in public, or to mask them (cover them with some other emotion). But females, he says, neutralize or mask anger.[10]

In the long run, though, women's facial expressivity (with their emotional expressivity) has been allowed a wider range than men's, encompassing within the sex stereotype not only pleasant expressions, but negative ones, like crying. This range only stops short at guilt-free anger. Men's emotional display is limited and according to some reports, reflects a paucity of feeling itself. This greater variability in women not only makes them vulnerable by virtue of giving personal information in one-sided fashion, but it is used to belittle them as emotionally unstable: the

---

* In actuality, children of both sexes are encouraged not to show negative emotion —e.g., pouting—as part of their subordination to adults, of which more will be said later. But the sex-typed training determines which types of negative emotions get more strongly restricted in either sex.

[10] Paul Ekman, "Universals and Cultural Differences in Facial Expressions of Emotion," in James K. Cole (ed.), Nebraska Symposium on Motivation, 1971 (Lincoln: University of Nebraska Press, 1971). See also P. Ekman and Wallace V. Friesen, Unmasking the Face (Englewood Cliffs, N.J.: Prentice-Hall, 1975).

Buck, et al., have suggested that females are "externalizers" of emotion, high in overt emotional expression, low in skin conductance response, while males are "internalizers," with little overt expression, large and frequent electrodermal changes. The data supporting this contention, however, are marginally significant. Ross Buck, V. J. Savin, R. E. Miller, and W. F. Caul, "Communication of Affect through Facial Expressions in Humans," Journal of Personality and Social Psychology, 1972, 23, 362–71; R. Buck, R. E. Miller, and W. F. Caul, "Sex, Personality, and Physiological Variables in the Communication of Affect via Facial Expression," Journal of Personality and Social Psychology, 1974, 30, 587–96.

hysterical female is common stock for dramatic presentations and comedies alike.

Despite the breadth of women's range, all emphasis is on the pleasant end of the emotional spectrum, with special attention to the smile. The smile is woman's badge of appeasement; many feminists have pointed out its special significance for women, and have attempted to change their own smiling habits. Firestone writes,

> In my own case, I had to train myself out of that phony smile, which is like a nervous tic on every teenage girl. And this meant that I smiled rarely, for in truth, when it came down to real smiling, I had less to smile about. My "dream" action for the women's liberation movement: *a smile boycott,* at which declaration all women would instantly abandon their "pleasing" smiles, henceforth smiling only when something pleased *them.*[11]

Facial expression—woman smiling at man.

Silveira too interprets women's smile to men as an appeasement gesture rather than a signal of pleasure or friendliness, and has suggested that women seem more likely to smile to a man (1) when a woman and man are greeting each other, and (2) when the two know each other only moderately well.[12] Chesler has written that both women and men "are

---

[11] Shulamith Firestone, *The Dialectic of Sex* (New York: Bantam, 1970), p. 90.
[12] Jeanette Silveira, "Thoughts on the Politics of Touch," *Women's Press* (Eugene, Ore.), 1, 13 (Feb. 1972), 13.

deeply threatened by a female who does not smile often enough and, paradoxically, who is not very unhappy." [13]

How do we know women smile more than men? We must check the notion against our own experience, because there is very little in the research literature to shed light on the matter. I searched seven recent books on nonverbal communication (all by men), as well as research papers on smiling, but failed to turn up any statistics or even estimates on the relative frequency of smiling by males and females. What hints there are, however, support the hypothesis of women's more frequent smiling. Bugental, Love and Gianetto, for example, don't report relative frequencies of smiling by mothers and fathers, but write, "It was very apparent to observers that parents (in particular, mothers) smiled a great deal when observed (videotaped) and very little when supposedly unobserved. . . ." [14] There is another hint in Mehrabian's reports on an experiment on persuasiveness, that males' "facial pleasantness and activity" were judged to be less than those of females.[15] If we interpret "facial pleasantness and activity" as probably signifying smiling, this also suggests more smiling in females.

And Kendon and Ferber, observing and filming nonverbal behavior in natural settings, report that males were less likely to show a smile with teeth than females were. Since they also report that smiles with teeth were overall more frequent than smiles without, we may hesitantly infer (but not conclude) that the females they observed smiled more than the males.[16]

Students in my classes have conducted informal studies in smile elicitation—they smiled at individuals (about 300 of them, half males and half females) in public and noted whether the other smiled back. Interestingly, people returned smiles about 76 percent of the time, equally to males and females. But there was a pattern of smile return that was determined by sex: females returned smiles more often than males did, about 89 percent of the time, and returned them more to males (93 percent) than to other females (86 percent). Males only smiled back at 67 percent of the elicitations by females, and were very inhibited at

[13] Phyllis Chesler, *Women and Madness* (New York: Doubleday, 1972), pp. 278–79.

[14] Daphne E. Bugental, Leonore R. Love, and Robert M. Gianetto, "Perfidious Feminine Faces," *Journal of Personality and Social Psychology,* 1971, 17, 314–18. Quote is from p. 317.

[15] Albert Mehrabian, *Nonverbal Communication* (Chicago: Aldine-Atherton, 1972).

[16] Adam Kendon and Andrew Ferber, "A Description of Some Human Greetings," in R. P. Michael and J. H. Crook, eds., *Comparative Ecology and Behavior in Primates* (London: Academic Press, 1973), pp. 591–668.

returning smiles to males, which they did but 58 percent of the time. In the land where smiles are a commodity in trade between the sexes, then, women are exploited by men—they give 93 percent but receive in return only 67 percent. Firestone's call for a boycott in smiles is well conceived.

Women and men smile differently, as we saw above (females supposedly being more toothy); there are other differences, which are also related to the power differences between the sexes.

In one smile classification system one of the five basic smiles is the lip-in smile, which has special relevance to women:

> The lip-in smile is often seen on the faces of coy girls. It is much the same as the upper smile [in which upper teeth are showing, the mouth slightly open] except that the lower lip is drawn in between the teeth. "It implies that the person feels in some way subordinate to the person she is meeting." [17]

It seems to me, also, that this particular smile might be the result of women's attempting to meet the contradictory demands to give a great big smile and to keep the mouth shut.

There is other evidence that males and females use smiling differently. In a communication study, subjects were either to tell the truth—present materials consonant with their beliefs, or lie—present materials contrary to their own strongly-held beliefs. Male subjects showed greater facial pleasantness in the "deceit" condition than they did in the "truth" condition, though females' facial pleasantness wasn't affected by whether they were speaking truthful or deceptive material.[18] Perhaps women have developed greater facial image management than men. Recall the contradiction noted by Chesler, that women (not men) are expected to be both frequently smiling, and very unhappy.

The study by Bugental and her associates throws some light on this question. These investigators studied smiling in family interaction, and found more consistency between verbal message and facial expression in fathers than in mothers: "When fathers smiled at their children, they were saying something relatively friendly or more approving than if they were not smiling. When mothers smiled at their children, their verbal message was no more positive in evaluative content than if they were not smiling." [19] This behavioral difference is responded to by children: in other research, Bugental and her colleagues found that young children

---

[17] Nierenberg and Calero, *How to Read a Person Like a Book*, p. 32. The system described is attributed to Ewan Grant.

[18] In Mehrabian, *Nonverbal Communication.*

[19] Bugental, Love, Gianetto, "Perfidious Feminine Faces," p. 317.

respond to women's smiles as relatively neutral, compared with men's smiles, and are particularly put off by a woman's negative statement accompanied by a smile.[20] The authors interpret this sex difference in parents' smiling in terms of women's culturally-prescribed role:

> The traditional female role demands warm, compliant behavior in public situations; the smiling facial expression may provide the mask to convey this impression. If the smile serves this function for women, there may be little or no relationship between smiling and the evaluative content of verbal messages. For her, the smile may be situationally or role defined, rather than being relevant to the immediate verbal interchange.[21]

There is a good illustration of smiling as part of woman's role in the description of women's status at a TV network, in *Rooms with No View:*

> . . . The duty of morale-booster is assigned to NBC women and the role is essential in keeping male producers, executives, and brass on their feet. The unspoken command is "Smile!" and the woman who doesn't smile each time her boss enters the office (or elevator or cafeteria) and who doesn't smile regularly (God forbid she should actually frown!) in the presence of her boss is chided with "Don't look so sullen," "Whatsamatter, Sourpuss?" and similar remarks.[22]

But not all women do a lot of smiling. The researchers who studied smiling between parents and children cautioned that their findings are limited to middle-class families—not because they didn't also observe lower-class families, but "because the majority of lower-class mothers in this sample did not smile at all."

[20] D. E. Bugental, J. W. Kaswan, and L. R. Love, "Perception of Contradictory Meanings Conveyed by Verbal and Nonverbal Channels," *Journal of Personality and Social Psychology,* 1970, 16, 647–55. D. E. Bugental, et al., "Child versus Adult Perception of Evaluative Messages in Verbal, Vocal, and Visual Channels," *Developmental Psychology,* 1970, 2, 367–75.

[21] Bugental, Love, Gianetto, "Perfidious Feminine Faces," p. 315.

[22] Ethel Strainchamps, ed., *Rooms with No View: A Woman's Guide to the Man's World of the Media* (New York: Harper & Row, 1974), p. 15.

chapter eleven
BODY POLITICS AND BEYOND

At this point we will ask several questions: What do the facts presented add up to? What are their implications beyond the immediately available information? How may the knowledge gained through this study be applied to change the distribution of power? Let's take up summation, implications, and applications one at a time.

SUMMATION

In the course of this book I have attempted to put forward and document the following points:

1. **Nonverbal behavior is a major medium of communication in our everyday life.**

2. **Power (status, dominance) is a major topic of nonverbal communication; and nonverbal behavior is a major avenue for social control on a large scale, and interpersonal dominance on a smaller scale.**

3. **Nonverbal power gestures provide the micropolitical structure, the thousands of daily acts through which nonverbal influence takes place, which underlies and supports the macropolitical structure.**

4. **Because our culture considers trivial, ignores, and doesn't educate its members to nonverbal behavior, it constitutes a vague stimulus situation. Its interpretation is then highly susceptible to social influence (e.g., explanations utilizing sex stereotypes) which further maintain the status quo.**

179

5. Nonverbal control is of particular importance to women, who are more sensitive to its cues and probably more the targets of such control.

6. Many nonverbal behaviors have the dual function of expressing either dominance or intimacy, according to whether they are asymmetrically or symmetrically used by the partners in a relationship.

7. The behaviors expressing dominance and subordination between non-equals parallel those used by males and females in the unequal relation of the sexes.

Looking over all the evidence presented in the foregoing chapters, we may develop Table 5, summarizing nonverbal behaviors used between equals (close and distant) and nonequals (superior and subordinate).

From this table we readily see that:

The same behaviors may be used to express relationships of different sorts, of solidarity and status, between equals and between nonequals.

The same behaviors exhibited by superior to subordinate are those exhibited by men to women; and women exhibit to men the behaviors typical of subordinate to superior.

The first six categories show completely parallel structure (except where unknown) in the three pairs of columns, illustrating the generalizability of Brown's "universal norm": the form used between intimates is used to inferiors and the form used between strangers is used to superiors.[1]

The last three categories—facial expression, emotional expression, and self-disclosure—seem to violate this universal norm: though the forms used between status nonequals and between the sexes are parallel, they don't square with the order of forms used between equals. Here, the form used between intimates is that shown to superior (smiling, showing emotions), and the form used between strangers (hiding emotions and personal information) is that shown to subordinate. This seeming reversal may be explained by an examination of the dialectic of friendship: friendship is a mixture of privilege and vulnerability. Friends may take liberties with each other, and they may exhibit their weaknesses to each other. All ten categories illustrate behaviors of privilege, but in the first six, the friendly option is for exercising one's privilege; in the last three, the option is for revealing one's vulnerability.

In the case of eye contact, I have attempted to reduce the complex data to two simple rules that may be extracted. Here again we have a parallel between status nonequals and male/female behaviors, but the

[1] Roger Brown, *Social Psychology* (New York: Free Press, 1965).

TABLE 5

GESTURES OF POWER AND PRIVILEGE. EXAMPLES OF SOME NONVERBAL BEHAVIORS WITH USAGE DIFFERING FOR STATUS EQUALS AND NONEQUALS, AND FOR WOMEN AND MEN.

	Between Status Equals		Between Status Nonequals		Between Men and Women	
	Intimate	Nonintimate	Used by Superior	Used by Subordinate	Used by Men	Used by Women
1 Address	Familiar	Polite	Familiar	Polite	Familiar? *	Polite? *
2 Demeanor	Informal	Circumspect	Informal	Circumspect	Informal	Circumspect
3 Posture	Relaxed	Tense (less relaxed)	Relaxed	Tense	Relaxed	Tense
4 Personal space	Closeness	Distance	Closeness (option)	Distance	Closeness	Distance
5 Time	Long	Short	Long (option)	Short	Long? *	Short? *
6 Touching	Touch	Don't touch	Touch (option)	Don't touch	Touch	Don't touch
7 Eye contact	Establish	Avoid	Stare, Ignore	Avert eyes, Watch	Stare, Ignore	Avert eyes, Watch
8 Facial expression	Smile? *	Don't smile? *	Don't smile	Smile	Don't smile	Smile
9 Emotional expression	Show	Hide	Hide	Show	Hide	Show
10 Self-disclosure	Disclose	Don't disclose	Don't disclose	Disclose	Don't disclose	Disclose

* Behavior not known

parallel of status equals and nonequals is less straightforward. Establishment of eye contact between intimates, and avoidance between strangers, is similar to the stare/avert of nonequals, but there is no parallel to the ignore/watch of nonequals. However, it may be that with eye contact we have another example of the unity of privilege and vulnerability in friendship: looking at the other may be both an expression of the stare privilege, and of the watching vulnerability.

The "Human Beast" or the Human Best?

We have demonstrated not only parallels between different aspects of human behavior, but also, at times, between human and other animal behavior. There is easy temptation to speculate on innate tendencies and evolutionary development of these behaviors. It is not within the scope of this book either to examine thoroughly what the human/animal parallels are, or to look at the deeper question of their origin and relationship. Readers are referred, however, to the works of ethologists (students of natural animal behavior) such as Eibl-Eibesfeldt [2] for intriguing and careful scientific evidence and discussion.

Some points made by Eibl-Eibesfeldt are worth repeating here (they have been made as well by other writers). First, we must distinguish between behaviors which are *analogous* and those which are *homologous*. These terms are applied to anatomical structures which are similar in different species, but which may achieve that similarity in different ways. Homologous structures are those which are based on a common genetic link; thus, for example, the forelimbs of the whale, bat, and human being, which are all rather dissimilar in appearance, can be shown to have evolved from the same common ancestor. Analogous structures, on the other hand, may be similar in outward appearance—for example, the digging legs of the mole and the mole-cricket, or the sleek body forms of fishes, penguins, fish-lizards, and whales—but they develop as independent adaptations to similar conditions.

The question that arises, then, is whether the similarities between behaviors of other animals and humans are due to common ancestors, or to common adaptations to similar conditions. Such similar conditions affecting many forms of animal life may be environmental conditions—crowding, scarcity of food, danger to life—which act on natural tendencies to bond, to reject, to protect (self, young, territory, possessions), or to

[2] Irenäus Eibl-Eibesfeldt, *Love and Hate: The Natural History of Behavior Patterns* (trans., Geoffrey Strachan) (New York: Holt, Rinehart, and Winston, 1972). See also his *Ethology: The Biology of Behavior* (New York: Holt, Rinehart, and Winston, 1970).

dominate. There are means for investigating this question—for example, mapping out the similarities according to family relations among different species, observing *all* species of an evolutionary grouping for a behavior (or its variant). Obtaining such knowledge requires much more systematic and time-consuming investigation than has yet been possible, but we may hope that those currently laboring in this field, and those who follow, will attack such questions.

Furthermore, it will be most enlightening to look more closely, if possible, at the evolution of gesture within our own species. Eibl-Eibesfeldt has made some progress in this direction by looking at: (1) the universality of body expressions in different cultures, and (2) the similarity of certain of our expressions to those exhibited among people whose forms of social organization (e.g., nomadic, tribal) stand in the prehistory of our own culture. He also cites historical evidence for the origin of various expressions.

The Hit Is Gone, But the Hurt Lingers On. From a historical viewpoint, we may note the preponderance of dominance behaviors that seem to be remnants of actual physical conflict. Moving close to or towering over another, staring, pointing, touching, leaning forward—all are elements of actual combat, and may be residuals of an earlier time when dominance was settled in more direct and overt physical ways. (Some behaviors of dominants—leaning back, turning away, relaxing—do not carry this suggestion of aggression, but rather indicate the posture of one secure in the hierarchy. In such situations, the behaviors of subordinates —tension, physical lowering, smiling, head and eye lowering—take on the characteristics of defensive and submissive postures.)

When so much of our nonverbal dominance behavior carries a subtle physical threat, whose meaning may be perceived on our lowest stages of awareness, women will be at a distinct disadvantage. Because of their socialization to avoid physical contact, and their lack of training in physical ability and self-defense, and the environmental situation in which many of their number are indeed attacked physically, women may be unconsciously and readily intimidated and controlled. In addition, they will most likely fail themselves to utilize dominance signals which have physical connotations; their socialization away from physical contact may include the avoidance of physically-related dominance signals.

Does Distinctive Mean Instinctive? In considering the "instinctiveness" of nonverbal behaviors, we should keep in mind Birdwhistell's comments about male–female differences in behavior (cited in Chapter 1): Human beings are hardly differentiated by sex in the first place; and in the second, we necessarily organize much gender display in body expression. Therefore,

8. **The overwhelming bulk of sex-differentiated behavior is learned and is developed to display otherwise unobtrusive differences.**

But even if certain behaviors are instinctive, what then? Are they evidence that human behavior is immutable, biologically determined? Eibl-Eibesfeldt stresses the point that

. . . if a certain behavior pattern or disposition is inherited, this by no means implies that it is not amenable to conditioning, nor must it be regarded as natural in the sense that it is still adaptive (i.e., conducive to survival). . . .[3]

Tendencies to behavior forms *may* be genetically based—but still not necessarily good for the species or unchangeable.

Eibl-Eibesfeldt goes to pains to save the name of ethology from the ideology of the new biologists of the "human beast"—those who wish to portray humanity as basically aggressive and engaged in intra-species struggle. He admits that the aggressive drive has at times been over-emphasized in animal study, though less by ethologists than by their interpreters, especially the mass media. He makes the essential point that humans display as much love as hate, as much bonding, warmth, supportiveness, and attraction as hostility, aggression, rejection, and war.

In a similar way, I wish to make it clear that my arguments in this book are not for the existence of any "natural" dominance or hierarchical behavior, "natural" antagonism of women and men, or "natural" dominating tendencies on the part of males. We are undeniably the victims of a patriarchy, but how we got to where we are is a complex matter, a subject for not only psychologists and ethologists, but for historians, anthropologists, sociologists, political scientists, and others. As a psychologist, and as a human being before and after that, I have seen ample demonstration of the potentiality and mutability of human behavior and relationships. I maintain an unswerving faith in people's ability to grow and to change both themselves and their world for the better (actively, not passively).

What I have attempted to show here is NOT that humans are locked in a timeless struggle, great against small, warring race against peaceful race, male against female. On the contrary, I believe that such pseudo-scientific sensationalisms are a *smokescreen to hide the fact that the distribution of power in our society is very unevenly patterned.* It is not

[3] Eibl-Eibesfeldt, *Love and Hate,* p. 3.

biologically distributed, but socially distributed. We are being diverted to the wrong patterns, to entertaining stories that merely reflect to us the ideologies that were laid in our minds by the culture of a hierarchical system.

Gestures of Dominance and Submission

We have looked at a wide variety of nonverbal signs and symbols. Can we call any of them gestures of dominance or submission similar to those identified among animals? A gesture of dominance is exhibited by a dominant animal in conflict with a subordinate one, and the submissive gesture is exhibited in return. The function of these gestures is considered to be regulation of conflict within a species, to preserve its members from full-scale battles to the death over dominance.

What criteria shall we demand for such signals among humans? Such a gesture should be one whose meaning is agreed upon by the majority

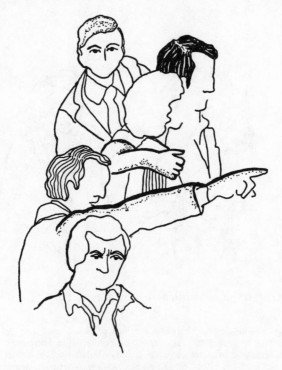

Gestures of dominance.

of the interactive community. Since we have seen that nonverbal actions affect and regulate behavior but are not a large part of our conscious repertoire of communication, I would not require that the gesture be *knowingly* sent or received. We would demand, however, that it be used in conflict situations, by appropriate actors (e.g., attempts at dominance, attempts to call off aggression). And furthermore, that it have the desired effect on the receiver of the communication.*

Gestures of dominance and submission may be tentatively identified among humans from the set of behaviors which are correlates of power, status or dominance, or are seen to serve as threats. Table 6 lists some behaviors from this category, paired as reciprocals of threat and corresponding submissive response.

It should be noted that although these dominance and submission ges-

Gestures of submission—lowering eyes, cuddling, smiling.

---

* We may also distinguish between *symbols of dominance* and *gestures of dominance*. The former would be cues from the nonverbal environment, such as overwhelming height, authoritative clothing, and symbols of office, which while not gestures have much of the effect of dominance gestures—defusing aggression, maintaining a hierarchy.

TABLE 6

PROPOSED GESTURES OF DOMINANCE AND SUBMISSION
AMONG HUMANS

Dominance	Submission
Stare	Lower eyes, avert gaze, blink
Touch	"Cuddle" to the touch
Interrupt	Stop talking
Crowd another's space	Yield, move away
Frown, look stern	Smile
Point	Obey, stop action (or stop talk); move in pointed direction

tures correspond in that they are reciprocals of similar types of behavior, one does not necessarily imply the other. Both seem to have almost universal application. A touch may be met with lowered eyes, frowning and pointing may make one stop talking, a smile may be submitted to any dominance gesture.

Do these gestures correspond to gestures of dominance and submission among animals? Strict criteria identifying them as such might demand better demonstrations of clear communication, maybe stereotyped or exaggerated behavior on the part of the sender, perhaps universal potential of sending the signal within the sub-class (dominants or subordinates), and correlation with other actions of sender and receiver. While in the aggregate I feel that enough of these have been demonstrated to justify classifying these behaviors as such gestures, others may wish to wait on further evidence.

The particular terms given the behaviors, and additional information the terms imply, do not unduly concern me at this point in our overview. They are at least gestures associated with persons in dominant and subordinate positions. There is enough to provoke thought, to suggest direction for further investigation, to allow individuals to inspect their own behavior and think of other such behaviors. Of particular interest, we may observe that much of men's behavior seems to consist of gestures of dominance, and much of women's, gestures of submission.

Power Meets Sex, and Vice Versa

This book may have seemed to you to be overconcerned with power. Surely, you may say, power is not everything. Well, if I have emphasized power and diminished other aspects of human interaction, it is a deliberate bias which does not begin to counterbalance the hundreds of books and papers on nonverbal communication that emphasize emotional expression, internal motivation, interaction between supposed equals, and behavior outside real human context. I do not write of power as an alien force that occasionally intrudes on our lives, and therefore should command a corner of psychological study; rather, I see it as the context in which our lives are lived, the oxygen of our social life, as unnoticed but as encompassing as the ocean to the fish. This view is the end result of a slow awakening to the inadequacies of my own and others' lives which are due to *other people's* obsessions with power (i.e., among those who have power and oppress others to maintain it), and to a social organization that embodies power vacuums and power high pressure areas.

Power has emerged in my investigation of nonverbal behavior, especially differences between males and females, as the most parsimoniously explanatory and useful concept by which to organize this behavior. It has particularly illuminated the relationships between men and women, including those often considered sexually based. As for sex differences that seem not to be based on power, as I have previously pointed out (Chap. 8),

9. **Many nonverbal behaviors that seem meaningless and non-power-related in fact are aspects of sex privilege or reflect societal biases ultimately founded in power differences.**

And those that do not so obviously fall into these categories, at the least emphasize the female-male distinction and serve to keep the sexes farther apart, unnaturally different, and even hostile and warring.

Are there "innocent" gesture differences between the sexes, ones that have no meaning in the pattern of inequality and struggle? If women drink a beverage looking over the cup, while men do so looking into it (or vice versa), does this harm anybody? If men and women hold cigarettes differently, what does this express about power? The answer to these questions is that as long as one group is privileged at the expense of the other, everything that contributes to that privilege is damaging, no matter how innocent-seeming. We cannot know what differences are "natural," either instinctual or based on non-power situational differences, until the power difference is removed.

There are no gesture differences I am ready at this time to dismiss. Whether it is that every difference has been (or can be) seized upon and made into a symbol of power, or the other way around, that power has been translated into myriad symbols (meaningless in themselves) to make itself public and visible, makes little difference. While the tiniest gesture is a prison bar or a grenade in the war, it cannot be called innocent.

The "vive la différence" school will ask, Do you want to eliminate all sex difference, so that you can't distinguish between men and women? Are you against sex? My answer is that I think it will take a lot more than ideas like this to eliminate sex, it being rather pleasurable and seemingly necessary to the survival of the species. If you're getting your pleasure from the manufactured and power-oriented differences described here, perhaps you should examine what you really take pleasure in. These differences have engendered hostility that has kept women and men apart, not brought them together.

Nonverbal at the Crux

The points about power developed in this book have been:

10. **Power is the capability of influencing or compelling others, based on the control of desired resources. (Power, status, and dominance are different, though related and often confounded, concepts.)**

11. **The ultimate underpinning of power is force. The resources on which power is based are in demand and those who control them must defend them from others' claims. However, force is the last-ditch, not front-line defense.**

12. **Power is exercised along a continuum, from least to greatest application of force. This continuum involves at least the following points:**

    a. *Internalized controls.* This is colonization of the mind, achieved through socialization. The easiest way to ensure we don't challenge the establishment is to have us stop ourselves, by implanting police officers inside our heads (through childhood teaching).

    b. *Environmental structuring.* Should our internal police be asleep, and we forget ourselves, strategically-placed reminders in our surroundings can stop us, one point further along the way to break through control.

    c. *Nonverbal communication.* Should the environmental reminders fail to stop us, other people—both "friend" and "foe"—will make us aware of our place and what we're doing, by subtle cues.

    d. *Verbal communication.* Are we ignoring even the nonverbal communication? Words are certainly now in order. These, too, have their spectrum, from mild surprise, cajoling, and joking through straightforward explanations and strong threats of consequences.

    e. *Mild physical sanctions.* When verbal communication fails to restrain us, our fellows must restrain us physically. A girl holds back her friend's arm from throwing a snowball at a disliked teacher, the wife holds the husband back from beating the child, buddies hold back two men from fighting, the police line holds back the angry crowd from approaching the government figure. People take us by the hand and lead us away from our contemplated action, hold our arms and hands down, place hands on our shoulders to keep us sitting, kick us under the table or put their hand over our mouth (or wash it with soap) for saying the wrong thing, hold us by the upper arms or around the waist to keep us back from somewhere, slap our faces or punch us or beat us up. Such physical sanctions take two main forms, temporary restraint and mild punishment.

f. *Long-term restraint and its ramifications.* When ordinary citizens, or nonpersonally applied police power fails, the state is allowed to retain, imprison, isolate, and apply physical and mental punishment to its members should they break the legal/social code (or threaten it, or be suspected of it). The main tools of this enforcement are jails, prisons, and mental hospitals.

g. *Weapons, death, war.* At this point it is clear that neither reminders, nor punishments, nor threats nor restraints will work to deter the person moving against the norms. All the stops are out, and those in power will attempt to stop the behavior at all costs. (And at this point the behavior will be harder to stop.)

Two things are to be noted in this continuum: first, the constraints in the mildest and strongest extremes are mass remedies, mass-produced, so to speak, to work on whole populations. Those in the middle are more often individual and intimate, personalized to handle the deviant (at the extremes we are not dealing with individual deviants). By this same token, the middle areas are not avenues commonly open to persons to complain against aggregates larger than individuals, such as institutions or companies.

Second, as we move from mild to forceful application of power, we move from the common and familiar to the rare and strange:

13. Generally speaking, the mildest form of force which is effective will be used.

Simple violations are handled by moving up the ladder a step, then another step, to the point of control. When steps are skipped, for example, when a police officer kills a suspected robber, or a citizen protest group seems to skip earlier forms of restraint against an institution and inflicts physical damage, we feel something is wrong. (Of course, as I have pointed out above, the middle areas are hardly open to opponents of institutions.)

It is not always so that the mildest forms of control are the ones in constant use. Obviously, against the most oppressed groups in a society, the state operates at stronger levels. Curfews, police harassment and brutality, ghettoes, concentration camps—all have been (and are) the daily life of oppressed people within societies dominated by another political group.

There is a major observation about this power spectrum that concerns nonverbal behavior:

14. Nonverbal behavior occupies a crucial point in the continuum, between covert and overt control (and between covert and overt resistance).

It is used to influence another, but when attention is called to it, it's denied. It is used to resist power, but when the resister is accused, it is denied. (This ability to deny nonverbal behavior makes it adaptable to protest by the relatively powerless.) Or more often, it may escape detection: it is subtle enough to influence us without our knowledge, and subtle enough for us to resist influence without making outright defiance. It is at the point where people *must* be controlled, for the social structure to remain intact. It is a traffic point for the exchange of much reminder information even when people have not slipped out of their internal controls; in many ways it acts as the reins of the state.

THE POLITICS OF CASTE: IMPLICATIONS

Throughout this book I have written of "sex differences" in behaviors. It is time to look more closely at the assumptions that underlie that label, and the other common label applying to actions of males and females, "sex roles." We must be wary when broad categories of social phenomena are ascribed to biological conditions such as gender. William Ryan's landmark book *Blaming the Victim* made it clear, through statistics and explication, that social phenomena ascribed to race—for example, illegitimacy, broken families, delinquency among blacks—are actually due to economic factors.[4] At the same economic levels, blacks and whites are undifferentiated in their participation in such "social problems." It has been a convenience of white supremacy to identify a "Negro problem," as it was the convenience of Nazism to identify a "Jewish problem" and of male supremacy to identify a "woman problem." These may be better identified as the "white problem," the "Gentile problem," and the "man

[4] William Ryan, *Blaming the Victim* (New York: Random House, 1971).

problem," or more precisely, racism, anti-Semitism, and misogyny. Or, even more precisely, caste oppression.

The results of oppression are ever blamed on its victims, as Ryan so brilliantly demonstrates. We now recognize that these problems are not legitimately identified by their victims' ethnic or biological traits, but by their real origins in oppression. In the same way, behaviors that arise from the power differential in our society, which are shown to be similar to behaviors in other situations of power difference, are not legitimately ascribed to gender. *They are not sex differences, they are power differences.*[5] *There is no "woman problem," there is an oppression problem. There is no "battle of the sexes," there is class and caste war.*

The popular term "sex roles" is generally thought to be a more liberal explanation of observed sex differences, clearly denying biology and pointing to socialization and social norms as the origin of behavioral differences. (In this respect it is not unlike "liberal" social theories which blame not black heredity, but black "family structure," or ghetto culture and environment, for blacks' problems.) Thorne has stated the case against the concept "sex roles" with the following arguments: 1. Role terminology is not fully applicable to gender. 2. "Sex roles" terminology tends to mask questions of power and inequality. 3. It is significant that sociologists do not use the terms "race roles" or "class roles." 4. Much of "sex roles" literature is fraught with reification.[6] If we ascribe differences in female and male nonverbal behavior to "sex roles" without clarifying the power positions underlying those "roles," we are muddying up the term *role* to the point of meaninglessness.

These ways of labeling gender-associated aspects of behavior may determine the approach that one takes to research. Hochschild has identified the following four types of research perspective commonly adopted: (1) sex differences, (2) sex roles, (3) women as a minority group, (4) the politics of caste.[7] This book may be seen in the arena of the politics of caste. While those concerned with women as a minority group often deal with prejudice and discrimination, and may draw parallels with other minorities, the politics of caste emphasizes "power, the different kinds of

[5] Kathleen Grady has made a similar point, in "Angrogyny Reconsidered," presented at the Eastern Psychological Association meetings, 1975.

[6] Barrie Thorne, "Is Our Field Misnamed? Towards a Rethinking of the Concept 'Sex Roles,' " *Newsletter, American Sociological Association Section on Sex Roles,* 1976 (Summer), 4, 2, 4–5.

[7] Arlie Hochschild, "A Review of Sex Role Research," *American Journal of Sociology,* 1973, 78, 1011–29. In Joan Huber, ed., *Changing Women in a Changing Society* (Chicago: University of Chicago Press, 1973), pp. 249–67.

power, its distribution, use, and expression, in the parlor and in the marketplace." [8]

The understanding of the politics of caste, and development of a psychology of oppression, are priorities of the first order for psychology and social science in general. There are two types of benefits from focusing on women within a caste-political context: on the one hand, observing similarities to other situations of inequality illuminates the behaviors and relations of men and women; on the other hand, analyses developed with regard to sex-based power may be applied to other power arenas. Toward that development, I wish to demonstrate further points that the study of nonverbal behavior may clarify not only in the situation of women, but in that of other powerless groups also. My discussion will focus again on women: it will look at (1) parallel treatment of children and women, (2) reaction to women's adoption of "male" gestures, and (3) major issues of the women's movement, including "brain-washing."

Women and Children Last

The fact that women and children have so often been treated as a unit has more than their physical connection at heart. Society's treatment of women, as many theorists have observed, is similar to the treatment of children; indeed, not just popular ideology, but law and social science make women into children. Children are probably the group whose oppression and control are most readily justifiable to the majority of society. If women may be shown to be like children (and, in fact, if other oppressed groups can), then their inferior position may be more readily explained to, and accepted by, those who may question it.

Eibl-Eibesfeldt has noted that "In commercial art the childish attributes of women are frequently exaggerated as well as the sexual attributes." [9] He illustrates this point with a commercial drawing of a bikini-clad adult female with large head, extremely wide eyes, tiny nose, pony-tail hairdo, and puckered lips. "This childishly puckered mouth," he writes, "has a very strong appeal and is especially exaggerated in drawings as a childlike feminine characteristic." [10] In a similar vein, a popular song (sung by male to female) proclaims, "You look just like a baby in a cradle to me, I just can't keep my hands off of you." Other aspects of female appearance, which may be manipulated by social demands, emphasize childish features: rouge gives the appearance of full cheeks, fashions frequently

8 Hochschild, "Review of Sex Role Research," p. 258.
9 Eibl-Eibesfeldt, *Love and Hate*, p. 22.
10 Eibl-Eibesfeldt, *Love and Hate*, p. 137.

return to the childish form—pinafores, "baby dolls," empire dresses, flat breasts, short skirts, and so on. Beauty for women in our culture is bound up with the simulation of youth.

There is likewise striking similarity between the prescribed nonverbal behaviors for children and for women. Children are told, for example:

Kinesics: Don't point; don't touch; sit up straight (i.e., be tense); don't put your feet up; don't lean back; don't turn the chair around backward.

Both children and women must be circumspect in behavior (both are under more social control) and are omitted from the handshake culture. Both are subjected to trivializing gestures such as the pat on the head or rear, or finger to the nose.

Facial expression: Don't stare; don't pout; don't frown; let's see a smile. Both women and children are expected to show emotion, "allowed" to cry (though made to feel guilty for it), expected to lower eyes and head before authority; display of anger is prohibited in both.

Space and time: Both children and women have small spaces, shared with others, invadable, lower, towered over, and less preferred. They are likely to be below and behind others; and as smaller beings move in an environment intimidating and often structured for larger persons. Their time is mostly in others' control, assumed valueless, curfewed.

Here we see social controls being enforced similarly on two groups.

We now know that the behaviors that are denied are just those which are often used in asserting power, such as pointing, touching, and staring. Why should children not be allowed to stare or point, actions which harm no one and are allowed to adult males? Apparently because they are signs of dominance, and their use by children would constitute insubordination in our society.

For children, the enforcement of these controls is an introduction to adult rules, especially those pertaining to class-based deference. At adolescence, young males break out of them: they become initiated more and more into the male handshake club; they most defiantly violate sanctions against certain postures—leaning back in a chair, slumping, sitting with the chair backwards; and they begin to assert male prerogative toward females—most notably, in excessive (often awkward) attempts at touching. Adolescent females, on the other hand, continue being treated as children nonverbally, making the shift from one powerless group to another almost imperceptibly. The one power they do gain in reaching adulthood is that of asserting control over children, their comrades in oppression. And women are, unfortunately, the avenue for a great deal of society's oppression of children.

Through such cueing socialization processes guarantee not only a future adult with the cultural norms of body behavior, but one that learns compliance at an early age, the better to fit into the adult demands of a hierarchical social system. (Those who follow orders also learn well how to give them.) Children are born into this world without any observable notions of hierarchy, superiority, or subordination; this training prepares them to take their place in a society of petty tyrants and half-slaves, to dominate or to be made into second-class citizens. We begin by making them feel inferior to a "master race," a feeling that is a prime building block of fascism.

When Power Becomes Sex

It doesn't take a genius to note that power and sexuality are often confused in our society. In nonverbal behavior we can see two major effects of this, in which power gestures are explained as sexual, but for different reasons.

Sexual intimacy as an explanation for men's power gestures. Touching isn't the only nonverbal power gesture whose greater use by men is attributed to their sexiness. Other prerogatives of the powerful—for example, familiar address, encroachment on personal space, staring—are claimed to be only results of sexual attraction * (in the words of another popular song, "You're just too good to be true, can't keep my eyes off of you").

The dual nature of these gestures, as expressions either of intimacy or dominance, makes such ambiguities both possible and likely. As we observed with regard to touching, a sexual attraction explanation cannot explain the asymmetry of the gesture, since women have to be considered to have strong sexual drive as well as men. Contrary to widespread propaganda, *men are not oversexed, they are overprivileged.*

15. **Sexual attraction cannot sufficiently explain men's greater usage of gestures which indicate both intimacy and dominance.**

When women protest male gestures which they feel have gone too far, they are likely to be answered with an attack to an even more vulnerable section of their psychological anatomy—their caring. "I was only being friendly, you're too sensitive," the attack begins. The woman has caused hurt feelings in another, made someone feel rejected, and is made to pay for it in the coin of guilt—and, of course, by backing down in her analysis of the situation and her self-defense. Another form of attack on such occasions is to accuse a woman who does not accept unwanted intimacies of being "frigid."

Violating genderpower. That's what happens when power gestures are interpreted as such in men. What happens when women emit these gestures? There are several types of response to such violations:

16. **Usurpation of the nonverbal symbols of power by women (and other powerless people) may be ignored, denied, or punished by others, rather than accepted.**

17. **Denial of nonverbal power gestures made by women often takes the form of attributing the gesture to sexual advance rather than dominance.**

A woman who puts her hand on a male colleague's shoulder, or gives him a dominance stare in a meeting, or approaches males as close as a man does, may meet with the following responses:

a. *Ignoring.* She and her gesture are treated as if they didn't happen, presumably in the hope that ignoring them will make them go away.

b. *Denial.* If the gesture itself can't be ignored, its power aspect can be de-

* An extreme example of this rule is that very frequently physical violence—the ultimate show of strength between males—against women by men is explained as a gesture of love.

nied. Rather than being interpreted as an assertion of dominance, or prerogative of power, it is frequently interpreted as sexual invitation. Many women who have attempted to equalize nonverbal behavior with men have gotten much more sexual response than they bargained for, and much more than the parallel behavior would have gotten for men. A touch, a stare, a closeness, a loosening of demeanor, even huskiness of the voice—all are perceived as sexiness in women. In the vagueness of knowledge that even the senders have about their own nonverbal behavior, it's understandable that such definitions of the situation are accepted by women as well as men. Having their movements interpreted sexually will inhibit women in making gestures of power. Moreover, attribution of sexual aggressiveness to a woman does two things to ensure the power balance remains the same: it compliments the man, and it disarms the woman, placing her back in her familiar unthreatening role of sex object. It can be quite disconcerting to have sex thrown at you in the middle of an intellectual discussion, as many women will testify. Their intellectual content is trivialized and if they protest, their anger may be trivialized and sexualized also: "You're so cute when you're mad, baby."

c. *Punishment.* If, on the other hand, a woman's gesture is unmistakably nonsexual (in itself or because of another gesture which "tags" it), and those around perceive she is usurping male privilege, punishment may follow. This punishment can be physical or psychological, verbal or nonverbal, and from men or from other women. There are many ways to stick woman back in "her place" for exhibiting "male" characteristics: she may be labeled as deviant and abhorrent, domineering, castrating bitch, lesbian. It's interesting to note that the latter two terms specifically imply a denial of sexuality to men (through either threat to their own "potency," or withholding women's sexuality from them), since much of men's sexuality has been tied to their power.

d. *Acceptance.* A dominance gesture from a woman that is met with resentment and anger by a man has probably been accepted at face value. Another response that shows such acceptance is an attempt to restore the balance of power—which is, most often, to restore it to overbalance on the male's side. A male who has been touched by a woman will often find a way within the next few minutes to touch back, to claim some of the toucher's space, to handle the toucher's property, or to score verbal if not nonverbal points.

Yes, there is another response to women's violation of nonverbal sex norms.

e. *Submission.* Men (or women) may show submissive gestures and obedience, signifying acceptance of dominance or recognition of legitimate authority in a woman.

NONVERBAL POWER AND WOMEN'S LIBERATION

Just as insights from the women's liberation movement have added to our understanding of nonverbal communication as social control, so the study of nonverbal behavior can give insight to questions of women's liberation. In the past decade, women have again turned to an examination of power as a key to understanding and changing their situation in society; many of their fundamental questions have been directed to the workings of power. Thus, questions related here to women's liberation are of interest to those who wish to study power in any context.

"The personal is political" is a statement of the movement that has been taken in many ways, but basically it refers to the position that there is nothing we do—no matter how individual and personal it seems—that does not reflect our participation in a power system: our politics are reflected in the way we deal with others in our personal lives; they *are* the way we live, as well as what we profess. This belief takes on new dimension when viewed with regard to nonverbal communication, in which we see just how much of the seemingly personal is truly political.

But additionally, it raises further questions of interest to social scientists: What is the relationship between *institutionalized* power and *interpersonal* power relationships (the macropolitical and the micropolitical)? How is the study of personal power related to questions of social control? (And how "trivial" and diversionary is the study of personal power?)

Another question in the study of power concerns its manifestations: What are the *forms* power takes, and the *dynamics* by which it works? What forms and dynamics find particular application to relationships in which women are involved?

In the women's movement different women, and different schools of thought, see different *goals* to be obtained through studying power. Do we learn about power in order to recognize and defend against it, or to gain acceptance into the halls of power—or seize power fully—ourselves? What can the study of nonverbal assertion tell us about *power to defend* and *power to control?* Does power exercised in defense lead to power exercised in dominance? Will power that is openly known and acknowledged (e.g., when nonverbal communication is widely understood) necessarily lead to corruption (as much as power that is wielded more covertly)?

Parallels have been drawn in this book, as elsewhere, between the behaviors of women and of other minority and oppressed groups. It is of value to ask what *analogies* can be drawn, what *similarities* seen, between the exercise of power over women and its exercise over other groups, such as blacks, homosexuals, other national and racial minorities, working class people, children, etc. And what *differences* exist that make for different power forms and dynamics exerted toward these groups? What are the similarities and differences in their responses to nonverbal power?

Finally, the question of "brainwashing" has also occasioned much debate in the women's movement. In this discussion, women's position in society may be laid either to *socializaion* (internalization of sex norms and biases, characteristic passivity, self-hate—brainwashing) or to *external factors* (e.g., economic dependence and threat of punishment).* While the socialization position has held most attention and support, some women have consistently disagreed with it. They have pointed out that to speak, for example, of women's nonassertiveness as self-instigated is a pseudo-psychological diversion from very concrete issues of control. One writer puts it:

> There are real consequences a woman must suffer every time she steps out of line. By talking about brainwashing we can avoid recognizing these consequences and instead focus on the so-called "emotional damage" done to her as a child and the need to "free her mind." [11]

While the nation delves deeper into women's crippled minds, the power relationships and concrete punishments and deprivations of our society do not change. This question, then, is a fundamental one for the study of nonverbal communication: How much of power over women is *internal,* and how much is *external?* How do the external and internal interact?

Nicole Anthony has illuminated the fundamental link between the internal and the external, in her "Open Letter to Psychiatrists":

> Sometimes, in the middle of a heated discussion with a man, a strong woman finds herself acting chimp-like [submitting]. I'm oppressing myself, she thinks, why do I act like a schmuck, I don't need to act like this, the psychiatrist says I oppress myself, I internalize, etc.
>
> *If we filmed the scene we would see that what really happened was that he gave a gesture of dominance and she submitted in fear.*
>
> There's no need to submit, the psychiatrists say. Another lie. If a woman refuses to respond to the gestures of dominance she is frequently physically

---

* Related forms of this debate have taken place in discussions of other social movements. The question of "false consciousness" among workers, for example, is also one of brainwashing vs. external conditions.

[11] Redstocking Sister, "Brainwashing and Women," in Radical Therapist Collective, eds. (J. Agel, producer), *The Radical Therapist* (New York: Ballantine, 1971), p. 122. See also Ann Battle-Sister, Review of *A Tyrant's Plea,* etc., *Journal of Marriage and the Family,* 1971, 33, pp. 592–97.

attacked. A wife needs only to be hit by a husband larger and heavier than she. Thereafter the most fleeting subliminal gesture will serve to remind her of the costs of rebellion.

The moments of "internalization" are really the moments when we respond to gestures of dominance. They are not inside of our heads.[12]

Similarly, Lynn O'Connor points out,

The forms of female behavior that our contemporary ideologues have called internalized self hate or masochism are usually just a logical response to a man's gesture of dominance. Women have spent years on the psychiatric couch hunting down a nonexistent internal enemy.[13]

Thus the covert/overt position of nonverbal behavior in the power continuum is also crucial to the individual: nonverbal communication may be seen as the link between internalized and externalized control.

18. Much of women's behavior which is interpreted as self-limiting may in reality be the end of a sequence in which assertion was attempted, and suppressed, on the nonverbal level.

The experiment by Word, Zanna, and Cooper (in Chapter 2), in which white interviewees who were treated like blacks reacted with inferior performance, has shown us that subtle behavior can indeed be powerful enough to evoke behavioral submission.

This view proposes, in a sense, a mediating response that includes both elements of the controversy: the threat is there, and the socialization (or learned response) is there; nonverbal cues mediate between them. Here is furthermore the healthy reminder that a psychology that looks at a single individual acting, outside the social context, is liable to incomplete and distorted interpretations. The interactive model best accounts for submissive behavior, even in people who have been shown to have conditioned submission.

Training in self-assertion or self-blame? The movement for women's training in self-assertiveness which has mushroomed in recent years relates directly to this question of brainwashing vs. external controls. While I don't dispute the effects of socialization in women, having struggled with

---

[12] Nicole Anthony, "Open Letter to Psychiatrists," *Radical Therapist*, 1970, 1, 3, 8; presented at 1970 Convention of the American Psychiatric Association.

[13] Lynn O'Connor, "Male Supremacy: A Theoretical Analysis," reprint available from KNOW, Inc., P.O. Box 86031, Pittsburgh, Pa. 15221.

the monsters of passivity, self-doubt and self-hatred in my own head, I am wary of a broad social program whose ultimate effect is a re-education process for victims rather than oppressors.

Much assertive training has emphasized nonverbal cues and responses, and at times it has been suggested that making these behaviors assertive will alter the social condition not only of individual women, but of women as a whole. People interested in nonverbal communication, especially in its relation to women, must be concerned with this movement. As I have pointed out, use of the symbols of power does not guarantee their acceptance as such. And, rather than making women powerful or changing the social structure, such a training program may tend to divide women and strengthen the existing class structure.*

Furthermore, to focus on women's own minds and interaction styles as the source of their oppression is the most vicious sort of blaming the victim, right up there with curfews for women to save them from attack. To suggest, as many have, that women *choose* to use self-deprecating speech, gestures, postures—"women are their own worst enemies"—is implying that they pick these behaviors as they would pick clothes to wear for the day. It simplistically implies much more control over the situation, its rewards and punishments, than exists, and places blame and guilt on women's own heads. Certainly part of women's problems has been their socialization and nonverbal style; but this is evidenced in interaction (not just action), it doesn't exist in a vacuum. Women's consciousness-raising groups have constituted in themselves a form of assertiveness training—which has generally been meant to serve as a prelude to action, not as an end in itself. Combating this "slave psychology" is a smaller part of the problem than many people think it is. The real problem in "slave psychology" is, after all, *slavery*.

Of course, the goal is not for women to blame themselves, or to use their new assertiveness against others oppressed by the system, but to create the conditions in which people's natural assertiveness will not be suppressed, and assertion training will no longer be necessary.

* While the assertive training movement is vaguely understood by many to be advancing women's cause, we may ask which women it is helping: because of the expenditure in time, transportation, and fees, the poorest women will not be trained in assertion. And would it help them if they were? "Uppity behavior" loses jobs. Even middle and upper-middle class women, who will form the core of trainees, can't economically or politically "afford" to assert themselves to those more powerful than they. It's more likely that their assertiveness will be directed at those of equal and less power—for example, other women and service workers. Indeed, many of the examples given from the training deal with just such people and often women are told to practice assertiveness in just such "low risk" situations.

APPLY GENEROUSLY AS NEEDED: APPLICATIONS

If knowledge is sterile and meaningless without application, as I believe it is, then what can be done concretely with the knowledge presented in this book? One application can be to the gathering of other information, and to that end I have provided an Appendix suggesting research directions. Since body politics, like other politics, is unfortunately not amenable to the vote, we must look for other avenues of change.

Good scientists are universally hesitant to make application of their findings until they are certain of them. There are some who would hold back at this point, to wait until "all the facts are in." Conservatism and caution are commendable attitudes, indeed, the only ones for a responsible science to take, but they can be misapplied. To those who would argue that we don't yet know enough to apply findings from nonverbal study, I would answer:

1. On individual questions there may be incomplete data, but extrapolation, analogy, and theory, judiciously applied, may fill in many of the gaps. At this point we have facts that interlock in intriguing patterns—perhaps enough to make a "periodic table" whose blanks then lead to new truths to be pursued.

2. Theory binds together our body of knowledge, and is intimately related to practical application that tests it. Research is one limited area of practice; real-life application (with feedback) will provide even richer data to inform theory.

3. To keep demanding further research can postpone application indefinitely and serve as a diversionary tactic to *keep* people from learning anything. As lawyer-activist Florynce Kennedy observes, research only amounts to measuring the size of the turds they throw at you. Powerless people have no time to waste on this.

4. The application I suggest is in a spirit of open inquiry. Test ideas from experimentation against your own experience—do they ring true? Apply them in your daily life—do they work? If not, why not? If so, what more can be learned? How are they best applied? (Often people who have read my papers or heard me speak on touching have written me to tell of such application, in the spirit of "That seems to hit home—let's check it out.")

Breaking the Bodypower Barrier

The applicability of the studies reported in this book is varied, and will be more evident to many readers in particular ways than it will be to me. Here are some obvious conclusions for personal change:

Women can stop: smiling unless they are happy; lowering or averting their eyes when stared at; getting out of men's way in public; allowing interruption; restraining their body postures; accepting unwanted touch.

Women can start: staring people in the eye; addressing them by first name; being more relaxed in demeanor (seeing it's more related to status than morality); touching when it feels appropriate.

There's an especially important thing women can do: support their sisters, nonverbally. Women are notorious for disliking each other, a typical effect of oppression; I believe their subtle gestures communicate this rejection, even when the women do not wish to. In this competitive society, we haven't learned gestures of solidarity. Nevertheless, women are in the best position to develop these, having long taken responsibility for shoring up faltering members of humanity. (As Phyllis Chesler has pointed out, this supportive energy has usually gone to men and been denied other women.) [14]

At a party, the value women place on male company is often visibly displayed in rapt gazing, smiling, hovering near, and listening to men, and laughing at their jokes. Women who value women will gravitate toward *them,* listen to them with interest, orient toward them without gazing around the room watching men, ask interested questions, and so forth. Besides the obvious signs of nodding, smiling, and touching, supportive gestures can take the form of watching concernedly while another woman is speaking, leaning forward, not making distracting noises or gestures, and adopting the same (or mirror-image) posture to communicate agreement. Respect can be shown to other women by according them space, not interrupting them, and defending their space and speech for them when others invade.

Men can stop: invading women's personal space; touching them excessively; interrupting; taking up extra space; sending dominance signals to each other; staring.

Men can start: smiling; losing their cool, displaying emotion; confiding in other men; sending gestures of support; being honest when they are unsure of something; condensing their bodies.

Parents and teachers of children have a particular responsibility for change. *Parents and teachers can stop:* teaching boys to charge through the world as if they own it, get what they want by pushing others around, interrupt, touch, and crowd with impunity, to withhold their smile, suppress all emotional expression; showing young girls how to take up little space, drop their eyes, back down in conversation, move out of everyone's way, be hesitant to touch others, smile at any and everything. *Parents and teachers can start:* Helping boys to limit their territories—spatial, verbal,

[14] Phyllis Chesler, *Women and Madness* (New York: Doubleday, 1972), especially Chaps. 1 and 10.

visual—where they impinge on those of others (especially of females), encouraging them to express positive and tender emotions; accepting assertiveness, expansiveness, and anger in girls; modeling for both girls and boys self-respect and respect for others nonverbally, with neither subservience or dominance.

You Can Get There from Here. If you're serious about personal change, you can sit down and make out a list. Put down the behaviors exhibited by your sex (or other reference group), then mark those you believe you display and those you don't display. (You may need to spend some days monitoring your own behavior to know this.) Then, of those you display, mark which you want to keep and those you want to get rid of; of those you don't display, mark any you would like to acquire. List the characteristic behaviors of the other sex, or group you feel disadvantaged by (and perhaps spend some time observing whether these are displayed to you). Which ones do you yourself exhibit? Do you want to keep them? Which ones which you don't exhibit would you like to acquire? From these intentions, begin practicing the behaviors, perhaps one at a time, and cross them off your list as you acquire them. See if you like your behavior better, or find it more effective, after you have done this. See if you have brought about reciprocal changes in those who interact with you.

The Limits of Personal Change

Where will personal change get us? I don't see it as the road to changing the social order, by any means. But it is a first step, and a consciousness-raising one, and insofar as the micropolitical gives support and rationalization to the macropolitical, undermining that support ought to make inroads on the social structure. Awareness is a major key to action—the more we know of what's going on, the better we know what to do about it. Being able to resist influence and dominance from others can be greatly enhanced by awareness of nonverbal tactics. Being alert and responsive to nonverbal cues, we may serve as models for others, as well as educate them to this hidden world. In the future, I hope the vocabulary of people facing the powerful is as quick to label such silent power ploys as the hand on the shoulder, lowered pitch, straying eyes, and elevated position, as it is to label blatant threats and bribes.

Some people will contend that changing nonverbal behavior *is* the way to achieve social change—if every individual is changed, we will have changed the social structure. This philosophy pops up in different contexts among well-meaning people, but I cannot accept it. This slow-but-sure idea, favored because it is nonviolent and legal and involves a minimal bucking of the system, like other such plans has weaknesses in its non-disruptiveness and its direction of energies to individual (rather than social) solutions for what are really social problems. And we seldom if ever come into face-to-face contact with those who have the most power over us, anyway.

Is this a contradiction to my contention that nonverbal communication is a major influence in our lives and operates to maintain the power structure? No—it's a recognition that there is a macrostructure as well as a microstructure. They work together and must be attacked together. A combination of these approaches will be the strongest in achieving real change.

Should women change their nonverbal style? More attention has been given to the inadequacies of women's submissive style than to those acts and facts that cue it, or to women's nonverbal strengths. Many women do want to change how they come on. But in thinking about these inadequacies we have to be cautious of overvaluing male behaviors and undervaluing female ones. It's dead wrong to think that female body language is *all* self-belittling or without value. We must consider the different behaviors according to what they express, and decide whether we want to keep them. Emotional expressiveness and self-disclosure are good examples: just because they make a person more vulnerable with respect to nonexpressive others, are the behaviors to be abandoned? Better (in my opinion) that they should be developed in men, and valued by the society as a whole, than that emotional/social cripples be made of the lot of us. Until this happens, women can try to use these disadvantages as strengths—and as openings to demand expressiveness in others.

There has always been pressure to imitate the oppressor in every oppressive situation. Too often it has taken the form of imitating the oppressor's worst characteristics—such as devaluing our own kind, attacking others of our class, acting overbearing. Any valuable qualities displayed by those in power must be carefully separated from the ugly characteristics that come with power.

If you think that this book in illuminating the workings of power is pessimistic, then I have not been clear. Neither the history, nor the pervasiveness, nor the intricate workings, nor seeming inexorableness of power make it immutable. The history of power in fact shows us that victims of unfathomable oppression have arisen to claim their rights, that power is persistently being broken down and overturned. Every new insight into its workings may provide a new road to its overthrow. I am one who believes in the human ability through striving to transform political organization and social relations continually for the better. Let's not settle for less.

appendix

ON INTO THE UNKNOWN:

Further Research

It should be clear from the survey presented in this book that there is much still to learn. The research that needs to be carried out is sometimes obvious from the gaps and questions remaining in the reports I have presented. Here are some examples pertaining especially to nonverbal communication and the sexes:

- Fill in details on partially known phenomena, for example, interruption and touching: what happens in different settings? Between only women?
- Control status and sex in experimentation, to look at them separately.
- Check out informal observations, especially ones that supply the "missing link" for an analysis: Do women smile more than men? Do they avert the eyes more, and under what circumstances? Do women show more signs of uncertainty than men, such as "palms up" is supposed to be?
- Map the interactional *dynamics* of nonverbal power (see Word, Zanna, and Cooper in the black-white interview study, Chapter 2).
- Look for ties between women's culture and their body language; study women's nonverbal communication as of interest in its own right.
- Examine reactions (internal and external) to violation of nonverbal norms for the sexes.
- Look at power signals *within* sex groupings (especially among females, whose power interaction has been little studied) as well as *between* sex groups.

These are straightforward tasks, and readers can (and I hope by this time, have) come up with many more questions of interest themselves.

What is more important is to rethink our overall approach to nonverbal research. Old biases and premises must be cast out and new ones—yes, both new premises and new biases (for example, egalitarian and non-sexist)—must be the ground we stand on.

DON'TS

Nonverbal research must *avoid:*

- Blaming the victim. Because the actions of the powerless differ from those of the powerful, the conclusion is often that the actions are the source of the power difference, and the powerless need only change their actions to become powerful. There are even social programs with this kind of thinking; they are worse than a waste of money, they are an attack on human dignity.

- Rationalizing the status quo. Exploring the inner recesses of the mind, illuminating the parallels between humans and animals, or demonstrating historical and cross-cultural similarities can be important aids to understanding origins and processes of oppression, but they need not turn into social science apologism.

- Seeing racial and sexual groups as different species. William Ryan shows in *Blaming the Victim* that differences between whites and blacks are created by economic position, not by racial inheritance. Blacks and whites are alike; so are women and men. There are many more similarities between the sexes than differences; and the differences are created much more by circumstance than by biology. When finding differences between the sexes, look for *differences in situations.*

- Cultural, racial, sex and power biases. The Western white male status-quo-biased norm looks at certain groups—women, blacks, "primitive" cultures, poor people—as "different" (from the investigator) and attempts to describe and give reasons for the difference of the "other." I look forward to the day a research report begins,

This research was planned, executed, and is reported all from the perspective of the Anglo-Saxon male. Although we studied as many females as males, and just as many males differed from females as females differed from males, we choose to continue the time-honored tradition of social science, of considering the female as deviant. Thus, we conclude that women are emotional, have a strange reaction to being stared at, and don't know how to use power—not that men are unemotional, or that women and men react differently to staring and to power.

DO'S

Then, there are things that nonverbal research must *do:*

- Watch for unconscious biases throughout the research process: in the composition of the research team; the framing of research questions; subjects, objects, and settings of research; procedures; interpretation, writeup and distribution of results. You will have scientifically sounder research through these processes, which can serve as a model for others. Make sure to point out your differences and how they are achieved; use unbiased language, and point out that it was not difficult or ineloquent to do so. Don't stop with publication in professional journals, but get your results out to the community most affected by them; who has the knowledge helps to determine who has the power. Feedback and the interaction of theory and practice will make your research program even sounder scientifically.
- Broaden your research sample. Study social class *and* sex as factors. Don't limit study to the college population, with its class homogeneity. In nonverbal research, overattention to this group, at a stage of life in which society demands concern with mating, may have given undue emphasis to concern with emotional expression and disregard of dominance and power. Study older adults as well as young ones.
- Study power/status as well as solidarity expressed in nonverbal behavior. Look at this variable especially in interaction between the sexes. Document the volume, and breadth, of dominance gestures.
- Look at parallels to language, for example:

Genderlects: Is there a "women's language" and a "men's language" of nonverbal communication? Or different body *genderlects,* as the parallel phenomena in spoken language have been termed?

Acquisition: Linguists and psychologists have speculated that because of the central role of women in child-rearing, both male and female children learn "women's language" as a first tongue, and that boys must later learn "men's language." Is this true? And does the same thing happen for nonverbal communication? Do males then become bilingual, so to speak, in body language?

Bilingualism: In bilingual regions, generally one language is dominant, because of its speakers' political dominance. Speakers of the other language are forced to become bilingual in order to both retain their own language and speak to those in command. If males become bilingual in the socialization process, it reverses the usual correlation with power. Is either male or female nonverbal bilingualism the case? Do males retain the bilingualism? Or do females pick it up, as a matter of survival?

Sex difference and sexism: As we saw in Chapter 10, our language is not only spoken differently by females and males, but in its usage it systematically reduces the status and humanity of women. Does this happen too in nonverbal language? What form would sexism take nonverbally? (See the discussions in Chapters 7 and 8 of the female-excluding handshake, and of obscene gestures.)

- Avoid simplistic conceptions of personality factors. Look at environmental as well as personality determinants of nonverbal behavior, as was done in the Stanford Prison Study.*

- Above all, critically appraise the research of others. Has previous research been absorbed in the intricacies of the scale structure of red herrings? What does it mean to report "race differences" or "sex differences" in an area of behavior? The researcher who reports such differences without comment on their context is like a scientist who puts rats with short whiskers in one Skinner box programmed to reward a response to red light, and long-whiskered rats in another box, which rewards a response to green light, and later describes to the world the stunning findings on "whisker differences in rats."

* In this study, Zimbardo and his colleagues placed normal, healthy male college students in a simulated prison setting as either guards or prisoners, and soon found they developed prisoner and guard "personalities" to such a pathological degree that the experiment had to be called off. But these "personality" manifestations were not traits the students began with—psychological testing, and randomly assigning them to either role, eliminated this possibility (see "The Pathology of Imprisonment," in Zick Rubin's *Doing Unto Others* (Englewood Cliffs, N.J.: Prentice-Hall, 1975).

INDEX

SUBJECT INDEX

Abigail Van Buren (column), 60-1
Address, terms of, 4-5, 67-8, 72, 78, 107
Afro-Americans (*See* Blacks)
Aggression, 27, 183-4
  kinesic, 126, 129, 146-50
  and touch, 121-2
  visual, 153-4, 162, 163n
Animal behavior, 182-3, 185
  eye contact, 154, 166
  facial expression, 169
  and space, 27-9
  and time, 43-4
Ann Landers (column), 1
Approach, angle of, 41
Assertiveness, 199-201
Authority, 20, 128

Beetle Bailey (comic), 102
Blacks (*See also* Interaction, Interracial; Race)
  Black English, 71, 132
  eye contact, 158-60
  facial expression, 170, 173
  kinesics, 132-5
  space, 35-6, 38, 41
Blaming the victim, 12, 63, 201, 207
Boundary behavior, 103, 115
Burger, Warren, Chief Justice, 57

Change, 202-5
Children, 6, 16n
  facial expression, 170-1
  kinesics, 130
  space, 30, 33-4, 39
  touch, 97, 108, 114, 119, 121-2
  and women, 193-5
Chivalry, 64-5, 110n
Circumspection, 84-6
  and women, 91
Clothing
  men's, 87-8, 90
  women's, 1, 89-90
Comics, 115, 168-9
Competition, 126-7
Congruity, principle of, 87
Crowding, 39-40

Dance, 145, 150
Demeanor, 1, 4, 82-93 (*See also* Circumspection; Clothing; Disruption; Height, personal; Looseness; Relaxation; Tension; Tightness)
  sex differences, 38, 89-93
Disruption, 82-3
Distance, interpersonal, 28, 32-3, 36
Dominance, 2, 3, 5 (*See also* Authority; Power; Status)
  among animals, 28-9
  definition, 19-20
  facial expression, 169-71
  gestures, 6, 28, 125-9, 140, 145, 185-7
    physical threat, 126, 129, 183
Door ceremony, 64
Dreiser, Theodore, 93n

Ehrlichman, John, 69, 87-8
Emotion, restriction of, 83, 172-4

Environment, 55-66, 189
  restriction, 62-4
  sex differences, 60, 65-6
  and women, 59-66
Eye contact, 128-30, 151-67, 181-2 (*See also* Staring; Visibility)
  affiliation, 161-2
  age status, 155, 158
  attention, 154-5, 159, 161-3, 166
  aversion, 154, 163-5
  and conversation, 155-6, 158-61, 163
  cultural/racial factors, 158-60
  dominance, 152-3, 155-6
  sex differences, 158, 160-7

Facial expression, 168-78, 194 (*See also* Eye contact; Smiling; Visual behavior)
  black, 170, 173
  sex differences, 173-8
Field dependence, 162
Films, 115-6
Ford, Gerald, 87, 124-5

Gender display, 135-6, 139-40, 174 (*See also* Sex differences, under different nonverbal behaviors)
Gestural slang, 146-7
Gesture, 127 (*See also* Kinesics; Touch; Steepling)
  obscene, 146-7

Haldeman, H. R., 69, 70, 87, 88
Handshake, 110, 111, 114, 129
Haptics (*See* Touch)
Head movement, 128, 136-8
Height
  personal, 88-9, 128
    and women, 91-2
  spatial, 3, 55, 58-9, 128, 148-9
Heloise, Hints from (column), 53
Homosexuals, 141
Housework, 53, 64
Humor, 71, 77-8, 84

Immediacy, 10-12
Impression formation, 92-3
Individuality, loss of, 40
Inequality, 21-3
Information, 73, 157, 172-4
Insubordination, gestures of, 132-3, 170, 173
Interaction
  female/male, 37, 109, 111n, 114, 137-9, 147-50, 161, 164, 166-7, 175
  interracial, 9-13, 35, 38, 41, 159-60
  sexual, 15-7
Interruption, 69
  sex differences, 74-5

Jesus, 96n

Kennedy, John, 33
Kinesics, 124-50, 194 (*See also* Gesture; Head movement; Posture)

211

Submission, gestures of, 34, 140, 145, 185-7
Synchrony, 128

Tension, 85, 130 (*See also* Tightness)
  and women, 91
Territory, 27-32, 36, 38, 58, 127
  women's, 61-2
Tightness, 84-5, 132
Time, 43-54, 194
  among animals, 43-4
  restrictions, 53
  and social class, 47-9
  and space, 43-9
  and women, 51-4
  zones, 44-5
Touch, 5, 94-123 (*See also* Handshake)
  affiliative, 101, 104, 106, 122
  age differences, 103-4
  avoidance, 98-9, 123
  body regions, 111-2, 118
  cultural/racial factors, 100, 111, 113
  and dominance, 105-6, 118-9, 127
  hostile, 121-3
  magic/religious aspects, 96-7
  meaning, 117-8, 122
  and men, 109-110, 123
  metaphor, 98
  in popular culture, 115-6
  and sex, 99, 101, 109, 117-20
  sex differences, 103, 105-6, 109-16, 118-9, 122
  and status, 95, 102-5, 116
  types, 118
  and women, 108-10, 123
Transvestites, 141

Unobtrusive measures, 108

Vanderbilt, Amy, 142
Visibility, 3-4, 157-8, 166-7
Visual behavior, 170, 173 (*See also* Eye contact)

Waiting, 45-52, 54 (*See also* Time)
Watergate, 68, 70, 85-8
Women, 13-18, 183, 202, 205 (*See also* Chivalry; Misogyny; Sex differences)
  in advertisements, 59-60
  and children, 193-5
  and demeanor, 89-93
  and environment, 59-66
  and passivity, 65
  and space, 36-42
  and territory, 36, 39
  and time, 51-54
  and touch, 108-10, 123
Women's liberation, 198-201

AUTHOR INDEX

213